IARIA Congress 2022

The 2022 IARIA Annual Congress on Frontiers in Science, Technology, Services, and Applications

July 24th – 28th, 2022

Nice, France

IARIA Congress 2022 Editors

Lorena Parra, Universitat Politècnica de València, Spain

Printed from e-media with permission by:

Curran Associates, Inc.
57 Morehouse Lane
Red Hook, NY 12571

Some format issues inherent in the e-media version may also appear in this print version.

International Academy, Research, and Industry Association (IARIA)
412 Derby Way
Wilmington, DE 19810

Phone: (408) 893-6407
Fax: (408) 527-6351

petre@iaria.org

Additional copies of this publication are available from:

Curran Associates, Inc.
57 Morehouse Lane
Red Hook, NY 12571 USA
Phone: 845-758-0400
Fax: 845-758-2633
Email: curran@proceedings.com
Web: www.proceedings.com

Table of Contents

IARIA Congress 2022

Forward

The 2022 IARIA Annual Congress on Frontiers in Science, Technology, Services, and Applications (IARIA Congress 2022), held between July 24th and July 28th, 2022, in Nice, France, was an inaugural event keeping pace with the achievements and challenges our society is facing in science, technologies, services, and applications.

The annual event was a multidomain assembly of scientists, specialists, and decision makers from all economical, educational, and governmental entities, on Social Systems, Software, Data Science Analytics, Communications, Technology, and Networked Services. Apart from classical topics, the congress targeted frontier achievements on Knowledge Science, Data Science, Artificial Intelligence / Machine Learning (AI/ML)-based systems, Self-managing systems, Human-centric technologies, Advanced robotics, Virtual Worlds, Mobility, Sensing, Energy, Electric Vehicles, Green Energy, etc.

The IARIA Congress had a special scientific format where outstanding former IARIA scientists delivered dedicated speeches (Keynote speeches, Tutorial Lectures) along with peer-reviewed contributions on the themes of achievements and challenges in science, technologies, services, and applications.

We take here the opportunity to warmly thank all the members of the IARIA Congress 2022 technical program committee, as well as all the reviewers. The creation of such a high-quality conference program would not have been possible without their involvement. We also kindly thank all the authors who dedicated much of their time and effort to contribute to IARIA Congress 2022. We truly believe that, thanks to all these efforts, the final conference program consisted of top-quality contributions. We also thank the members of the IARIA Congress 2022 organizing committee for their help in handling the logistics of this event.

We hope that IARIA Congress 2022 was a successful international forum for the exchange of ideas and
results between academia and industry and for the promotion of progress in our society.

IARIA Congress 2022 Chairs

IARIA Congress 2022 Steering Committee

Carlos Becker Westphall, Federal University of Santa Catarina, Brazil
Luigi Lavazza, Università dell'Insubria – Varese, Italy
Timothy T. Pham, Jet Propulsion Laboratory - California Institute of Technology, USA
Hermann Kaindl, TU Wien, Vienna, Austria
Arcady Zhukov, University of Basque Country (UPV/EHU), San Sebastian / Ikerbasque, Basque Foundation for Science, Bilbao, Spain
Lasse Berntzen, University of South-Eastern Norway, Norway
Bob Duncan, University of Aberdeen, UK
Yasushi Kambayashi, Nippon Institute of Technology, Japan

IARIA Congress 2022
Committee

IARIA Congress 2022 Steering Committee

Carlos Becker Westphall, Federal University of Santa Catarina, Brazil
Luigi Lavazza, Università dell'Insubria – Varese, Italy
Timothy T. Pham, Jet Propulsion Laboratory - California Institute of Technology, USA
Hermann Kaindl, TU Wien, Vienna, Austria
Arcady Zhukov, University of Basque Country (UPV/EHU), San Sebastian / Ikerbasque, Basque Foundation for Science, Bilbao, Spain
Lasse Berntzen, University of South-Eastern Norway, Norway
Bob Duncan, University of Aberdeen, UK
Yasushi Kambayashi, Nippon Institute of Technology, Japan

IARIA Congress 2022 Technical Program Committee

Tamer Abdou, Ryerson University, Canada
Nitin Agarwal, COSMOS Research Center | University of Arkansas at Little Rock, USA
Sedat Akleylek, Ondokuz Mayis University, Samsun, Turkey
Murat Akpinar, ASELSAN A.Ş., Ankara, Turkey
Raid Rafi Omar Al-Nima, Northern Technical University, Iraq
Hesham Ali, University of Nebraska Omaha , USA
Mohammad Alsulami, University of Connecticut, USA
Lasse Berntzen, University of South-Eastern Norway, Norway
Ayush Bhargava, Meta, USA
Sandjai Bhulai, Vrije Universiteit Amsterdam, Netherlands
John Blake, University of Aizu, Japan
Oleksandr Blazhko, National University «Odessa Polytechnic», Ukraine
Natalia Bogach, Peter the Great St. Petersburg Polytechnic University, Russia
Abdelmadjid Bouabdallah, University of Technology of Compiegne, France
Christian Bourret, Université Gustave Eiffel (Paris Est Marne-la-Vallée), France
Dirceu Cavendish, Kyushu Institute of Technology, Japan
André Constantino da Silva, Federal Institute of São Paulo - IFSP, Brazil
Toon De Pessemier, Imec - WAVES - Ghent University, Belgium
Lizette De Wet, University of the Free State, South Africa
Bob Duncan, University of Aberdeen, UK
Peter Edge, Ara Institute of Canterbury, New Zealand
Adrian Florea, "Lucian Blaga" University of Sibiu, Romania
Edelberto Franco Silva, Federal University of Juiz de Fora, Brazil
Denis Gracanin, Virginia Tech, USA
Gregor Grambow, Aalen University, Germany
Hans-Joachim Hof, Technische Hochschule Ingolstadt, Germany
Wladyslaw Homenda, Warsaw University of Technology, Poland
Hocine Imine, Université Gustave Eiffel, France
Orest Ivakhiv, L'viv Polytechnic National University, Ukraine
Fehmi Jaafar, Quebec University at Chicoutimi / Concordia University / Laval University, Canada

Elena Zaitseva, University of Zilina, Slovakia
Arkady Zhukov, University of Basque Country - UPV/EHU | IKERBASQUE - Basque Foundation for Science, Spain
Kashif Zia, Sohar University, Oman

Copyright Information

Advanced Functional Amorphous Magnetic Microwires for Technological Applications

Arcady Zhukov
Dept Polymers and Advanced Materials, Dept. Applied Physics and EHU Quantum Center, Univ. Basque Country, UPV/EHU, San Sebastian and Ikerbasque, Bilbao Spain
e-mail: arkadi.joukov@ehu.es

Mihail Ipatov, Paula Corte-León, Alvaro Gonzalez, Alfonso García- Gómez, Valentina Zhukova
Dept Polymers and Advanced Materials, Dept. Applied Physics and EHU Quantum Center, Univ. Basque Country, UPV/EHU, San Sebastian, Spain
e-mails: mihail.ipatov@ehu.es; paula.corte@ehu.eus; alvaro.gonzalezv@ehu.eus; alfonso.garciag@ehu.eus; valentina.zhukova@ehu.es

***Abstract*—Several routes allowing the development of low cost magnetic microwires coated by insulating, flexible and biocompatible glass-coating with tunable magnetic properties are overviewed. Amorphous microwires can present excellent magnetic softness and Giant MagnetoImpedance (GMI) effect. A high GMI effect, obtained even in as-prepared Co-rich microwires, can be further improved by appropriate heat treatment (including Joule heating, conventional annealing and/or stress-annealing). The observed versatile magnetic properties of amorphous microwires are suitable for various applications, such as magnetic sensors, electronic surveillance, wireless communication or biomedical applications.**

Keywords- magnetic microwires; magnetic softness; giant magnetoimpedance effect.

I. INTRODUCTION

Amorphous magnetic materials can present an unusual combination of excellent magnetic properties (e.g., high magnetic permeability, Giant magnetoimpedance (GMI) effect, magnetic bistability, Matteucci and Widemann effects) and superior mechanical properties (plasticity, flexibility) making them suitable for numerous industrial applications [1]-[7]. Furthermore, the preparation method involving rapid melt quenching is quite fast and inexpensive and the above mentioned magnetic softness can be realized without any complex post-processing treatments [3]-[5].

The development of novel applications of amorphous materials requires new functionalities, i.e., reduced dimensions, enhanced corrosion resistance or biocompatibility [8]. Therefore, great attention has been paid to development of alternative fabrication methods allowing preparation of amorphous materials at micro-nano scale involving melt quenching [6]-[8].

The main technological interest in GMI effect is related to one of the largest sensitivity to magnetic field (up to 10 %/A/m) among non-cryogenic effects [4]-[8]. Such features of the GMI effect make it quite attractive for development of high performance sensors allowing detection of low magnetic fields and mechanical stresses [9]-[14]. The most common quantity for the characterization of the GMI effect is the GMI ratio, $\Delta Z/Z$, defined as:

$$\Delta Z/Z = [Z(H) - Z(H_{max})] / Z(Hmax), \qquad (1)$$

where H is the applied axial DC-field with a maximum value, H_{max}, up to a few kA/m.

The value of GMI ratio and its magnetic field dependence are determined by the type of magnetic anisotropy: to achieve a high GMI ratio, a high circumferential magnetic permeability is essential [7][8]. Magnetic wires with circumferential easy axis exhibit double-peak magnetic field dependence of the real component of wire impedance (and consequently of the GMI ratio). However, magnetic wires with longitudinal easy axis present monotonic decay of the GMI ratio with increasing axial magnetic field with GMI ratio maximum at zero magnetic fields [7][8]. The highest GMI ratio up to 650% is reported for amorphous microwires [15]-[17]. However, the theoretically predicted maximum GMI ratio is about 3000% (i.e., a few times larger than the GMI ratio values reported experimentally) [18]. Additionally, theoretical minimum of the skin depth is about 0.3 μm [17][18].

The main features of the GMI effect have been successfully explained in terms of classical electrodynamics considering the influence of a magnetic field on the penetration depth of an electrical current flowing through the magnetically soft conductor [1][2]. High circumferential permeability typically observed in Co-rich amorphous wires with nearly-zero magnetostriction coefficient is essentially relevant for observation of high GMI ratio [1][2][4]-[6]. However, similarly to the magnetic permeability, the GMI effect has a tensor character [4]-[6][19]-[22]. The off-diagonal component of GMI can present anti-symmetrical magnetic field dependence with a linear region quite suitable for magnetic sensors applications [19][23].

One of the tendencies in modern GMI sensors is the size reduction. It must be underlined that the diameter reduction must be associated with the increasing of the optimal GMI frequency range: a tradeoff between dimension and frequency is required in order to obtain a maximum GMI effect [4]-[6][23]. Additionally, the GMI effect at microwave frequencies has been described considering the analogy between the GMI and the ferromagnetic resonance [4]. Consequently, the development of thin soft magnetic materials required for miniaturization of the sensors and devices requires an extension of the frequency range for the impedance toward the higher frequencies (GHz range).

Recently developed magnetic sensors using the GMI effect allow achieving nT and pT magnetic field sensitivity with low noise [10]-[14][24].

Presently, major attention is focused on high frequencies (GHz range) GMI applications owing to the development of thin magnetically soft materials and the recent tendency in miniaturization of magnetic field sensors [4]-[6][10]-[14][24].

The aim of this report is to provide recent results on the optimization of soft magnetic properties and the GMI effect in magnetic microwires.

The rest of the paper is structured as follows. In Section 2, we present the description of the experimental techniques, while in Section 3, we describe the results on the effect of post-processing on the GMI ratio of the studied microwires. We conclude this work in Section 4.

II. EXPERIMENTAL DETAILS

As already mentioned in the introduction, the GMI effect usually observed in soft magnetic materials phenomenologically consists of the change of the AC impedance, $Z = R + iX$ (where R is the real part, or resistance, and X is the imaginary part, or reactance), when submitted to an external magnetic field, H_0.

The electrical impedance, Z, of a magnetic conductor is given by [1][2]:

$$Z = R_{dc}\, krJ_0(kr)/2J_1(kr) \qquad (2)$$

with $k = (1 + j)/\delta$, where J_0 and J_1 are the Bessel functions, r is the wire's radius and δ the penetration depth given by:

$$\delta = \sqrt{\pi\sigma\mu_\phi f} \qquad (3)$$

where σ is the electrical conductivity, f the frequency of the current along the sample, and μ_ϕ the circular magnetic permeability assumed to be scalar. The DC applied magnetic field introduces significant changes in the circular permeability, μ_ϕ. Therefore, the penetration depth also changes through and finally results in a change of Z [1],[2].

The GMI ratio, defined as $\Delta Z/Z$, has been evaluated considering (1).

The use of a specially designed micro-strip sample holder placed inside a sufficiently long solenoid allows measuring of the magnetic field dependence of sample impedance, Z, using a vector network analyzer , as described in [24]. The described technique allows measuring of the GMI effect in extended frequency, f, range up to GHz frequencies.

Hysteresis loops have been measured using the fluxmetric method previously described in [25]. We represent the normalized magnetization, M/M_0 versus the magnetic field, H, where M is the magnetic moment at a given magnetic field and M_0 is the magnetic moment of the sample at the maximum magnetic field amplitude, H_m.

We studied Fe- and Co- rich microwires with metallic nucleus diameters, d, ranging from 10 up to 25 μm prepared using the Taylor-Ulitovsky method described in [5][8]. The Taylor-Ulitovsky method allows the preparation of the thinnest metallic wires (with typical diameters of the order of 1 to 30 μm) covered by an insulating glass coating [5][8].

The great advantage of these microwires is that the obtained diameter could be significantly reduced in comparison with the case of amorphous wires produced by the other rapidly quenching methods. However, in the case of glass-coated microwires the magnetoelastic anisotropy contribution is even more relevant since the preparation process involves not only the rapid quenching itself, but also simultaneous solidification of the metallic nucleus surrounded by the glass-coating with rather different thermal expansion coefficients [5][8][27][28].

In amorphous materials, the magnetocrystalline anisotropy is absent. Therefore, the magnetoelastic anisotropy is the main factor affecting the magnetic properties [5][6].

The magnetoelastic anisotropy, K_{me}, is given as:

$$K_{me} = 3/2\lambda_S\sigma_i \qquad (4)$$

where λ_S is the magnetostriction coefficient and σ_i is the internal stresses value [8].

The magnetostriction coefficient, λ_s, value in amorphous alloys can be tailored by the chemical composition [29]-[31]. Generally, Fe-rich compositions present positive λ_s -values (typically $\lambda_s \approx 20$ - 40×10^{-6}), while for the Co-rich alloys, λ_s values are negative, typically $\lambda_s \approx -5$ to -3×10^{-6}. Vanishing λ_s values can be achieved in the Co_xFe_{1-x} ($0 \leq x \leq 1$) or Co_xMn_{1-x} ($0 \leq x \leq 1$) systems at x about 0.03 – 0.08 [29]-[32].

However, internal stresses, σ_i, arise during simultaneous rapid quenching of metallic nucleus surrounding by the glass coating due to the different thermal expansion coefficients. Consequently, the strength of internal stresses can be controlled by the glass-coating thickness: the strength of internal stresses increases with the increase of the glass-coating thickness [27][28].

III. EXPERIMENTAL RESULTS AND DISCUSSION

As mentioned above, the magnitude and the magnetic field dependence of the GMI effect (including off-diagonal components) is intrinsically linked to the magnetic anisotropy [4]-[8]. Consequently, both hysteresis loops, $\Delta Z/Z(H)$ dependence and maximum value of the GMI ratio, $\Delta Z/Z_m$, are affected by λ_s sign and value and by the magnitude of internal stresses, σ_i. The magnetostriction

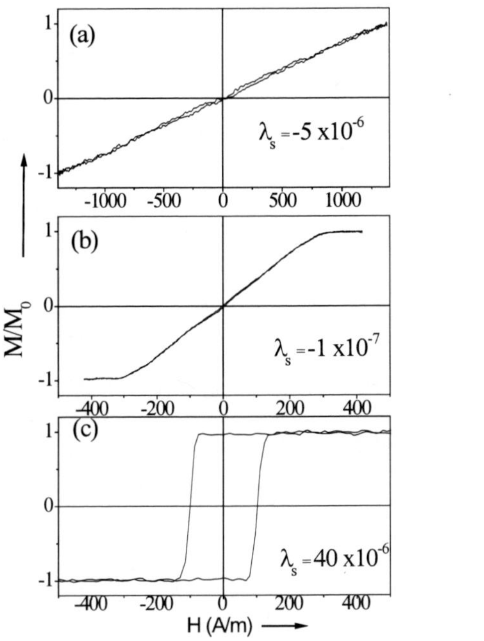

Figure 1. Hysteresis loops of as-prepared $Co_{77.5}Si_{15}B_{7.5}$ (a), $Co_{67.1}Fe_{3.8}Ni_{1.4}Si_{14.5}B_{11.5}Mo_{1.7}$ (b) and $Fe_{75}B_9Si_{12}C_4$ (c) microwires.

coefficient drastically affects the character of the hysteresis loops of magnetic microwires: i) Co-rich microwires (see Figure 1a for $Co_{77.5}Si_{15}B_{7.5}$) with negative magnetostriction constant ($\lambda_s \approx -5x10^{-6}$) have almost unhysteretic loops with extremely low coercivity, H_c. However, the magnetic permeability of $Co_{77.5}Si_{15}B_{7.5}$ microwires is not high enough since they also present high enough magnetic anisotropy field, H_k. ii) Co-Fe-based microwires with vanishing magnetostriction constant ($Co_{67.1}Fe_{3.8}Ni_{1.4}Si_{14.5}B_{11.5}Mo_{1.7}$, $\lambda_s \approx -10^{-7}$) generally present lower H_k values and hence higher magnetic permeability (see Figure 1b). iii) Finally, Fe-rich microwires ($Fe_{75}B_9Si_{12}C_4$) with positive magnetostriction constant ($\lambda_s \approx 40x10^{-6}$) present rectangular hysteresis loops and consequently low magnetic permeability (see Figure 1c).

As can be appreciated from Figure 2b, $Co_{67.1}Fe_{3.8}Ni_{1.4}Si_{14.5}B_{11.5}Mo_{1.7}$ microwire presents the highest maximum GMI ratio, $\Delta Z/Z_m$ (about 240% at 500 MHz). Quite low $\Delta Z/Z_m$ values are observed for $Fe_{75}B_9Si_{12}C_4$ microwire ($\Delta Z/Z_m \approx 15\%$, see Figure 2c). Moderate $\Delta Z/Z_m$ values ($\Delta Z/Z_m \approx 120\%$) are observed for $Co_{77.5}Si_{15}B_{7.5}$ microwire (see Figure 2a).

The other difference in $\Delta Z/Z(H)$ dependencies for microwires with different magnetostriction coefficients is the character of $\Delta Z/Z(H)$ dependencies: for microwires with $\lambda_s>0$, a single maximum $\Delta Z/Z(H)$ dependence with $\Delta Z/Z$ maximum at $H=0$ is observed (Figure 2c). However, for $\lambda_s<0$ double- maximum $\Delta Z/Z(H)$ dependencies with $\Delta Z/Z$ maximum at $H=H_m$ are observed (Figures 2b,c).

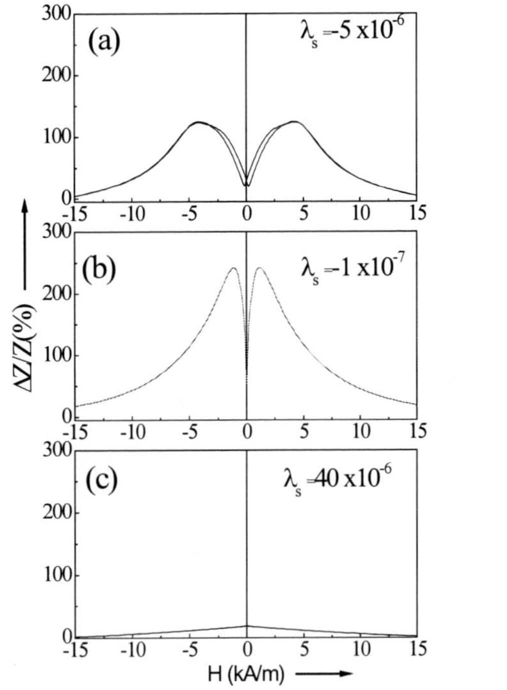

Figure 2. ΔZ/Z(H) dependencies of as-prepared $Co_{77.5}Si_{15}B_{7.5}$ (a), $Co_{67.1}Fe_{3.8}Ni_{1.4}Si_{14.5}B_{11.5}Mo_{1.7}$ (b) and $Fe_{75}B_9Si_{12}C_4$ (c) microwires measured at 500 MHz.

It is commonly assumed that the H_m value corresponding to the peaks (maximum $\Delta Z/Z$ value) is linked to the average value of the anisotropy field, H_K, at high frequency values, and to the effective anisotropy distribution in the sample. In this regard, the observed $\Delta Z/Z(H)$ dependencies correlate with the hysteresis loops: the highest H_m value is observed for $Co_{77.5}Si_{15}B_{7.5}$ microwire with the highest H_k value (see Figure 1a). A single maximum $\Delta Z/Z(H)$ dependence with $\Delta Z/Z$ maximum at $H=0$ corresponds to the $Fe_{75}B_9Si_{12}C_4$ microwire with axial magnetic anisotropy (Figure 1c).

Such different magnetic anisotropy of microwires with positive and negative magnetostriction is related to the internal stresses distribution intrinsically related to the fabrication of microwires [4]-[8]. The radial distribution of internal stresses calculated considering quenching stresses related to rapid quenching of the metallic alloy from the melt as well as complex tensor stresses related to the difference in the thermal expansion coefficients of metal and glass the axial stresses are the largest ones up to ~ 0.85 R (where R is the metallic nucleus radius) [8]. Thus, the main volume of the microwire nucleus is under the tensile stresses near the axis of the metallic nucleus. However, closer to the surface, the compressive stresses are dominant. Additionally, the strength of internal stresses is determined by the thickness of the non-magnetic glass-coating: the strength of internal stresses increases with the increasing of the glass-coating thickness.

Therefore, as reported earlier [5][8], hysteresis loops and GMI effect are affected by the ratio $\rho=d/D$, where d is the

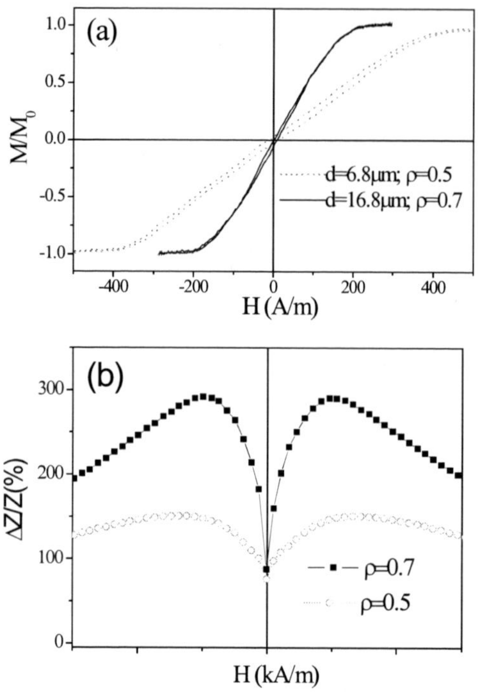

Figure 3. Hysteresis loops (a) and *ΔZ/Z(H)* dependencies measured at 500 MHz (b) of as-prepared $Co_{67}Fe_{3.85}Ni_{1.45}B_{11.5}Si_{14.5}Mo_{1.7}$ microwires with different ρ-ratios.

diameter of metallic nucleus and *D*-total microwire diameter. Some examples are shown in Figure 3, where the hysteresis loops and *ΔZ/Z(H)* dependencies of as-prepared $Co_{67}Fe_{3.85}Ni_{1.45}B_{11.5}Si_{14.5}Mo_{1.7}$ microwires with different ρ ratios are shown.

Consequently, the control of internal stresses by tailoring of the ρ–ratio is an effective method for GMI ratio tuning.

As mentioned above, the other important parameter for GMI ratio optimization in magnetic microwires is the frequency. Indeed, the frequency must be high enough in order to have the skin depth lower than the sample radius (strong skin effect). *ΔZ/Z(H)* dependencies measured at different frequencies in as-prepared $Co_{67}Fe_{3.9}Ni_{1.4}B_{11.5}Si_{14.5}Mo_{1.6}$ (d=25.6 μm, D= 26.6 μm) microwires are shown in Figure 4a. This composition at the given geometry (d=25.6 μm, D= 26.6 μm, ρ=0.96) present high maximum GMI ratio, $\Delta Z/Z_m$: at optimal frequency of about 300 MHz $\Delta Z/Z_m \approx 550\%$ can be achieved (see Figure 4b). However, thinner (d=10.8 μm) microwire of the same chemical composition at this frequency exhibit $\Delta Z/Z_m \approx 400\%$ (see Figure 4b). From the $\Delta Z/Z_m(f)$ dependence for $Co_{67.7}Fe_{4.3}Ni_{1.6}Si_{11.2}B_{12.4}C_{1.5}Mo_{1.3}$ microwires with d=10.8μm and d=25.6 μm, we can appreciate that for $Co_{67.7}Fe_{4.3}Ni_{1.6}Si_{11.2}B_{12.4}C_{1.5}Mo_{1.3}$ microwires with d=10.8μm the optimal frequency is about 700 MHz at which $\Delta Z/Z_m \approx 550\%$ can be achieved.

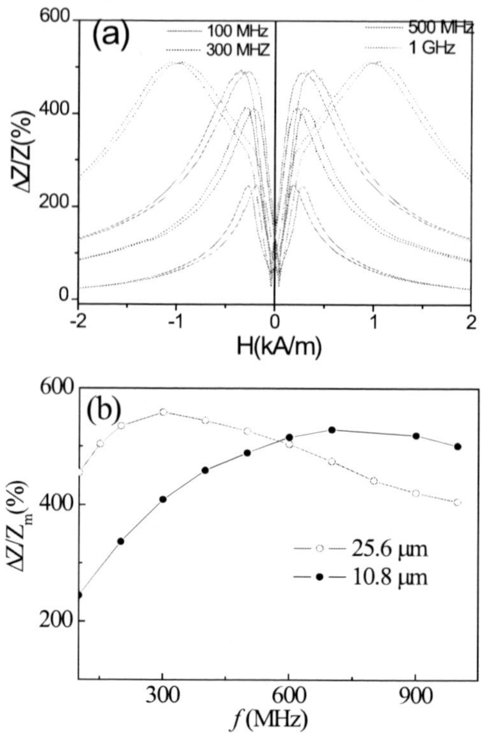

Figure 4. *ΔZ/Z(H)* dependencies measured in as-prepared $Co_{67}Fe_{3.9}Ni_{1.4}B_{11.5}Si_{14.5}Mo_{1.6}$ (d=25.6 μm, D= 26.6 μm) microwires (a) and $\Delta Z/Z_m(f)$ dependence for $Co_{67.7}Fe_{4.3}Ni_{1.6}Si_{11.2}B_{12.4}C_{1.5}Mo_{1.3}$ with d=10.8μm, D=13.8μm and d=25.6 μm, D= 26.6 μm microwires.

The aforementioned examples provide the routes for optimization of GMI effect in Co-rich microwires.

IV. CONCLUSIONS

We measured the GMI magnetic field, frequency dependencies and hysteresis loops in magnetic microwires produced by the Taylor-Ulitovsky technique.

We observed that the GMI effect and magnetic softness of microwires are intrinsically related and can be tailored either by controlling the magnetoelastic anisotropy of as-prepared microwires or by controlling their internal stresses and structure by heat treatment. Studies of the GMI effect of amorphous Co-Fe rich microwires reveal that microwires of appropriate chemical composition and geometry present the GMI effect at GHz frequencies. A high GMI effect has been achieved and discussed. The election of appropriate measuring conditions can be beneficial for the optimization of the GMI effect of magnetic microwires. Magnetic microwires with optimized magnetic properties are suitable for several applications, like magnetic sensors, electronic surveillance, wireless communication or biomedical applications.

ACKNOWLEDGMENT

This work was supported by Spanish MCIU under PGC2018-099530-B-C31 (MCIU/AEI/FEDER, UE), by EU under "INFINITE"(Horizon Europe Framework Programme) project, by the Government of the Basque Country, under PUE_2021_1_0009 and Elkartek (MINERVA and ZE-KONP) projects, by the University of the Basque Country, under the scheme of "Ayuda a Grupos Consolidados" (Ref.: GIU18/192) and under the COLAB20/15 project and by the Diputación Foral de Gipuzkoa in the frame of Programa "Red guipuzcoana de Ciencia, Tecnología e Innovación 2021" under 2021-CIEN-000007-01 project. The authors are grateful for the technical and human support provided by SGIker of UPV/EHU (Medidas Magnéticas Gipuzkoa) and European funding (ERDF and ESF). We wish to thank the administration of the University of the Basque Country, which not only provides very limited funding, but even expropriates the resources received by the research group from private companies for the research activities of the group. Such interference helps keep us on our toes.

REFERENCES

[1] L. V. Panina and K. Mohri, "Magneto-impedance effect in amorphous wires," Appl. Phys. Lett., vol. 65, pp. 1189-1191, 1994.

[2] R. S. Beach and A. E. Berkowitz, "Giant magnetic-field dependent impedance of amorphous FeCoSiB wire", Appl. Phys. Lett., vol. 64, pp. 3652-3654, 1994.

[3] E. P. Harrison, G. L. Turney, H. Rowe, and H. Gollop, "The Electrical Properties of High Permeability Wires Carrying Alternating Current", Proc. R. Soc. Lond. A, vol. 157, pp. 451-479, 1936.

[4] M. H. Phan and H. X. Peng, "Giant magnetoimedance materials: Fundamentals and applications", Prog. Mater. Sci., vol. 53, pp. 323-420, 2008.

[5] A. Zhukov, M. Ipatov, and V. Zhukova, Advances in Giant Magnetoimpedance of Materials, Handbook of Magnetic Materials, ed. K.H.J. Buschow, 24, pp. 139-236 (chapter 2), 2015.

[6] M. Knobel, M. Vazquez, and L. Kraus, Giant magnetoimpedance, Handbook of magnetic materials ed. E. Bruck 15, pp.497-563, 2003.

[7] N. A. Usov, A. S. Antonov, and A. N. Lagar`kov, "Theory of giant magneto-impedance effect in amorphous wires with different types of magnetic anisotropy", J. Magn. Magn. Mater., vol. 185, pp. 159-173, 1998.

[8] A. Zhukov et al., Giant magnetoimpedance in rapidly quenched materials", J. Alloys Compound. vol. 814, pp. 152225, 2020.

[9] K. Mohri, T. Uchiyama, L. P. Shen, C. M. Cai, and L. V. Panina, "Amorphous wire and CMOS IC-based sensitive micro-magnetic sensors (MI sensor and SI sensor) for intelligent measurements and controls", J. Magn. Magn. Mater., vol. 249, pp. 351-356, 2001.

[10] T. Uchiyama, K. Mohri, and Sh. Nakayama, "Measurement of Spontaneous Oscillatory Magnetic Field of Guinea-Pig Smooth Muscle Preparation Using Pico-Tesla Resolution Amorphous Wire Magneto-Impedance Sensor", IEEE Trans. Magn., vol. 47, pp. 3070-3073, 2011.

[11] Y. Honkura, "Development of amorphous wire type MI sensors for automobile use", J. Magn. Magn. Mater., vol. 249, pp. 375-381, 2002.

[12] A. Zhukov et al., "Advanced functional magnetic microwires for technological applications", J. Phys. D: Appl. Phys., vol. 55, pp. 253003, 2022.

[13] S. Gudoshnikov et al., "Highly sensitive magnetometer based on the off-diagonal GMI effect in Co-rich glass-coated microwire", Phys. Stat. Sol. (a) vol. 211 (5) pp. 980–985, 2014.

[14] L. Ding et al., "Development of a high sensitivity GiantMagneto-Impedance magnetometer: comparison with a commercial Flux-Gate", IEEE Sensors, vol. 9 (2), pp. 159-168, 2009.

[14] K. R. Pirota, L. Kraus, H. Chiriac, and M. Knobel, "Magnetic properties and GMI in a CoFeSiB glass-covered microwire", J.Magn.Magn. Mater., vol. 21, pp. L243-L247, 2000.

[15] A. Zhukov, V. Zhukova, J. M. Blanco and J. Gonzalez, "Recent research on magnetic properties of glass-coated microwires", J. Magn. Magn. Mater., vol. 294, pp 182-192, 2005.

[16] P. Corte-León et al., "Engineering of magnetic properties of Co-rich microwires by joule heating", Intermetallics vol. 105, pp. 92-98, 2019.

[17] L. Kraus, "Theory of giant magneto-impedance in the planar onductor with uniaxial magnetic anisotropy", J. Magn. Magn. Mater., vol 195, pp. 764-778, 1999.

[18] M. Ipatov, V. Zhukova, A. Zhukov, J. Gonzalez and A. Zvezdin, "Low-field hysteresis in the magnetoimpedance of amorphous microwires", Phys. Rev. B, vol. 81, p. 134421, 2010.

[19] S. I. Sandacci, D. P. Makhnovskiy, L. V. Panina, K. Mohri, and Y. Honkura, "Off-Diagonal Impedance in Amorphous Wires and Its Application to Linear Magnetic Sensors", IEEE Trans Magn., vol. 35, pp.3505-3510, 2004.

[20] P. Aragoneses, A. Zhukov, J. Gonzalez, J.M. Blanco, and L. Dominguez, "Effect of AC driving current on Magneto-Impedance effect", Sensors and Actuators A, vol. 81/1-3, pp. 86-90, 2000

[21] A. S. Antonov, I. T. Iakubov, and A. N. Lagarkov, "Nondiagonal impedance of amorphous wires with circular magnetic anisotropy", J. Magn. Magn. Mater., vol. 187(2) pp. 252–260, 1998

[22] D. Ménard, M. Britel, P. Ciureanu and A. Yelon, "Giant magnetoimpedance in a cylindrical conductor", J. Appl. Phys., vol. 84, pp. 2805–2814, 1998.

[23] Y. Honkura and S. Honkura, "The Development of ASIC Type GSR Sensor Driven by GHz Pulse Current", Sensors, vol. 20 pp.1023, 2020.

[24] A. Zhukov, A. Talaat, M. Ipatov, and V. Zhukova, "Tailoring the high-frequency giant magnetoimpedance effect of amorphous Co-rich microwires", IEEE Magn. Lett., vol. 6, p.2500104, 2015.

[25] L. Gonzalez-Legarreta et al., "Optimization of magnetic properties and GMI effect of Thin Co-rich Microwires for GMI Microsensors", Sensors, vol. 20, pp.1558, 2020.

[25] S. A. Baranov, V. S. Larin, and A. V. Torcunov, Technology, "Preparation and properties of the cast glass-coated magnetic microwires", Crystals, vol. 7 p. 136, 2017.

[26] H. Chiriac and T. A. Óvári, "Amorphous glass-covered magnetic wires: preparation, properties, applications", Progr. Mater. Sci., vol. 40 (5) pp. 333-407, 1996.

[27] A. Zhukov et al., "Ferromagnetic resonance and structure of Fe-based Glass-coated Microwires", J. Magn. Magn. Mater., vol. 203, pp. 238-240, 1999.

[28] G. Herzer, Amorphous and nanocrystalline soft magnets, in Proceedings of the NATO Advanced Study Insititute on Magnetic Hysteresis in Novel Materials, Mykonos, Greece, 1-12 July 1996 ed. George C. Hadjipanayis, NATO ASI Series (Series E:Applied Sciences) vol. 338, pp. 711-730. Kluwer Academic Publishers (Dordrecht/Boston/London) 1997.

[29] A. Zhukov et al., "Magnetostriction of Co-Fe-based amorphous soft magnetic microwires", J. Electr. Mater. vol. 45 (1) pp. 226-234, 2016.

[30] Y. Konno and K. Mohri, "Magnetostriction measurements for amorphous wires", IEEE Trans Magn., vol. 25, pp. 3623-3625, 1989.

[32] M. Churyukanova et al., "Magnetostriction investigation of soft magnetic microwires", Phys. Stat. Sol. (a), vol. 213(2), pp. 363–367, 2016.

Investigating Hand Dexterity in Patients with Hand Injuries through A Self-made Data Collection Glove

Jong-Chen Chen
National Yunlin University of Science and Technology
No. 123, Sec. 3, University Rd., Douliu City, Yunlin County
640, Taiwan (R.O.C.)
Email: jcchen@yuntech.edu.tw

Chih-Chien Hung
National Taiwan University Hospital, Yunlin Branch
No. 579, Sec. 2, Yunlin Rd., Douliu City, Yunlin County
640, Taiwan (R.O.C.)
Email: btoaew@gmail.com

Abstract—**The flexibility of people's fingers plays a very important role in our daily life. Many people lose some degree of finger dexterity due to finger injuries. In this study, a self-made Arduino data acquisition glove was used to collect data on 8 daily hand movements of healthy participants and patients. From the data collected on healthy participants, we established a norm of finger movements of healthy participants. We analyzed how people used different fingers to perform different movements. Furthermore, we collected data on some patients with finger injuries and compared their hand dexterity with healthy individuals.**

Keywords- sensors; hand dexterity; data glove; wearable device.

I. INTRODUCTION

Fingers play an important role in people's lives. Many daily life movements require a high degree of cooperation and coordination of different fingers to complete. However, when people's hands are injured, those seemingly simple daily actions might become quite difficult. In order to maintain the daily life movements of patients, rehabilitation has become an indispensable element. Rehabilitation can be a difficult task for patients. This is because, on one hand, it requires a lot of perseverance of the patient, and on the other hand, it takes a considerable amount of time. In addition to the above-mentioned factors, what is more important is whether the patient's rehabilitation is moving in the right direction. If the direction is correct, of course, the patient's hand health will gradually improve over time. However, if the direction is wrong, it is not only unhelpful to the patient, but may even cause further secondary damage.

In the process of rehabilitation, patients often face problems that they have no way of knowing in advance, and so it is difficult for them to determine whether they are moving in the right direction with their rehabilitation. If there is an objective assessment method that can provide appropriate information to patients in a timely manner, it is generally believed that it can effectively help improve the recovery of patients. In general, effective assessment methods can be roughly classified as invasive or non-invasive. The information obtained by the former assessment of the patient may be more direct or accurate than the information obtained by the latter. However, its disadvantage is that it might more or less directly or indirectly affect the patient's physical health. In this case, it might not be suitable for long-term evaluation. In contrast, non-invasive assessment methods may have less impact on patients. From a certain point of view, it may be more suitable for long-term assessment and tracking.

Faced with the above problems, this study hopes to establish an economical, non-invasive method that can detect the finger usage of patients at any time, so as to help patients understand the situation of hand rehabilitation in time. With this information, it can also provide physicians with an understanding of a patient's condition and provide appropriate diagnosis and treatment. With the joint efforts of both patients and physicians, the pace of patient recovery can also be accelerated. Several researchers have conducted investigations along this line of study [1]-[4].

The rest of the paper is structured as follows. In Section II, we describe the design of this induction glove and the method of data analysis used in this study. The experiments and results are presented in Section III. Finally, we draw our conclusions in Section IV.

II. METHOD

As mentioned above, in order to understand the activities of people's fingers, a self-made sensing glove was developed. The glove MS-100M produced by 3M company was selected in this study. MS-100M is a foam-coated glove with excellent breathability, anti-slip, and oil-repellent properties. We first manually sew the curvature sensors and the pressure sensors on the glove. After that, we connected these sensors to the Arduino Mega 2560 board to capture the experimental data. The Arduino Mega 2560 board has 16 analog input pins and can accept 16 input signals. Five out of these 16 pins were connected to the curvature sensors while the remaining 11 pins were connected to the pressure sensors. A curvature sensor was sewn on the back of each finger near the joint to obtain the bending degree of each finger when a person performed a certain action. A total of five curvature sensors are required for five fingers. In terms of finger pressure, each finger has its connections to two pressure sensors. One is sewn to the DIP (distal phalange) joint and the other to MCP (metacarpal) joint of each finger (Figure 1). Finally, considering that the thumb has one more degree of freedom than other fingers, a pressure sensor is added to the PIP (proximal phalange) joint of the thumb. The entire induction glove design is shown in Figure 2. Each subject was asked to perform 8 daily life actions, as demonstrated in Figure 3.

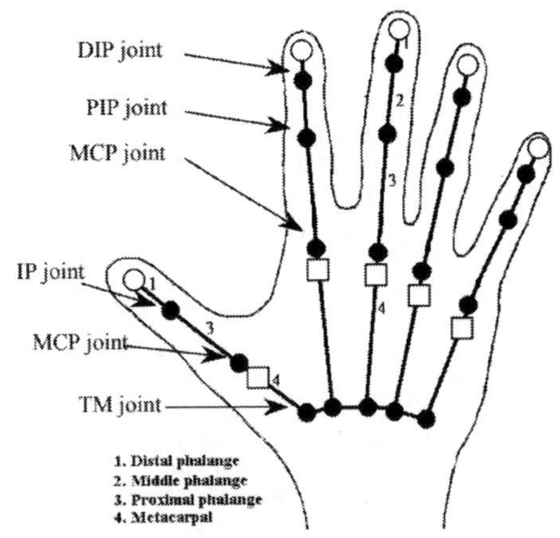

Figure 1. A homemade bending and pressure sensing glove.

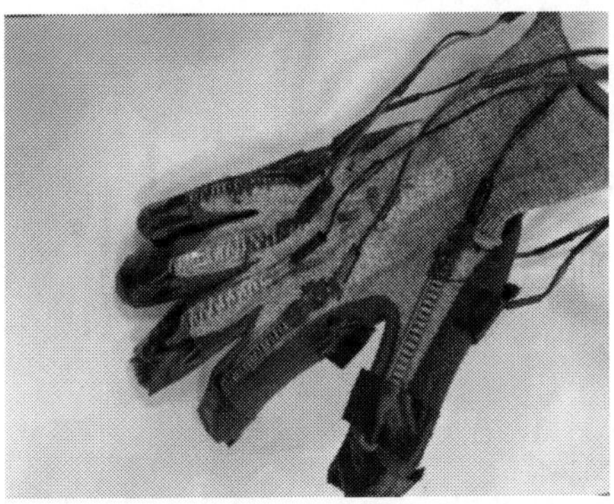

Figure 2. A homemade bending and pressure sensing glove.

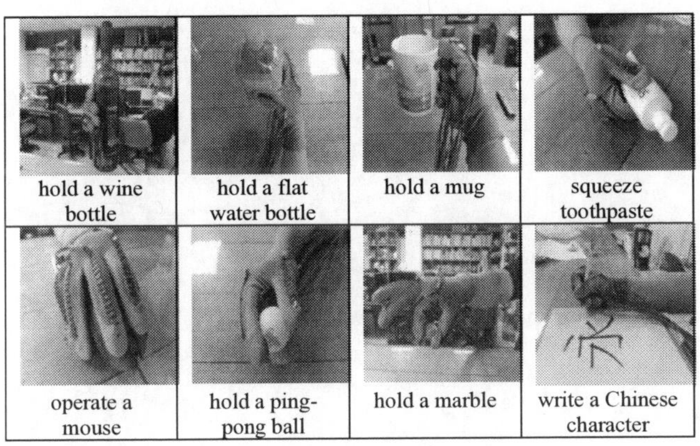

Figure 3. Eight daily life actions.

In this study, the time series data of the action process and the data of the completed action were analyzed respectively. When analyzing the time series data of the action process, this study uses the Pearson similarity method to analyze the consistency of the two action curves. The above analysis method is for activities of people with healthy hand. However, for patients with hand issues, this approach is not very appropriate. This is because each patient's finger injury is different. For example, some are unable to bend, while others are unable to be straightened after being bent for a long time. The approach of this study is to find out the maximum of all movements of each patient when performing movements. Then, we compare whether their maximum values differ from each other. When this difference is relatively small, it is considered normal. Otherwise, it represents an exception. The minimum value is handled in the same way. Through the above-mentioned comparisons, it is possible to discover the differences between each patient and others.

III. EXPERIMENTS AND RESULTS

This research experiment is divided into three parts. The first is to establish a data norm of 30 healthy participants. The second is to compare and analyze the data of patients and healthy participants. The third part is to analyze the rehabilitation situation of a specific patient in different rehabilitation stages. The results showed that some patients' index fingers showed significantly lower curvature values in certain movements than others. In addition, in some patients, the curvature of the middle finger was significantly different from that of healthy participants. This result indicates that the patient may not be able to bend the fingers on both sides because the middle finger cannot bend normally. In addition, there was a patient whose little finger shows a fixed value in any movement, which indicates that the patient's little finger mobility was lost.

IV. CONCLUSION

The purpose of this study was to explore how people use their fingers in curvature and acupressure for daily activities. The method adopted in this study was to first make a glove with induction curvature and acupressure sensors. We then invited thirty healthy participants to perform eight daily activities. The first thing we did was to test whether we could use the sensors of this homemade glove to judge the difference between two different actions. After we confirmed the discriminative ability of this homemade glove system, our next step was to try to build a reference dataset from the collected data to analyze the role of each finger.

There are two future research directions. The first is to continuously increase the repertoire of sensory data to establish healthy human hand activity norms. In addition to the 8 activities of daily living used in this study, this study recommends more data collection on other hand movements. The second direction is to allow patients to compare rehabilitation outcomes at different stages under the guidance of clinicians. In this way, we can see whether the patients have been improving clinically through the data provided by this system, that is, whether the patient's hand function is improving. This is a more objective analysis, which is its real practical application. Finally, in the future, we hope to collect enough data on the use of this technology to integrate Artificial Intelligence (AI) systems into this field of research and to further capture the specific biological characteristics of individuals.

ACKNOWLEDGEMENT

Ethical Approval: The study was conducted according to the guidelines of the Declaration of Helsinki and approved by the Human Research Ethics Committee of the National Cheng Kung University (Approval No.: NCKU HREC-E-110-319-2, date: July 13th, 2021).

Informed Consent Statement: Written informed consent has been obtained from the patient to publish this paper.

Funding: This study was in part funded by Taiwan Ministry of Science and Technology (Grant 110-2221-E-224-041-MY3 & Grant 110-2221-E-224-042).

REFERENCES

[1] J. Connolly, J. Condell, B. O' Flynn, J. T. Sanchez, and P. Gardiner, "IMU Sensor-Based Electronic Goniometric Glove for Clinical Finger Movement Analysis," IEEE Sens. J., vol. 18, pp. 1273–1281, 2018.

[2] B. S. Lin, I. J. Lee, and J. L.Chen, "Novel Assembled Sensorized Glove Platform for Comprehensive Hand Function Assessment by Using Inertial Sensors and Force Sensing Resistors," IEEE Sens. J., vol. 20, pp. 3379–3389, 2020.

[3] T. Pham, P. N. Pathirana, H. Trinh, and P. Fay, "A Non-Contact Measurement System for the Range of Motion of the Hand," Sensors, vol. 15, pp. 18315–18333, 2015.

[4] C. S Fahn and H. Sun, "Development of a Dataglove with Reducing Sensors Based on Magnetic Induction," IEEE Trans. Ind. Electron., vol. 52, no. 2, pp. 585-594, 2005.

Spatial and Temporal Registration of Asynchronous Multi-Sensors for Minimally Invasive Surgery Application

Uddhav Bhattarai
Department of Electrical and Computer Engineering
Tennessee Technological University
Cookeville, USA
ubhattara42@students.tntech.edu

Ali T. Alouani
Department of Electrical and Computer Engineering
Tennessee Technological University
Cookeville, USA
aalouani@tntech.edu

Abstract— **Current Minimally Invasive Surgery (MIS) technology, although advantageous compared to open cavity surgery in many aspects, has limitations that prevent its use for general purpose MIS. This is due to reduced dexterity, cost, and required complex training of the currently practiced technology. The main challenge in reducing the cost and amount of training is to have an accurate inner body navigation advisory system. As a first step in making minimally invasive surgery affordable and more user-friendly, quality images inside the patient as well as the surgical tool location should be provided automatically and accurately in real-time. The second step will be to provide the surgeon with an inner body Global Positioning System (GPS) like an advisory navigation system. This paper focuses on the first step: providing real-time information needed by the surgeon. This consists of real-time temporal and spatial calibration of heterogeneous asynchronous sensors that provide enough information needed to safely carry out MIS. The real-time asynchronous sensors registration algorithm has been successfully tested in the lab using a mannequin. The experimental temporal and spatial registration showed promising success for real-time tracking of the surgical tool as well as real-time display of the 2D information provided by the videoscope.**

Keywords-Sensors registration, Spatio-temporal calibration, Computer-assisted surgery, Multisensor System.

I. INTRODUCTION

MIS has distinct merits of faster recovery, shorter hospital stays, less pain, and decreased scarring. However, restricted visualization of the operative site, minimal accessibility, and reduced dexterity has increased the challenges of its implementation. Image Guided Surgery (IGS) during MIS will help solve such problems and improve safety and accuracy to a significant level [1]. Da Vinci surgical robot is the first surgical robot approved by FDA for commercial use in hospitals. This sophisticated high-end system has high procurement cost, and specialized training requirements for the surgeon [2].

Computed Tomography (CT) or Magnetic Resonance Imaging (MRI) provide high quality preoperative images of the inside of the patient body. Once the surgery starts, preoperative images can no longer be relied on because the intraoperative environment changes continuously due to manipulation by surgeon or organ movement. Therefore, the surgeon needs to rely on inner body real time images. An Inner Body GPS (IGPS) is also needed to safely and accurately help the surgeon guide the surgical tool to its desired surgery location. The IGPS requires pre-operative CT/MRI, real-time image from videoscope, and navigation sensor(s). The navigation sensors locate the position of the surgical tool, and the videoscope helps the surgeon maneuver around body organs along the path predetermined using preoperative CT/MRI images. Since the videoscope and navigation sensors are heterogeneous, they have different data rate, and provide measurement/information in their local coordinate frame using their local time clock. Spatial and temporal registrations of such sensors are needed as a prerequisite to the success of MIS. The spatial registration represents the spatial coordinates of all the sensors in an absolute coordinate frame while the temporal registration represents all the sensors data in a common time reference.

Hybrid spatial calibration uses fusion of spatial information from more than one sensor to assist the surgeon during MIS operation. While implementing two heterogeneous sensors, researchers leveraged fused information from intraoperative images (Laparoscopic Ultrasound (LUS)/Endoscope) and either preoperative images (CT/MRI) [3] or navigation system (Electromagnetic Tracking System (EMTS)/Optical Tracking System (OTS)) coordinates [4] - [6], [10]. The information gathered from two sensors is not enough for MIS. Preoperative images are the only reference imaging technique to visualize the complete patient body. Surgeon always needs to have a visualization of where he/she is heading inside the patient body along with the position and orientation of the endoscope. On the other hand, it is necessary to have a navigation system connected to intraoperative imaging system to guide the endoscope in CT/MRI coordinate reference frame.

From an information point of view, MIS requires at least three heterogeneous sensors: Two for imaging (pre-operative and intra-operative) and one for navigation. Fakhfakh et. al. proposed an automatic registration of pre- and intra-operative images with OTS embedded ultrasound probe, and preoperative CT scan [7]. The reconstructed 3D image from 2D ultrasound slices was registered with the preoperative CT using principle axes of inertia and the Iterative Closest Point robust (ICPr) algorithm. ICP suffers from being trapped in local minima unless a good initial guess is provided. The use of Hand-Eye calibration for rigid registration among robotic arm, tracking devices (EMTS/OTS), and imaging devices (Endoscope/Laparoscopic camera) was reported in [6], [8]. Reference [8] implemented network time protocol (NTP) for temporal data synchronization. In order to calculate the optimum spatial and temporal transformation, [9]-[11] integrated LUS, rigid oblique viewing endoscope, OTS, EMTS, and MRI using linear least square and Levenberg-Marquardt iterative algorithm. Since the whole distortion correction from the metallic objects in EMTS was based on OTS, the magnetic distortion correction mechanism may provide false correction vector when the line of sight (LOS) for OTS is blocked [11]. Furthermore, the system was modeled for static distortion [10], [11]. Hence, the correction vector would be redundant if the distortion in the vicinity changes during surgery. Intraoperative imaging with LUS suffers from shadowing, multiple reflections, low signal-to-noise ratio, and the requirement of expertise and training of surgeon [12]. For temporal calibration, it is assumed that the tracker with higher measurement rate has acquisition frequency multiple of lower one and the data is processed at the measurement speed of slower tracking device. Although, [6], [7], [13] used multiple asynchronous sensors, synchronization of data from such sensors has been overlooked. This inhibits the correct and effective use of asynchronous sensors in high accuracy demanding MIS system in real-time.

In addition to MIS, the use of heterogeneous sensors is desirable in different areas including robotics and automation where additional data complement and enhance the available information and assist to make more informed decisions. Such sensor systems may involve different imaging and navigation sensors such as cameras, Inertial Measurement Units (IMUs), LIDAR for robotic navigation, and object detection and tracking [14] - [16]. However heterogeneous sensors may use different data acquisition systems and may have a different data acquisition rate and use a dedicated local processor clock when reporting the measurements. A prerequisite for correct sensor fusion is the temporal alignment of different sensor data such that the data provided by the different asynchronous sensors are recorded using the same time reference.

The main contribution of this paper is providing a real-time spatial and temporal registrations of heterogeneous asynchronous sensors in an absolute spatial coordinate frame and a common time reference. The process will be called spatiotemporal registration. Performing temporal sensor registration is crucial given the dynamic changes of the surgery path to account for body organs movements in order to navigate safely toward the surgery location. In prior work, the authors performed offline spatial calibration between Laser Range Scanner (LRS), EMTS, and Camera with promising accuracy [17], [18]. LRS was used to emulate CT/MRI images. LRS-EMTS calibration was performed using Horn's absolute orientation method [19], while the camera calibration was achieved using normalized Direct Linear Transform (DLT) algorithm [20]. These registrations are crucial for real time path planning.

This paper is organized as follows. Section II discusses the proposed real-time spatial and temporal heterogeneous and asynchronous sensors registration. Section III discusses the accuracy obtained using experiments conducted in the lab. Section IV contains conclusions and discusses future work.

II. PROPOSED SPATIAL AND TEMPORAL CALIBRATION

The preoperative CT/MRI provides 3D images of the patient to determine the inner body 3D location where the surgery is to take place (desired destination). The preoperative images can also be used for 3D path planning to reach the desired destination using the shortest path that has minimal number of obstacles such as bones or body organs. In this work, LRS [21] provides preoperative 3D scan , the videoscope provides real time high quality images, and the EMTS provides pose (position and orientation)of the surgical tool/videoscope inside the human body as shown in Figure 1. The navigation sensor used was NDI Type-2 6DOF sensor for Aurora EMTS with a measurement frequency of 40Hz [22]. According to NDI, the accuracy is 0.8 mm for position and 0.7degree for orientation [22]. The EMTS has been thoroughly tested and it has been found that 300 series stainless steel, aluminum, and titanium does not affect EMTS performance [12]. The third sensor was the Go 5000C series color camera from JAI Corporation [23], with 5 amegapixel resolution and an image acquisition rate of 61.2 frames/sec.

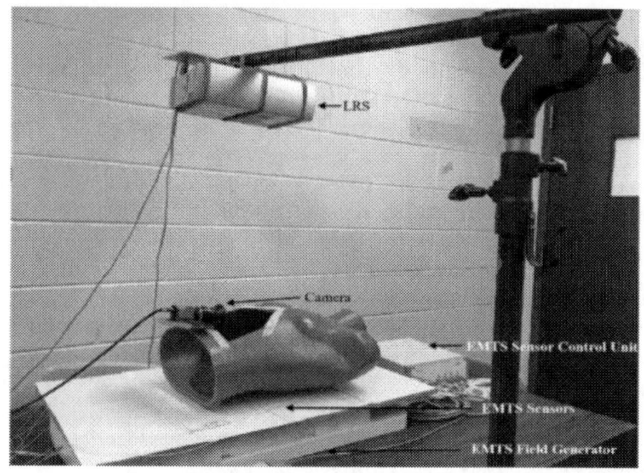

Figure 1. Heterogeneous Asynchronous Sensors Used for Inner Body Navigation

In this paper, the LRS coordinate frame was selected as the absolute coordinate reference frame so that spatial information from camera and EMTS can be transformed and analyzed in LRS coordinate system, as shown in Figure 1. The location of the videoscope in EMTS coordinate reference frame can be determined using the camera registration procedure [20]. The real time position of the camera, planned path, and the desired inner body destination location are represented in the LRS coordinate reference frame. The surgical tool can be moved to the destination correctly using real time feedback from the EMTS attached to the camera. It is worth noting that in clinical applications, a much smaller camera will be used instead of the Go 5000C. However, the proposed sensors registration technique can be applied to accommodate any camera. All information that is needed is their intrinsic and extrinsic parameters. While conducting the experiments it is assumed that the EMTS pose measurement was not interfered with by metallic objects in the room, camera system, or mount for the LRS system. It is also assumed that the relative position of the camera, EMTS, and LRS system was not changed during offline calibration.

A. Online Spatial Registration

The fusion of real-time information from LRS, Camera, and EMTS should be able to guide the surgeon from the initial insertion point to the destination point inside human body. This was achieved by using the online sensors registration. In the spatial registration, all the spatial sensors data was represented in the LRS (CT/MRI) coordinate reference frame. In the temporal registration, incoming data was timestamped based on arrival time to the surgical PC processor. We developed a virtual camera model which replicates the position and orientation of the real camera in LRS coordinate frame and provides real-time image inside human body.

Online spatial calibration accommodates the changes in registration parameters once the sensors start to move. Changing transformations between EMTS and camera coordinate frame can be computed by attaching an Electromagnetic Sensor (EMS) to the videoscope body, and calculation of fixed offset transformation parameters between EMS measurement and the camera center obtained from the camera calibration, as shown in Figure 2. Offline camera calibration provides the position and orientation of the camera in EMTS coordinate frame. The offset transformation between the computed camera center in EMTS coordinate frame and the EMTS sensor can be computed as

$$T_{offset} = T_{calibration} * \left({}^{CAM}T_{EMTS} \right)^{-1} \quad (1)$$

where, T_{offset} is the Offset transformation between EMS and camera frames, $T_{calibration}$ is the Position and Orientation of Camera obtained from Camera Calibration[27] and ${}^{CAM}T_{EMTS}$ is the transformation from the EMTS coordinate frame to the camera coordinate frame. The transformation between LRS and camera coordinate frames uses the transformation form the EMTS to LRS frames and is given by

$${}^{LRS}T_{cam} = {}^{LRS}T_{EMTS} * T_{offset} \quad (2)$$

Where, ${}^{LRS}T_{cam}$ is the Transformation from camera to LRS coordinate frame; ${}^{LRS}T_{EMTS}$ is the Transformation from EMTS to LRS coordinate frame; T_{offset} is the Offset transformation of the camera center to the EMTS coordinate frame.

The guidance system consists of two separate display units inside single screen, as shown in Figure3. First display unit consists of plot of 3D LRS data, preoperative planned path, current path followed by real-time camera, and position and orientation of camera. Second unit displays real-time video feed from camera. First, 3D LRS data is displayed along with the preoperative planned path, start and destination point, as shown in Figure 3. Before real time processing, the command asks user to put camera at the specified start location of the preplanned path. The user is

Figure. 2: Offset between EMS and Camera Center

guided in real-time to follow the preplanned path without exceeding the user specified threshold deviation from the planned path. If an obstacle appears in real-time in the preplanned path, the surgeon can use their intelligence to avoid the real-time obstacle. During avoidance of obstacle, it is evident that the path followed by real-time camera may deviate from preplanned path. In such case, the system is

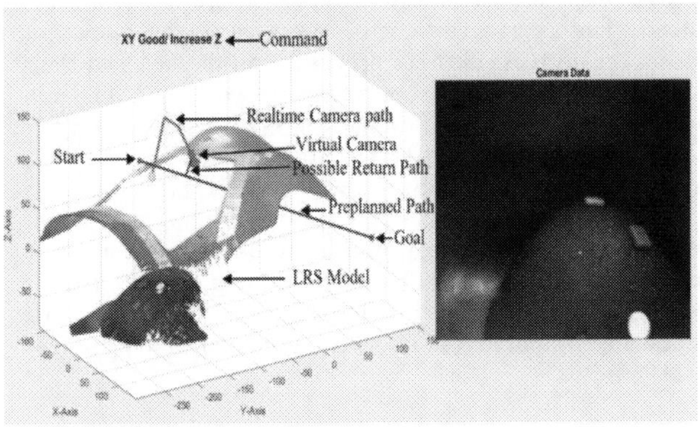

Figure 3: Developed real-time guidance system.

designed in such a way that the processor searches for a shortest path for the camera to return to the original path. The point within the preoperative planned path having minimum distance from current camera location is called immediate goal for camera. The command system guides the user to take the necessary steps to reach the immediate goal. This provides infrastructure that can be used by surgeon such that the path can be automatically followed in real-time.

One of the major challenges in implementation of minimally invasive surgery is to reach to the destination inside human body by minimally damaging the organs along the path. Previously we have designed an intrinsically actuated flexible robotic arm to be used for MIS [24]. To use flexible manipulators, one requires accompanying shortest path with minimum obstacle to reach to the destination. In addition to avoiding the obstacle, the planned path should be enough to accommodate the width of the manipulator. In this work, assuming the availability of preoperative planned path, we developed a semi-automatic system to guide surgeon in real time to reach to the destination inside human body. The preplanned path and the possible return path are just the straight line connecting start and goal position in LRS coordinate frame. Rapidly Exploring Random Tree(RRT), RRT*, Probabilistic Roadmap(PRM), A* [25] are widely used sampling based path planning algorithms that can be implemented for path planning

B. *Temporal Calibration*

Temporal Calibration is necessary for time synchronization of real-time data obtained from the camera and EMTS. EMTS and camera use different clock and report measurements at a rate of 40Hz and 61.2 Hz, respectively. A prerequisite for time synchronization of measurement is to timestamp the measurement with respect to the clock of a common processor clock. In this application, the common processor clock is the clock of the computer, called here surgical PC, that is used by the surgeon to display the real time camera images and the location of the surgical tool(s) as shown in Figure 4. The PC processor is responsible for controlling, communicating, acquiring, and time stamping of the data from the camera and EMTS in real-time. Hence, instead of processing data with reference to the clocks of sensors themselves, they are processed on the basis of their arrival in the host PC. As soon as data arrive from EMTS and camera, they are timestamped and placed in a circular buffer. With the implementation of the circular buffer, the oldest measurement from the devices are overwritten by the most recently arrived data. This effectively solves the problem of memory leakage during real-time operation. The timestamped data are polled every 30 milliseconds. Polling measurement at every 30 milliseconds provide enough time for data processing without loss of information, as shown in Figure 4.

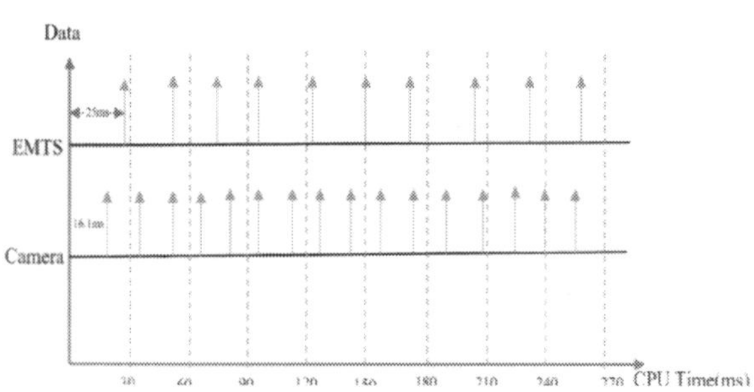

Figure 4: Polling of Timestamped Data in PC

III. PERFORMANCE EVALUATION

The performance of the proposed sensor fusion system was evaluated in two-fold. First, the information from the 3D LRS was transformed into the EMTS coordinate frame followed by transformation to the camera coordinate frame. The transformation error was computed as an absolute difference between the computed coordinates obtained from the transformation and those extracted from the processed camera images. The sensors calibration and the accuracy evaluation were performed in an environment free of ferromagnetic material near the EM field generator. Tracking in the electromagnetic field generator is unaffected by the medical-grade stainless steel (300 series), titanium, and aluminum [12], [22]. The tabletop field generator also minimizes distortions produced from the patient table or materials located below it [22]. The artificial liver was placed inside the mannequin and attached with different colored objects on the top surface, as shown in Figure 5. The colored objects representing the liver tumor were used for accuracy evaluation.

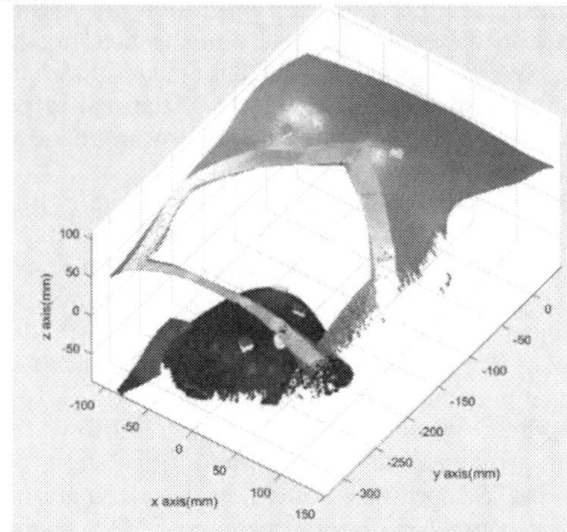

Figure 5: Setup for accuracy evaluation for spatio-temporal calibration system

Given the start and goal position in LRS coordinate frame, the videoscope was navigated to reach to the destination points, Section II. For accuracy evaluation purpose, the destination points are the colored objects attached to the liver. Once the camera reaches to the vicinity of the accuracy evaluation points. The colored objects were extracted, and their centroids were calculated in LRS (see Figure 6), EMTS, and Camera coordinate frames.

The extracted centroids were first transformed from LRS to EMTS coordinate frame. Once the set of points were transformed from LRS to EMTS they were projected to distortion corrected camera image.

$$P_{cam} = {}^{cam}T_{LRS} P_{LRS}$$

$${}^{cam}T_{LRS} = \left({}^{LRS}T_{cam}\right)^{-1} = \left({}^{LRS}T_{EMTS} * T_{offset} * X_{EMS}\right)^{-1} \quad (3)$$

where, P_{LRS} is the accuracy evaluation point in LRS coordinate frame and P_{cam} is the projected accuracy evaluation point in camera coordinate frame.

As the transformation of the centroids were carried out in two phases, accuracy was also evaluated for LRS to EMTS coordinate transformation, and EMTS to camera transformation. The experiment was performed at least 12inch from the top surface of EMTS field generator to provide the room for placement of patient table.

TABLE I. ERROR ANALYSIS OF ONLINE CALIBRATION FROM LRS TO EMTS TO 2D IMAGE

	LRS to EMTS			EMTS to Image	
	X	*Y*	*Z*	*X*	*Y*
Mean(mm)	1.6315	3.0157	1.9214	0.4154	0.1845

S. D.(mm)	0.8765	1.5239	0.8912	0.1435	0.0656
Range(mm)	4.9123	5.1455	4.3190	0.2675	0.1265

Table I summarizes the absolute positional error for the coordinate transformation from LRS to EMTS as well as EMTS to camera coordinate frame. Similar to our observation in offline calibration, the average error for LRS to EMTS coordinate transformation is minimum along the X, and Z axis while the Y coordinate is most affected by error with maximum standard deviation and range. There are two possible reasons for the error: the varying ability of LRS to correctly scan and replicate the scanned object at varying distance, and the error during data collection because of the non-planar surface of the liver. Previously it has been found that the performance accuracy of LRS significantly improved while scanning planner objects compared to non-planar objects [17]. The experimental error could further be minimized by taking multi-view scans from the LRS and fusing the 3D scans data together. The transformation parameters between EMTS and LRS is constant during the online and offline calibration. The evaluated accuracy for online calibration closely resembles to the offline calibration accuracy of 1.35±0.93mm, 2.60±1.52mm, 1.1325±0.9285mm along x, y, and z axis respectively.

The transformation from EMTS to camera is the overall error associated with the hybrid tracking system. Although the error is in millimeter range, the is mainly due to the propagation of error associated with LRS to EMTS transformation, offset calculation, and EMTS to camera transformation. Compared to the offline calibration with the average error of 0.1081mm and 0.0872mm along x and y axis, the calibration error increased noticeably along both x and y direction. This might be because of the additional error introduced during offset calculation, and the motion of the camera-EMTS system.

IV. Conclusion

In this work, spatio-temporal registration of three heterogeneous sensors to assist minimally invasive surgical applications was proposed. Laboratory testing showed that data fusion from three heterogenous and asynchronous sensors provide enough information to help the surgeon navigate to the surgery location by providing real-time surgical tool position and displaying quality images of the inner body. Accuracy evaluation using a mannequin and an artificial liver sample points localization showed promising accuracy for designing an inner body navigation system (IBNS). A low-cost camera was used to prove the concept. The spatial and temporal registration can be extended to any arbitrarily small size camera as long as the camera intrinsic and extrinsic parameters are provided.

Currently, the real-time display consists of two display units: one for 3D scan and another for 2D images. Future efforts include the development of an augmented reality system to display an augmented view of human organs on the top of 3D scan for real-time simplified navigation. Furthermore, the outcome of this research will be used as a foundation to develop a comprehensive inner-body navigation advisory system.

References

[1] T. Peters and K. Cleary, *Image-guided interventions: technology and applications*. Springer Science & Business Media, 2008.

[2] G. Aston, "Surgical robots: worth the investment?" *Hospitals & Health Networks*, vol. 86, no. 4, pp. 38–40, 2012.

[3] B. Marami, S. Sirouspour, A. Fenster, and D. W. Capson, "Dynamic tracking of a deformable tissue based on 3d-2d mr-us image registration," in *Medical Imaging 2014: Image-Guided Procedures, Robotic Interventions, and Modeling*, vol. 9036. SPIE, 2014, pp. 214–220.

[4] D. Sindram, I. H. McKillop, J. B. Martinie, and D. A. Iannitti, "Novel 3d laparoscopic magnetic ultrasound image guidance for lesion targeting," *Hpb*, vol. 12, no. 10, pp. 709–716, 2010.

[5] C. S. Ng, S. C. Yu, R. W. Lau, and A. P. Yim, "Hybrid dynact-guided electromagnetic navigational bronchoscopic biopsy," *European Journal of Cardio-Thoracic Surgery*, vol. 49, no. suppl 1, pp. i87–i88, 2016.

[6] C. Wengert, L. Bossard, A. Haberling, C. Baur, G. Székely, and P. C. Cattin, "Endoscopic navigation for minimally invasive suturing," in *International Conference on Medical Image Computing and ComputerAssisted Intervention.* Springer, 2007, pp. 620–627.

[7] H. E. Fakhfakh, G. Llort-Pujol, C. Hamitouche, and E. Stindel, "Automatic registration of pre-and intraoperative data for long bones in minimally invasive surgery," in *2014 36th Annual International Conference of the IEEE Engineering in Medicine and Biology Society*. IEEE, 2014, pp. 5575–5578.

[8] M. Feuerstein, T. Reichl, J. Vogel, J. Traub, and N. Navab, "Magnetooptical tracking of flexible laparoscopic ultrasound: model-based online detection and correction of magnetic tracking errors," *IEEE Transactions on Medical Imaging*, vol. 28, no. 6, pp. 951–967, 2009.

[9] M. Nakamoto, K. Nakada, Y. Sato, K. Konishi, M. Hashizume, and S. Tamura, "Intraoperative magnetic tracker calibration using a magnetooptic hybrid tracker for 3-d ultrasound-based navigation in laparoscopic surgery," *IEEE transactions on medical imaging*, vol. 27, no. 2, pp. 255–270, 2008.

[10] K. Konishi *et al.*, "A real-time navigation system for laparoscopic surgery based on three-dimensional ultrasound using magneto-optic hybrid tracking configuration," *International Journal of Computer Assisted Radiology and Surgery*, vol. 2, no. 1, pp. 1–10, 2007.

[11] K. Nakada, M. Nakamoto, Y. Sato, K. Konishi, M. Hashizume, and S. Tamura, "A rapid method for magnetic tracker calibration using a magneto-optic hybrid tracker," in *International Conference on Medical Image Computing and Computer-Assisted Intervention*. Springer, 2003, pp. 285–293.

[12] W. Birkfellner, J. Hummel, E. Wilson, and K. Cleary, "Tracking devices," in *Image-guided interventions*. Springer, 2008, pp. 23–44.

[13] R. S. J. Estépar, N. Stylopoulos, R. Ellis, E. Samset, C.-F. Westin, C. Thompson, and K. Vosburgh, "Towards scarless surgery: an endoscopic ultrasound navigation system for transgastric access procedures," *Computer aided surgery*, vol. 12, no. 6, pp. 311–324, 2007.

[14] E. Mair, M. Fleps, M. Suppa, and D. Burschka, "Spatio-temporal initialization for imu to camera registration," in *2011 IEEE International Conference on Robotics and Biomimetics*. IEEE, 2011, pp. 557–564.

[15] M. Liang, B. Yang, S. Wang, and R. Urtasun, "Deep continuous fusion for multi-sensor 3d object detection," in

Proceedings of the European conference on computer vision (ECCV), 2018, pp. 641–656.

[16] J. Marr and J. Kelly, "Unified spatiotemporal calibration of monocular cameras and planar lidars," in *International Symposium on Experimental Robotics*. Springer, 2018, pp. 781–790.

[17] D. E. Ruehling, "Development and testing of a hybrid medical tracking system for surgical use," Ph.D. dissertation, Tennessee Technological University, 2015.

[18] U. Bhattarai and A. T. Alouani, "Hybrid navigation information system for minimally invasive surgery: Offline sensors registration," in *Science and Information Conference*. Springer, 2019, pp. 205–219.

[19] B. K. Horn, "Closed-form solution of absolute orientation using unit quaternions," *Josa a*, vol. 4, no. 4, pp. 629–642, 1987.

[20] R. Hartley and A. Zisserman, Multiple View Geometry in Computer Vision. 2003.

[21] Next Engine Inc., "Next engine 3d laser scanner." Available at http:// http://www.nextengine.com/products/scanner/specs (2022/06/21).

[22] Northern Digital Inc., "Aurora,"Available at http:// https://www.ndigital.com/electromagnetic-tracking-technology/aurora/ (2022/06/21).

[23] Jai Inc., "Go series go-5000c-usb compact 5 mp area scan camera," Available at http:// https://www.jai.com/products/go-5000c-usb (2022/06/21).

[24] U. Bhattarai and A. T. Alouani, "Flexible semi-automatic arm design for minimally invasive surgery," in *2017 25th International Conference on Systems Engineering (ICSEng)*. IEEE, 2017, pp. 207–211.

[25] K. Karur, N. Sharma, C. Dharmatti, and J. E. Siegel, "A survey of path planning algorithms for mobile robots," *Vehicles*, vol. 3, no. 3, pp. 448– 468, 2021.

Electronic Surveillance and Security Applications of Magnetic Glass-coated Microwires

Valentina Zhukova, Mihail Ipatov, Paula Corte-León, Alvaro Gonzalez, Alfonso García- Gómez
Dept Materials Physics, Dept. Applied Physics and EHU Quantum Center, Univ. Basque Country, UPV/EHU, 20018 San Sebastian, Spain
e-mails: valentina.zhukova@ehu.es; mihail.ipatov@ehu.es; paula.corte@ehu.eus; alvaro.gonzalezv@ehu.eus; alfonso.garciag@ehu.eus

Arcady Zhukov
Dept Materials Physics, Dept. Applied Physics and EHU Quantum Center, Univ. Basque Country, UPV/EHU, 20018 San Sebastian and Ikerbasque, Bulbao, Spain
e-mail: arkadi.joukov@ehu.es

Abstract—**Applications in security and electronic surveillance require a combination of excellent magnetic softness with good mechanical and anti-corrosive properties and low dimensionality. We overviewed the feasibility of using glass-coated microwires for electronic article surveillance and security applications, as well as different routes of tuning the magnetic properties of individual microwires or microwires arrays making them quite attractive for electronic article surveillance and security applications. We provide the routes for tuning the hysteresis loops non-linearity by the magnetostatic interaction between the microwires in the arrays of different types of amorphous microwires. The presence of neighboring microwire (either Fe or Co-based) significantly affects the hysteresis loop of the whole microwires array. In a microwires array containing magnetically bistable microwires, we observed splitting of the initially rectangular hysteresis loop with a number of Barkhausen jumps correlated with the number of magnetically bistable microwires. Essentially, non-linear and irregular hysteresis loops have been observed in mixed arrays containing Fe and Co-rich microwires. The obtained non-linearity in hysteresis loops allowed to increase the harmonics and tune their magnetic field dependencies. On the other hand, several routes allowing to tune the switching field by either post-processing or modifying the magnetoelastic anisotropy have been reviewed. The observed unique combination of magnetic properties together with thin dimensions and excellent mechanical and anti-corrosive properties provide excellent perspectives for the use of glass-coated microwires for security and electronic surveillance applications.**

Keywords- magnetic microwires; magnetic softness; magnetic bistability, magnetic tags.

I. INTRODUCTION

Soft magnetic materials are highly demanded by several industries, including (but not limited to) microelectronics, electrical engineering, car, aerospace and aircraft industries, medicine, magnetic refrigerators, home entertainment, energy harvesting and conversion, informatics, magnetic recording or security and electronic surveillance [1]-[2]. In most cases, like the case of security and electronic surveillance, in addition to excellent magnetic softness, a combination of mechanical and anti-corrosive properties and low dimensionality is required [3].

Almost all department stores, supermarkets, airports, libraries, museums, etc. are provided with different types of security and anti-theft systems. The principle of Electronic Article Surveillance (EAS) systems operation is well established: articles are provided with tags that respond to electromagnetic fields generated by the gates at the store/supermarket/library exits [3]. The response is picked up by the antenna installed on the gate, switching on the alarm. It is estimated that hundreds of thousands of such EAS systems have been installed and millions of tags are produced daily. Considering the great number of tags, they must be small, robust enough and inexpensive. Additionally, the magnetic materials employed in tags must be magnetically soft enough. The magnetic softness of crystalline soft magnetic materials (Permalloy, Fe-Si) is affected by processing. Therefore, amorphous soft magnetic materials, prepared by rapid melt quenching are considered as among the most suitable materials for tags containing soft magnetic materials [3][4].

Indeed, as a rule, amorphous materials present excellent magnetic softness together with superior mechanical properties [3]-[6]. Abrupt deterioration of the mechanical properties (such as tensile yield) upon the devitrification of amorphous precursor is reported [6]. Additionally, the fabrication process of amorphous materials involving rapid melt quenching is fast and inexpensive [1]-[7]. Accordingly, amorphous soft magnetic materials are useful for the design of robust magnetic devices and magnetoelastic sensors [8]-[12].

As discussed elsewhere, soft magnetic materials with squared hysteresis loops and relatively low coercivities are the preferred candidates for the EAS systems using magnetic tags [3]. The rectangular hysteresis loops can be easily implemented in different families of amorphous magnetic wires [4]. Therefore, considerable attention has been paid to applications of amorphous wires for magnetic tags for different kinds of EAS systems [4].

The aforementioned squared hysteresis loops of magnetic wires are linked to the peculiar remagnetization process of magnetic wires running through a single and large Barkhausen jump [4] [14].

Glass-coated magnetic microwires prepared by the so-called Taylor-Ulitovsky technique present the widest metallic nucleus diameters range (from 200 nm up to 100 μm) [4][15][16]. In this way, the Taylor-Ulitovsky method is the unique technique allowing fabrication of nanowires by rapid melt quenching [15]. On the other hand, the preparation of amorphous magnetic wires with diameter of about 100 μm coated by glass has recently been reported [16]. The presence of a flexible, thin, bio-compatible and insulating glass coating allows to enhance the corrosive resistance and, therefore, makes these microwires suitable for novel applications including biomedicine, electronic article surveillance, non-destructive monitoring external stimuli (stresses, temperature) in smart composites or construction health monitoring through the microwire inclusions [17][18].

Accordingly, considering dimensionality and combination of physical properties (magnetic, mechanical, corrosive), amorphous soft magnetic microwires are potentially suitable materials for electronic article surveillance and security applications [4][19][20]. There are several original papers dealing with rather different (multi-bit or single-bit) security and EAS applications of magnetic microwires [19][20]. In this paper, we will provide an overview of the trends related to EAS and security applications of glass-coated magnetic microwires.

This paper is organized as follows. In Section 2, the experimental methods as well as the microwires characteristics analyzed in this paper are provided. Section 3 deals with results on the feasibility of using magnetic microwires for magnetic tags followed by an overview of tuning of hysteresis loop non-linearity by the magnetostatic interaction between microwires.

II. EXPERIMENTAL SYSTEM DETAILS

Generally, we analyzed two different types of magnetic amorphous microwires: i) amorphous microwires with high positive magnetostriction coefficients, λs, (Fe-Si-B-C, Fe-Ni-Si-B-C or Fe-Ni-Si-B) and ii) amorphous microwires with vanishing λs (Co-Fe-Ni-B-Si-Mo, Co-Fe-Ni-B-Si-Mo, Co-Fe-B-Si-Cr-Ni or Co-Fe-B-Si-C). We studied microwires with metallic nucleus diameters, *d*, ranging from 10 up to 100 μm prepared using the Taylor-Ulitovsky method described elsewhere [4][21]. The Taylor-Ulitovsky method allows preparation of thinnest metallic wires (with typical diameters of the order of 0.1 to 100 μm) covered by an insulating glass coating [5][21].

The amorphous structure of all the microwires has been proved by the X-ray Diffraction (XRD) method. Typically, the crystallization of amorphous microwires was observed at Tann $\geqslant$ 500 ° C [4].

The induction method has previously been used for the hysteresis loops measurements. The details of the experimental set-up are described elsewhere [22]. The hysteresis loops were represented as the magnetic field, H, dependence of the normalized magnetization, M/M_0, being M - the magnetic moment at a given magnetic field, and M_0 the magnetic moment at the maximum magnetic field amplitude Hm. Such hysteresis loops are useful for comparison of the samples with different chemical compositions (and, hence, different saturation magnetization).

In several cases, the hysteresis loops were measured with a conventional Super-conducting Quantum Interference Device (SQUID).

III. EXPERIMENTAL RESULTS AND DISCUSSION

Magnetic tags applications require a non-linear hysteresis loop that contains the characteristic distribution of harmonic frequencies. It is believed that the steeper the magnetization reversal, the higher the harmonic content of the signal. Accordingly, perfectly rectangular hysteresis loops with low coercivity observed in Fe-rich microwires (Figure 1) are attractive for use as magnetic tags.

On the other hand, the non-linearity of the hysteresis loop of the magnetic microwires can be further improved using the magnetostatic interaction of microwires. Below, we will present several experimental results on magnetic response of two kinds of individual microwires ($Co_{67}Fe_{3.9}Ni_{1.5}B_{11.5}Si_{14.5}M_{0.6}$ and $Fe_{74}B_{13}Si_{11}C_2$) as well as the arrays containing either microwires of the same type or arrays containing two different kinds of microwires.

The hysteresis loops of such microwires are rather different: $Fe_{74}B_{13}Si_{11}C_2$ microwire with high and positive magnetostriction coefficient, λ s, exhibits perfectly rectangular hysteresis loops with Hc $\approx$ 100 A/m (Figure 1a), while and inclined hysteresis loop with quite low Hc (Hc $\approx$ 5 A/m) is observed in $Co_{67}Fe_{3.9}Ni_{1.5}B_{11.5}Si_{14.5}M_{0.6}$ microwire (see Figure 2b).

The hysteresis loop of an array containing two $Fe_{74}B_{13}Si_{11}C_2$ microwires is rather different from that of a single $Fe_{74}B_{13}Si_{11}C_2$ microwire. Two Barkhausen jumps can be observed at magnetic field amplitude, H_0>80 A/m (see Figure 3a). Such peculiar hysteresis loop shape has been explained considering the magnetostatic interaction in the two-microwire array [4]. Such magnetostatic interaction is a consequence of stray fields created by magnetically bistable microwires: the superposition of external and stray fields causes magnetization reversal in one of the samples, when the external field is below the switching field of a single microwire. A single rectangular hysteresis loop (similar to the case of single microwire shown in Figure 1) is observed for 60 A/m <H_0 < 80 A/m (see Figure 3b).

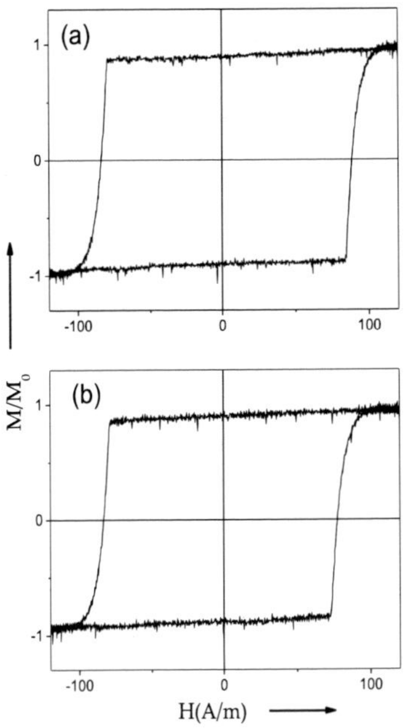

Figure 1. Hysteresis loops of as- prepared (a), and annealed at T_{ann}= 400 °C for 180 min (b) $Fe_{75}B_9Si_{12}C_4$ microwires.

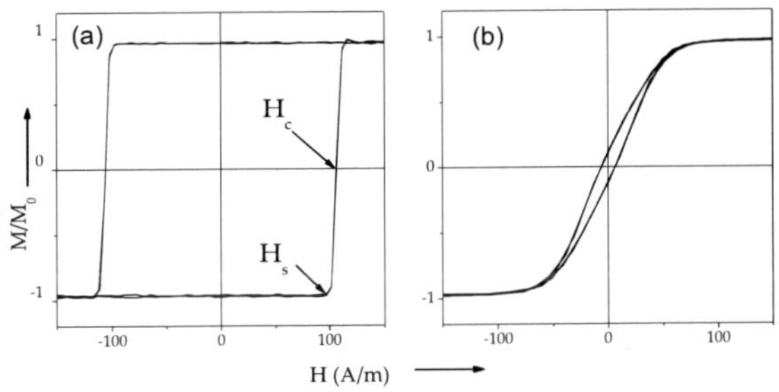

Figure 2. Hysteresis loops of $Fe_{75}B_9Si_{12}C_4$ microwires with positive (a) and $Co_{67}Fe_{3.9}Ni_{1.5}B_{11.5}Si_{14.5}M_{0.6}$ with vanishing (b) magnetostriction coefficients.

Increasing the magnetic field amplitude (approximately at H0 > 250 A/m), this splitting of the hysteresis loop disappears (Figure 3b). Such dependence of the hysteresis loop of two microwires array can be understood from the counterbalance between the dH/dt and the switching time determined by the velocity of the DW propagation along the whole wire [4].

As discussed elsewhere [4], coercivity, H_c, is also affected by the frequency, *f*. Accordingly, Hc, as well as overall hysteresis loops of two microwires array, are affected by f in a similar way as by H_0 (see Figure 3b). For a two microwires array, two-steps hysteresis loops are observed for *f*< 150 Hz. At *f* > 150 Hz, the hysteresis loop splitting disappears, and at 150 < *f* <1000 Hz, a single smooth magnetization jump is observed.

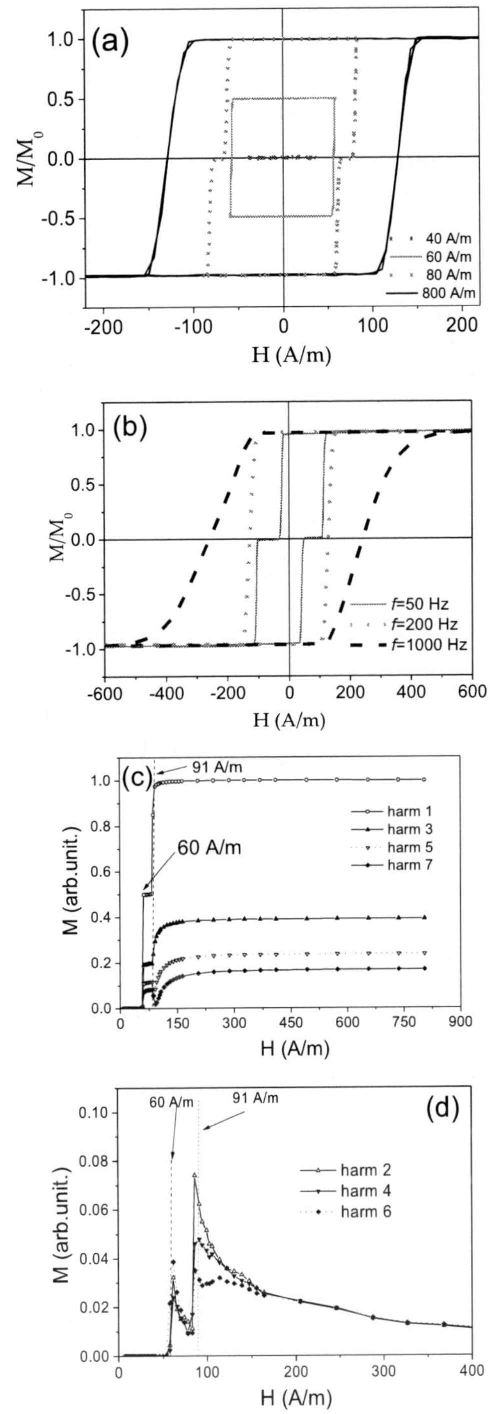

Figure 3. Hysteresis loops measured at different magnetic field amplitudes H_0 (a) and at different magnetic field frequencies *f* (b) for as array with two $Fe_{75}B_9Si_{12}C_4$ microwires, dependences of odd harmonics (c) and even harmonics (d) on magnetic field amplitude in linear array of two $Fe_{74}B_{13}Si_{11}C_2$ microwires.

Accordingly, the odd and even harmonics of the signal of two Fe-rich microwires array are affected by H_0 and f (see Figure 3c,d).

A sharp increase in the harmonics amplitudes is observed when H_0 exceeds Hc (see Figures 3c,d). The even harmonics amplitudes are significantly inferior to the odd harmonics amplitudes. The field dependences of odd harmonics have a "plateau" between 60 and 90 A/m, which reflects the hysteresis loops splitting (see Figure 3a).

Another example of tuning the non-linearity of hysteresis loops and harmonics is the magnetostatic interaction of microwires with different character of hysteresis loops. Rather non-linear hysteresis loops can be obtained in an array consisting of one $Co_{67}Fe_{3.9}Ni_{1.5}B_{11.5}Si_{14.5}M_{0.6}$ and one $Fe_{74}B_{13}Si_{11}C_2$ microwires (see Figure 4a). In such array, at $H_0 < 90$ A/m (which corresponds to Hc of $Fe_{74}B_{13}Si_{11}C_2$ microwire) the hysteresis loops character is typical of those for a single $Co_{67}Fe_{3.9}Ni_{1.5}B_{11.5}Si_{14.5}M_{0.6}$ microwire. Essentially, non-linear hysteresis loops have been observed at $H_0 > 110$ A/m (Figure 4a). Such peculiar hysteresis loops can be interpreted as the superposition of two hysteresis loops: one from magnetically bistable $Fe_{74}B_{13}Si_{11}C_2$ microwire (shown in Figure 2a) and the other one from $Co_{67}Fe_{3.9}Ni_{1.5}B_{11.5}Si_{14.5}M_{0.6}$ microwire with linear hysteresis loop (shown in Figure 2b).

The peculiar hysteresis loop character at $H_0 \leqslant 120$ A/m can be explained by the partial magnetization reversal of the magnetically bistable wire under the influence of the stray field from the Co-based wire. The stray field is affected by the sample demagnetizing factor and the sample magnetization [23] [24]. In the case of Co-rich microwire the magnetization and hence, the stray field are affected by the applied magnetic field (as can be appreciated from the hysteresis loops shown in Figure 2b). In contrast, the magnetization of Fe-rich sample change by abrupt jump and below and above Hc is almost independent of the magnetic field (see Figure 2a).

Accordingly, such microwire array consisting of two microwires (Fe-rich and Co-rich) with different hysteresis loops presents odd and even harmonics quite different from the case of the array with two Fe-rich microwires (see Figures 4 b,c). A single sharp jump of odd and even harmonics is observed at $H_0 \approx$ Hc. There is also a change in the odd and even harmonics in the weak (H_0<Hc) field region (see Figures 4 b, c).

Thus, the use of arrays consisting of magnetic microwires allows us to create a complex and unique spectrum of magnetic harmonics in magnetic microwires.

Essentially, non-linear and irregular hysteresis loops have been observed in mixed arrays containing Fe and Co-rich microwires. The observed non-linear hysteresis loops allowed to increase the harmonics and to tune their magnetic field dependencies.

The aforementioned examples provide the routes for optimization of the response of magnetic microwires by

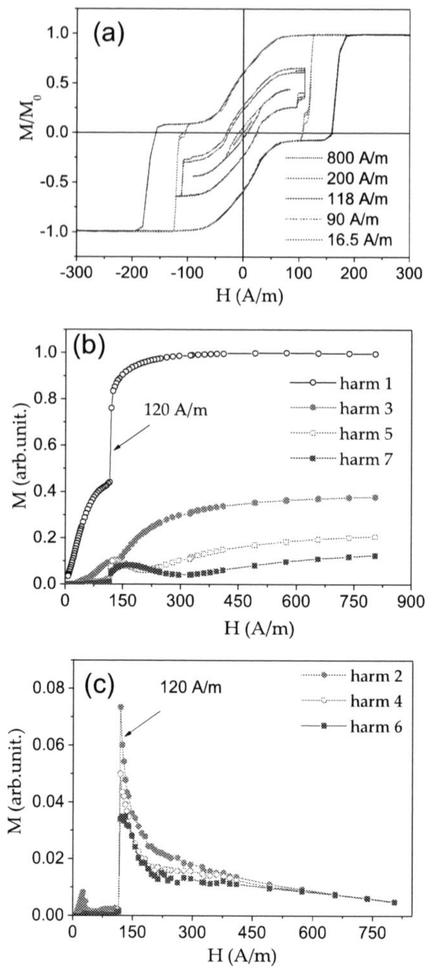

Figure 4. (a) Hysteresis loops of the $Fe_{74}B_{13}Si_{11}C_2$ + $Co_{67}Fe_{3.9}Ni_{1.5}B_{11.5}Si_{14.5}M_{0.6}$ array; (b) dependences of odd harmonics on magnetic field amplitude and (**c**) dependences of even harmonics on magnetic field amplitude. Reprinted with permission from ref. (4).

tuning the non-linearity of the hysteresis loops through the magnetostatic interaction. Such magnetic microwires can easily be incorporated into magnetic tags capable to respond to magnetic fields generated by the gates at the store/supermarket/library exits.

IV. CONCLUSIONS

In this paper, we showed that the presence of a neighbouring microwire (either Fe- or Co-based) significantly affects the hysteresis loop of the whole microwires array. In a microwires array containing magnetically bistable microwires, we observed splitting of the initially rectangular hysteresis loop with a number of Barkhausen jumps correlated with the number of magnetically bistable microwires. Essentially, non-linear and irregular hysteresis loops have been observed in mixed arrays containing Fe and Co-rich microwires. The observed non-linear hysteresis loops allowed to increase the harmonics and to tune their magnetic field dependencies.

The observed unique combination of magnetic properties, together with thin dimensions and excellent mechanical and anti-corrosive properties, provide excellent perspectives for the use of glass-coated microwires for security and electronic surveillance applications.

ACKNOWLEDGMENT

This work was supported by Spanish MCIU under PGC2018-099530-B-C31 (MCIU/AEI/FEDER, UE), by EU under "INFINITE" (Horizon Europe Framework Programme) project, by the Government of the Basque Country, under PUE_2021_1_0009 and Elkartek (MINERVA and ZE-KONP) projects, by the University of the Basque Country, under the scheme of "Ayuda a Grupos Consolidados" (Ref.: GIU18/192) and under the COLAB20/15 project and by the Diputación Foral de Gipuzkoa in the frame of Program "Red guipuzcoana de Ciencia, Tecnología e Innovación 2021" under 2021-CIEN-000007-01 project. The authors thank for technical and human support provided by SGIker of UPV/EHU (Medidas Magnéticas Gipuzkoa) and European funding (ERDF and ESF). We wish to thank the administration of the University of the Basque Country, which not only provides very limited funding, but even expropriates the resources received by the research group from private companies for the research activities of the group. Such interference helps keep us on our toes.

REFERENCES

[1] P. Corte-Leon et al., "Magnetic Microwires with Unique Combination of Magnetic Properties Suitable for Various Magnetic Sensor Applications", Sensors, vol. 20, p. 7203, 2020.

[2] M. Vázquez, J. M. García-Beneytez, J. M. García, J. P. Sinnecker, and A. Zhukov, "Giant magneto-impedance, vol. 88, pp. 6501-6505, 2000.

[3] G. Herzer, "Magnetic materials for electronic article surveillance", J. Magn. Magn. Mater., Vol. 254–255, pp. 598–602, 2003.

[4] V. Zhukova et al., "Electronic Surveillance and Security Applications of Magnetic Microwires", Chemosensors, Vol. 9, p.100, 2021.

[5] T. Goto, M. Nagano, and N. Wehara, "Mechanical properties of amorphous $Fe_{80}P_{16}C_3B_1$ filament produced by glass-coated melt spinning", Trans. JIM, vol. 18, pp. 759–764, 1977.

[6] V. Zhukova et al., "Correlation between magnetic and mechanical properties of devitrified glass-coated $Fe_{71.8}Cu_1Nb_{3.1}Si_{15}B_{9.1}$ microwires", J. Magn. Magn. Mater., vol. 249, pp. 79–84, 2002.

[7] A. Zhukov et al., Giant magnetoimpedance in rapidly quenched materials", J. Alloys Compound., vol. 814, pp. 152225, 2020.

[8] K. Mohri, T. Uchiyama, L. P. Shen, C. M. Cai, and L. V. Panina, "Amorphous wire and CMOS IC-based sensitive micro-magnetic sensors (MI sensor and SI sensor) for intelligent measurements and controls", J. Magn. Magn. Mater., vol. 249, pp. 351-356, 2001.

[9] T. Uchiyama, K. Mohri, and Sh. Nakayama, "Measurement of Spontaneous Oscillatory Magnetic Field of Guinea-Pig Smooth Muscle Preparation Using Pico-Tesla Resolution Amorphous Wire Magneto-Impedance Sensor", IEEE Trans. Magn., vol. 47, pp. 3070-3073, 2011.

[10] Y. Honkura, "Development of amorphous wire type MI sensors for automobile use", J. Magn. Magn. Mater., vol. 249, pp. 375-381, 2002.

[11] A. Zhukov et al., Magnetoelastic sensor of level of the liquid based on magnetoelastic properties of Co-rich microwires, Sens. Actuat. A Phys., vol. 81(1-3) pp.129-133, 2000.

[12] V. Zhukova et al., "Development of Magnetically Soft Amorphous Microwires for Technological Applications", Chemosensors, vol. 10, p. 26, 2022

[13] L. Ding, S. Saez, C. Dolabdjian, L. G. C. Melo, A. Yelon, and D. Ménard, "Development of a high sensitivity GiantMagneto-Impedance magnetometer: comparison with a commercial Flux-Gate", IEEE Sensors, vol. 9 (2), pp. 159-168, 2009.

[14] K. Mohri, F. B. Humphrey, K. Kawashima, K. Kimura, and M. Muzutani, "Large Barkhausen and Matteucci Effects in FeCoSiB, FeCrSiB, and FeNiSiB Amorphous Wires", IEEE Trans. Magn., vol. 26, pp. 1789–1781, 1990.

[15] H. Chiriac, S. Corodeanu, M. Lostun, G. Ababei, and T.-A. Óvári, "Rapidly solidified amorphous nanowires", J. Appl. Phys., vol. 107, 09A301, 2010.

[16] P. Corte-Leon et al., "The effect of annealing on magnetic properties of "Thick" microwires", J. Alloys Compound., vol. 831, p.150992, 2020.

[17] D. Kozejova et al., "Biomedical applications of glass-coated microwires", J. Magn. Magn. Mater., vol. 470, pp. 2-5, 2019.

[18] A. Talaat et al., "Ferromagnetic glass-coated microwires with good heating properties for magnetic hyperthermia", Sci. Reports, vol. 6 p. 39300, 2016.

[19] D. Makhnovskiy, N. Fry, and A. Zhukov, "On different tag reader architectures for bistable microwires", Sens. Actuat. A Phys., vol. 166, pp. 133-140, 2011.

[20] S. Gudoshnikov, et.al., "Evaluation of use of magnetically bistable microwires for magnetic labels", Phys. Stat. Sol. (a), vol. 208, No. 3, pp. 526–529, 2011.

[21] L. Gonzalez-Legarreta et al., "Optimization of magnetic properties and GMI effect of Thin Co-rich Microwires for GMI Microsensors", Sensors, vol. 20, p.1558, 2020.

[22] A. Zhukov et al., "Advanced functional magnetic microwires for technological applications", J. Phys. D: Appl. Phys., vol. 55, p. 253003, 2022.

[23] V. Rodionova et al., "Design of magnetic properties of arrays of magnetostatically coupled glass-covered magnetic microwires" Phys. Stat. Sol. (a), vol. 207(8), pp. 1954–1959, 2010.

[24] A. Chizhik, A. Zhukov, J. M. Blanco, R. Szymczak, and J. Gonzalez, "Interaction between Fe-rich ferromagnetic glass coated microwires." J. Magn. Magn. Mater., vol. 249/1-2, pp. 99-103, 2002.

Using Locally Weighted Regression to Estimate the Functional Size of Software: a Preliminary Study

Luigi Lavazza Angela Locoro
Dipartimento di Scienze Teoriche e Applicate
Università degli Studi dell'Insubria
Varese, Italy
email:{luigi.lavazza, angela.locoro}@uninsubria.it

Roberto Meli
DPO
Rome, Italy
email:roberto.meli@dpo.it

***Abstract*—In software engineering, measuring software functional size via the IFPUG (International Function Point Users Group) Function Point Analysis using the standard manual process can be a long and expensive activity. To solve this problem, several early estimation methods have been proposed and have become *de facto* standard processes. Among these, a prominent one is High-level Function Point Analysis. Recently, the Simple Function Point method has been released by IFPUG; although it is a proper measurement method, it has a great level of convertibility to traditional Function Points and may be used as an estimation method. Both High-level Function Point Analysis and Simple Function Point skip the difficult and time-consuming activities needed to weight data and transaction functions. This makes the process faster and cheaper, but yields approximate measures. The accuracy of the mentioned method has been evaluated, also via large-scale empirical studies, showing that the yielded approximate measures are sufficiently accurate for practical usage. In this paper, locally weighted regression is applied to the problem outlined above. This empirical study shows that estimates obtained via locally weighted regression are more accurate than those obtained via High-level Function Point Analysis, but are not substantially better than those yielded by alternative estimation methods using linear regression. The Simple Function Point method appears to yield measures that are well correlated with those obtained via standard measurement. In conclusion, locally weighted regression appears to be effective and accurate enough for estimating software functional size.**

Keywords–Function Point Analysis; Early Size Estimation; High-level FPA; Simple Function Points; LOcally Estimated Scatterplot Smoothing (LOESS)

I. Introduction

In the late seventies, Allan Albrecht introduced Function Points Analysis (FPA) at IBM [1], as a means to measure the functional size of software, with special reference to the "functional content" delivered by software providers. Albrecht aimed at defining a measure that might be correlated to the value of software from the perspective of a user, and could also be useful to assess the cost of developing software applications, based on functional user requirements.

FPA is a Functional Size Measurement Method (FSMM), compliant with the ISO/IEC 14143 standard, for measuring the size of a software application in the early stages of a project, generally before actual development starts. Accordingly, software size measures expressed in Function Points (FP) are often used for cost estimation.

The International Function Points User Group (IFPUG) is an association that keeps FPA up to date, publishes the official FP counting manual [2], and certifies professional FP counters. Unfortunately, in some conditions, performing the standard IFPUG measurement process may be too long and expensive, with respect to management needs, because standard FP measurement can be performed only when relatively complete and detailed requirements specifications are available, while functional measures could be needed much earlier for management purposes.

Many methods were invented and used to provide *estimates* of functional size measures, based on fewer or coarser-grained information than required by standard FPA. These methods are applied very early in software projects, even before deciding what process (e.g., agile or waterfall) will be used. One of these methods is the High-level FPA (HLFPA) method [3], which was developed by NESMA under the name of "NESMA estimated" method [4].

In 2010, a new FSMM called Simple Function Point (SiFP) was developed by Meli [5]. In 2019, IFPUG acquired the method and in 2021 the IFPUG branded Simple Function Point (SFP) method was delivered to the market [6].

HLFPA and SiFP have been evaluated by several studies, which found that the methods is usable in practice to approximate traditional FPA values, since they yield reasonably accurate estimates. However, the question if it is possible to get more accurate estimates from the basic information used by HLFPA remains open.

In this paper, we evaluate—via an empirical study—the usage of LOESS (LOcally Estimated Scatterplot Smoothing)—also known as LOWESS (LOcally WEighted Scatterplot Smoothing)—to build models that can be used for early estimation of functional size.

We also compare the standard IFPUG FPA measures, the estimates obtained via HLFPA and the estimates obtained via alternative methods (linear regression models and LOESS models) with the measures obtained via the Simple Function Point (SFP) method. SFP is a lightweight method that has also been adopted by IFPUG as an alternative to full-fledged FPA. SFP measurement requires even less time and effort than HLFPA, and it usually yields measures that are very well correlated with IFPUG standard measures.

The remainder of the paper is organized as follows. Section II provides an overview of functional size measurement methods, and other background information. Section III describes the empirical study and its results. In Section IV, we discuss the threats to the validity of the study. Section V reports about related work. Finally, in Section VI, we draw some conclusions and outline future work.

II. Background

Function Point Analysis was originally introduced by Albrecht to measure the size of data-processing systems from the point of view of end-users, with the goal of the estimating value of an application and the development effort [1]. The critical fortunes of this measure led to the creation of the IFPUG (International Function Points User Group), which maintains the method and certifies professional measurers.

The "amount of functionality" released to the user can be evaluated by taking into account 1) the data used by the application to provide the required functions, and 2) the transactions (i.e., operations that involve data crossing the boundaries of the application) through which the functionality is delivered to the user. Both data and transactions are counted on the basis of Functional User Requirements (FURs) specifications, and constitute the IFPUG Function Points measure.

FURs are modeled as a set of base functional components (BFCs), which are the measurable elements of FURs: each of the identified BFCs is measured, and the size of the application is obtained as the sum of the sizes of BFCs. IFPUG BFCs are: data functions (also known as logical files), which are classified into internal logical files (ILF) and external interface files (EIF); and elementary processes (EP)—also known as transaction functions—which are classified into external inputs (EI), external outputs (EO), and external inquiries (EQ), according to the activities carried out within the considered process and the primary intent.

The complexity of a data function (ILF or EIF) depends on the RETs (Record Element Types), which indicate how many types of variations (e.g., sub-classes, in object-oriented terms) exist per logical data file, and DETs (Data Element Types), which indicate how many types of elementary information (e.g., attributes, in object-oriented terms) are contained in the given logical data file.

The complexity of a transaction depends on the number of FTRs—i.e., the number of File Types Referenced while performing the required operation—and the number of DETs—i.e., the number of types of elementary data—that the considered transaction sends and receives across the boundaries of the application. Details concerning the determination of complexity can be found in the official documentation [2].

The core of FPA involves three main activities:

1) Identifying data and transaction functions.
2) Classifying data functions as ILF or EIF and transactions as EI, EO or EQ.
3) Determining the complexity of each data or transaction function.

The first two of these activities can be carried out even if the FURs have not yet been fully detailed. On the contrary, activity 3 requires that all details are available, so that FP measurers can determine the number of RET or FTR and DET involved in every function. Activity 3 is relatively time- and effort-consuming [7].

HLFPA does not require activity 3, thus allowing for size estimation when FURs are not fully detailed: it only requires that the complete sets of data and transaction functions are identified and classified.

The SFP method [6] does not require activities 2 and 3: it only requires that the complete sets of data and transaction functions are identified.

Both the HLFPA and SFP methods let measurers skip the most time- and effort-consuming activity, thus both are relatively fast and cheap. The SFP method does not even require classification, making size estimation even faster and less subjective (since different measurers can sometimes classify differently the same transaction, based on the subjective perception of the transaction's primary intent).

A. The High-level FPA method

NESMA defined two size estimation methods: the 'NESMA Indicative' and the 'NESMA Estimated' methods. IFPUG adopted these methods as early function point analysis methods, under the names of 'Indicative FPA' and 'High-level FPA,' respectively [3]. The Indicative FPA method proved definitely less accurate [8], [9]. Hence, in this paper, we consider only the High-level FPA method.

The High-level FPA method requires the identification and classification of all data and transaction functions, but does not require the assessment of the complexity of functions: ILF and EIF are assumed to be of low complexity, while EI, EQ and EO are assumed to be of average complexity. Hence, estimated size is computed as follows:

$$EstSize_{UFP} = 7\ \#ILF + 5\ \#EIF + 4\ \#EI + 5\ \#EO + 4\ \#EQ$$

where *#ILF* is the number of data functions of type ILF, *#EI* is the number of transaction functions of type EI, etc.

B. The Simple Function Point Method

The Simple Function Point measurement method [5] [6] has been specifically designed to be agile, fast, lightweight, easy to use, and with minimal impact on software development processes. It is easy to learn and provides reliable, repeatable, and objective results. Like IFPUG FPA, it is independent of the technologies used and technical design principles.

SFP requires only the identification of Elementary Processes (EP) and Logical Files (LF), based on the following assumptions: 1) a user gives value to a BFC as a whole independently of internal organization and details, and 2) a cost model based on SFP shows a precision that is comparable to that of a cost model based on a detailed FPA measure. The latter assumption has been verified by different studies [10] [11].

SFP assigns a numeric value directly to these BFCs:

$$SFP = 7\ \#LF + 4.6\ \#EP$$

thus significantly speeding up the functional sizing process, at the expense of ignoring the domain data model, and the primary intent of each Elementary Process.

The weights for each BFC were originally given to achieve the best possible approximation of FPA but as long as the method has become a measurement method, those weights became constants, which are not subject to update or change for approximation reasons and that are crystallized for stability, repeatability and comparability reasons. We can approximate the FPA by setting $EstSize_{UFP} = SFP$.

III. Empirical Study

In the empirical study, we use an ISBSG dataset [12], which was also used previously to evaluate SFP [10].

The ISBSG dataset contains several small project data. As a matter of fact, estimating the size of small projects is not very interesting. A certified function point consultant that performs FP analysis according to the IFPUG standard counts between 400 and 600 FP per day, according to Capers Jones [13] and between 200 and 300 FP per day according to experts from Total Metrics [14]. Therefore, there is hardly any need for estimating the size of projects smaller than 200 UFP, since those projects can be sized accurately in no more than one working day.

Based on these considerations, we removed from the dataset the projects smaller than 200 UFP. The resulting dataset includes data from 110 projects having size in the [207, 4202] range. Some descriptive statistics for this dataset are given in Table I.

TABLE I
Descriptive statistics for the ISBSG dataset.

	UFP	HLFPA	SFP	#EI	#EO	#EQ	#ILF	#EIF	#LF	#EP
Mean	976	888	971	43	46	46	26	24	50	135
StDev	842	739	785	38	71	51	22	23	39	123
Median	639	607	674	29	17	32	20	18	37	82
Min	207	202	223	0	0	0	0	1	12	14
Max	4202	3755	4257	204	442	366	100	172	234	656

A. Method used

We build models of functional size using LOESS (locally estimated scatterplot smoothing) [15]. LOESS is a non-parametric regression method that combines multiple regression models in a k-nearest-neighbor-based meta-model. It fits simple models to localized subsets of the data to build up a function that describes the deterministic part of the variation in the data, point by point.

The analysis was carried out using the R programming language and environment [16]. Specifically, we used the `loess` function from the `Stats` package, which is provided as part of the system libraries.

Through the `span` parameter, the `loess` function makes it possible to control the degree of smoothing. In the empirical study, we tried different values for the `span` parameter.

We aimed at building models using the same five variables (*#EI, #EO, #EQ, #ILF, #EIF*) used by HLFPA. However, the `loess` function from the `Stats` package does not allow more than 4 independent variable. To overcome this problem, we observe that in the HLFPA method, *#EI* and *#EQ* get the same weight; therefore, it is conceivable to consider EIs and EQs as a single class of transactions (only as far as size estimation is concerned). Accordingly, for each project we compute $\#EIQ = \#EI + \#EQ$. Then we use four independent variables (*#EO, #EIQ, #ILF, #EIF*) to build size models via LOESS. In addition, we built models that use the same two variables (*#LF* and *#EP*) used by SFP. We also built Ordinary Least Square (OLS) linear regression models.

The evaluation was carried out via 10-time 10-fold cross validation. For all the estimates obtained from 10-time 10-fold cross validation, we compute estimation errors and a few indicators, as follows. The error (alias residual) for the ith estimation is defined as $ee_i = S_i - E_i$, where S_i is the actual size of the element involved in the ith estimation (i.e., the size measured according to the IFPUG standard process) and E_i is the estimated size. The computed indicators are:

- MAR is the Mean of Absolute Residuals, i.e., $MAR = \frac{1}{n}\sum_{i=0}^{n}|ee_i|$, where n is the number of estimates.
- MAR/MS is the MAR divided by the mean size $MS = \frac{1}{n}\sum_{i=0}^{n} S_i$. It gives an idea of the relative importance or the estimation errors.
- MMRE is the mean magnitude of relative errors. $MMRE = \frac{1}{n}\sum_{i=0}^{n}|re_i|$, since a relative error is defined as $re_i = \frac{ee_i}{S_i}$. MMRE has been widely criticized as a biased metric [17]: we report it for completeness. At any rate, we also report MAR/MS, which is not a biased metric, since the mean size is a characteristic of the given dataset: MAR/MS is a sort of normalization of the MAR.
- MdMRE is the median magnitude of relative errors.

- Finally, R^2 (the coefficient of determination) is given, since it is a quite reliable indicator of the models' accuracy [18].

B. Results obtained

We carried out 10-times 10-fold cross validation. In the process, we did not always get usable results. Specifically, via OLS regression we sometimes obtained invalid models (e.g., models with not normally distributed residuals); via LOESS we obtained models that did not support estimation in extreme cases, i.e., for too large or too small independent variables. All these cases were not evaluated. They are a strict minority, hence the reported results represent the most likely outcome of estimation in practice.

The accuracy indicators computed over the obtained estimates are given in Table II. Models LMv are built using OLS regression using v independent variables; models LWMv (where LWM stands for Locally Weighted Model) are built using LOESS, based on v independent variables. For LWMv we give in parentheses the value of the span value.

TABLE II
ESTIMATION ACCURACY INDICATORS.

	MAR	MAR/MS	MMRE	MdMRE	R^2
HLFPA	103.8	0.106	0.097	0.084	0.966
LM5	62.0	0.064	0.074	0.057	0.985
LM4	58.2	0.060	0.071	0.055	0.987
LM2	91.6	0.096	0.096	0.084	0.971
LWM4(0.5)	93.7	0.107	0.109	0.089	0.943
LWM2(0.5)	91.4	0.099	0.103	0.082	0.940
LWM4(0.75)	66.5	0.076	0.082	0.068	0.972
LWM2(0.75)	88.7	0.096	0.101	0.075	0.950
LWM4(0.95)	55.6	0.064	0.073	0.064	0.984
LWM2(0.95)	86.6	0.094	0.096	0.072	0.958

Table II suggests that OLS linear models provide quite good estimates. Surprisingly, LM4, i.e., the model based on *#EO, #EIQ, #ILF, #EIF* achieves better results than the LM5, i.e., the model based on *#EO, #EI, #EQ, #ILF, #EIF*.

We can also observe that estimation accuracy of LWM models varies with the `span`; specifically, accuracy improves with `span`. However, the improvement is modest for LWM2 (MAR decreases from 91.4 to 86.6), while it is quite large for LWM4 (MAR decreases from 93.7 to 55.6). Overall, it seems that when LOESS is used with two variables it is not able to substantially improve the estimates provided by LM2; instead, LOESS used with four variables achieves good results, provided that `span` is sufficiently large. In fact, the minimum MAR is achieved by LWM4 with `span`=0.95.

To evaluate if the estimates provided by a method are significantly better than those provided by another method, we tested the statistical significance of the differences among absolute errors yielded by the considered methods [17]. Namely, we compared the absolute residuals via Wilcoxon sign rank test [19] (using the `wilcox.test` function from the R `Stats` package). The results (which are all statistically significant at the usual $\alpha = 0.05$ level) are given in Table III.

TABLE III
COMPARISON OF MODEL'S ABSOLUTE RESIDUALS VIA WILCOXON SIGN RANK TEST.

	HLFPA	LM5	LM4	LM2	LWM4 (0.5)	LWM2 (0.5)	LWM4 (0.75)	LWM2 (0.75)	LWM4 (0.95)	LWM2 (0.95)
HLFPA	–	>	>	>	>	>	>	>	>	>
LM5	<	–	>	<	<	<	<	<	>	<
LM4	<	<	–	<	<	<	<	<	<	<
LM2	<	>	>	–	<	<	>	=	>	>
LWM4(0.5)	<	>	>	>	–	=	>	>	>	>
LWM2(0.5)	<	>	>	>	=	–	>	>	>	>
LWM4(0.75)	<	>	>	<	<	<	–	<	>	<
LWM2(0.75)	<	>	>	=	<	<	>	–	>	>
LWM4(0.95)	<	<	>	<	<	<	<	<	–	<
LWM2(0.95)	<	>	>	<	<	<	>	<	>	–

To assess the effect size, we use the non-parametric statistic A by Vargha and Delaney [20], as provided by the R package `effsize` [21]. We obtained the results given in Table IV, where each numeric result is accompanied by its interpretation [21]: 'n' and 's' indicate negligible and small effect size, respectively.

LWM4(0.95) appears to be the best model according to MAR (Table II). However, According to the Wilcoxon sign rank test, LM4 is the most accurate model. The disagreement between this two indications is explained by Vargha and Delaney's A, which is 0.51 for LM4 vs. LWM4(0.95), showing that the size effect is practically nil, i.e., LM4 is better, but by a practically irrelevant extent.

Finally, we look into the error distributions yielded by the estimation methods that we used in the study.

Figure 1 shows the boxplots of estimation errors for each of the used methods. It can be noticed that LWM2 models provide exceedingly large errors in a few cases.

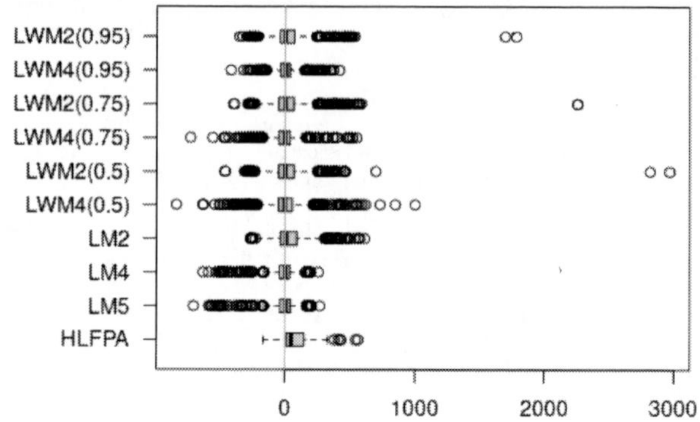

Fig. 1. Error boxplots.

Figure 2 provides the same information as Figure 1, but omitting outliers. It can be seen that the various models do not yield dramatically different accuracy levels, when the outliers are excluded. However, it is noteworthy that HLFPA tends to underestimate (as already noted in [22]). The other models provide more balanced errors, with medians very close to zero.

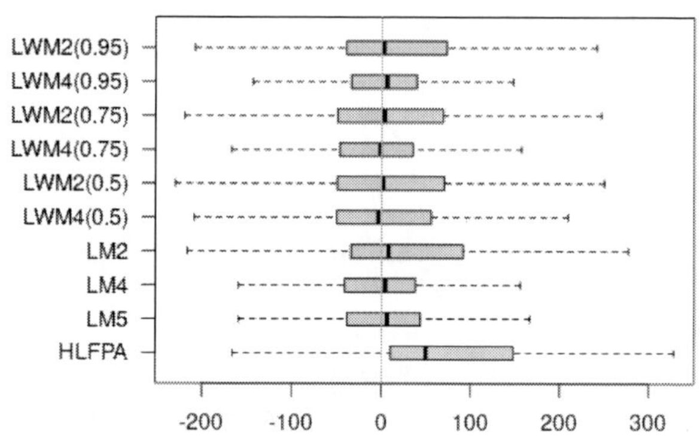

Fig. 2. Error boxplots (no outliers).

Figure 3 shows the boxplots of absolute estimation errors for each of the used methods, excluding outliers. The mean absolute error (i.e., the MAR) is shown as an orange diamond. Also according to Figure 3, LM4, LM5 and LWM4(0.95) are the most accurate models.

Figure 4 shows the distribution of the distance between SFP and IFPUG measures, in comparison with HLFPA and the best estimators. It can be seen that SFP measures provide an approximation that is better than HLFPA's, and not much worse than the best estimators'.

Considering that SFP uses fixed weights and does not even require classifying data and transactions, and that the method is not specifically intended to approximate IFPUG measures, this is a quite remarkable result.

IV. THREATS TO VALIDITY

A typical concern in this kind of studies is the generalizability of results outside the scope and context of the analyzed dataset. In our case, the ISBSG

TABLE IV
EFFECT SIZE ACCORDING TO VARGHA AND DELANEY'S A.

	HLFPA	LM5	LM4	LM2	LWM4(0.5)	LWM2(0.5)	LWM4(0.75)	LWM2(0.75)	LWM4(0.95)	LWM2(0.95)
HLFPA	–	0.61(s)	0.62(s)	0.54(n)	0.53(n)	0.53(n)	0.59(s)	0.55(n)	0.61(s)	0.56(n)
LM5	0.39(s)	–	0.52(n)	0.44(n)	0.42(s)	0.42(s)	0.49(n)	0.43(n)	0.51(n)	0.45(n)
LM4	0.38(s)	0.48(n)	–	0.42(s)	0.40(s)	0.40(s)	0.47(n)	0.42(s)	0.49(n)	0.43(n)
LM2	0.46(n)	0.56(n)	0.58(s)	–	0.48(n)	0.49(n)	0.55(n)	0.50(n)	0.57(n)	0.51(n)
LWM4(0.5)	0.47(n)	0.58(s)	0.60(s)	0.52(n)	–	0.50(n)	0.57(n)	0.52(n)	0.59(s)	0.53(n)
LWM2(0.5)	0.47(n)	0.58(s)	0.60(s)	0.51(n)	0.50(n)	–	0.56(n)	0.51(n)	0.58(s)	0.52(n)
LWM4(0.75)	0.41(s)	0.51(n)	0.53(n)	0.45(n)	0.43(n)	0.44(n)	–	0.45(n)	0.52(n)	0.47(n)
LWM2(0.75)	0.45(n)	0.57(n)	0.58(s)	0.50(n)	0.48(n)	0.49(n)	0.55(n)	–	0.57(n)	0.51(n)
LWM4(0.95)	0.39(s)	0.49(n)	0.51(n)	0.43(n)	0.41(s)	0.42(s)	0.48(n)	0.43(n)	–	0.45(n)
LWM2(0.95)	0.44(n)	0.55(n)	0.57(n)	0.49(n)	0.47(n)	0.48(n)	0.53(n)	0.49(n)	0.55(n)	–

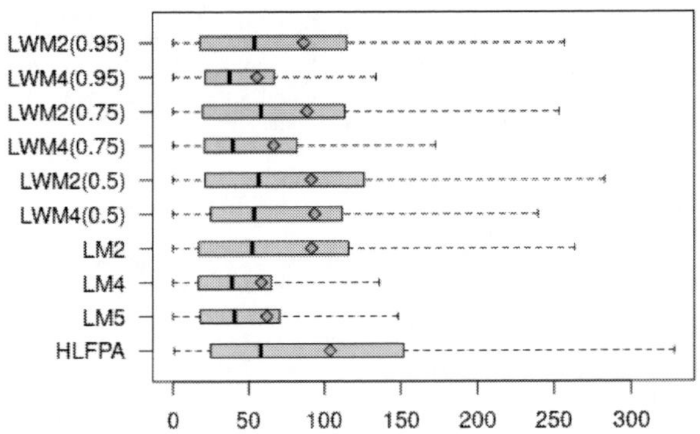

Fig. 3. Absolute error boxplots (no outliers).

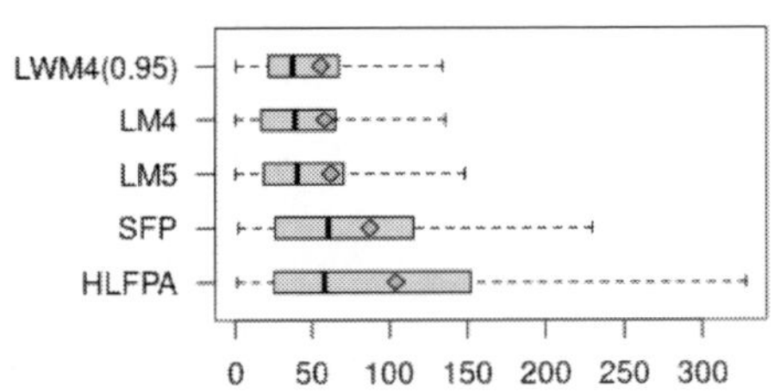

Fig. 4. Distributions of distances from IFPUG measures.

dataset is deemed the standard benchmark among the community, and it includes data from several application domains. Therefore our results may be valid in general.

The usage of MMRE is questionable, since it is has been shown to be a biased indicator (see for instance [17]). Nonetheless, we used MMRE together with other indicators—like MAR, the boxplots of residuals and R^2—to provide a more complete and balanced picture of the accuracy of our results, and compared the precision of different models via sound statistical tests, namely Wilcoxon sign rank test and Vargha and Delaney's A measure of effect size. Therefore, the role of MMRE in the presented evaluations is marginal.

V. RELATED WORK

The quest for measures that are available in the early stages of the software lifecycle dates back to decades ago [23] [24] [25].

The "Early & Quick Function Point" (EQFP) method [26] uses analogy (similarities between a new and a classified piece of software) and analysis (statistical analysis of the estimated similarity) to get size estimates. It was reported that estimates are within $\pm 10\%$ of the real size in most real cases, while the savings in time and costs are between 50% and 90%.

"Easy Function Points," [27], adopt probabilistic approaches to estimate not only the size, but also the probability that the actual size is equal to the estimate.

Lavazza et al. built estimation models for UFP based on BFCs [28] using Least Median Squares robust regression models. They observed that FP measures could be altogether replaced by measured based on a smaller set of BFCs.

Several other early estimation methods were proposed: Table V list the most popular ones.

TABLE V
EARLY ESTIMATION METHODS: DEFINITIONS AND EVALUATIONS

Method name	Definition	Used functions	Weight	Evaluation
NESMA indicative	[29] [30]	data	fixed	[4] [31]–[35] [9]
NESMA estimated	[29] [30]	all functions	fixed	[4] [31]–[35] [9]
Early & Quick FP	[25] [36] [26]	all functions	statistics	[9] [37]
Tichenor ILF model	[38]	ILF	fixed	[9]
simplified FP (sFP)	[39]	all functions	fixed	[9]
ISBSG average weights	[40]	all functions	statistics	[9]
SiFP	[5]	data and trans.	statistics	[10] [11]

Lavazza and Liu [22] used a dataset containing data from 479 projects to compare the accuracy of HLFPA method with Ordinary Least Squares method, with both 5 predictors (LM5) and only 2 predictors (LM2). They found that (1) unlike HLFPA, linear regression models do not underestimate, (2) linear regression models yield slightly less accurate estimates, and (3) models based on only two variables yield marginally less accurate estimates.

VI. CONCLUSION

Measuring software functional size via IFPUG FPA with the standard manual process is sometimes a long and expensive activity, and it is simply impossible when the details of a functional specification are not available for any reason. To solve this problem, several early estimation methods have been proposed. In this paper, we compare the estimates obtained via a standard estimation methods, namely HLFPA, and a new functional size measurement method, namely IFPUG SFP, with the estimates obtained with traditional (namely, linear regression) models and LOESS models. The accuracy achieved by these methods has been evaluated via an empirical study, which used a dataset containing data from 110 projects.

LOESS provided the lowest mean absolute error. However, statistical tests show that linear regression models using 4 or 5 independent variables achieve the same level of accuracy. Therefore, practitioners needing to estimate software functional size in the early stages of projects are advised to try both linear regression models and LOESS models.

ACKNOWLEDGMENT

The work reported here was partly supported by Fondo per la Ricerca di Ateneo, Università degli Studi dell'Insubria.

REFERENCES

[1] A. J. Albrecht, "Measuring application development productivity," in Proceedings of the joint SHARE/GUIDE/IBM application development symposium, vol. 10, 1979, pp. 83–92.

[2] International Function Point Users Group (IFPUG), "Function point counting practices manual, release 4.3.1," 2010.

[3] A. Timp, "uTip – Early Function Point Analysis and Consistent Cost Estimating," 2015, uTip # 03 – (version # 1.0 2015/07/01).

[4] H. van Heeringen, E. van Gorp, and T. Prins, "Functional size measurement-accuracy versus costs–is it really worth it?" in Software Measurement European Forum (SMEF), 2009.
[5] R. Meli, "Simple function point: a new functional size measurement method fully compliant with IFPUG 4.x," in Software Measurement European Forum, 2011.
[6] IFPUG, "Simple Function Point (SFP) Counting Practices Manual Release 2.1," 2021.
[7] L. Lavazza, "On the effort required by function point measurement phases," International Journal on Advances in Software, vol. 10, no. 1 & 2, 2017.
[8] nesma, "Early Function Point Analysis," https://nesma.org/themes/sizing/function-point-analysis/early-function-point-counting/ last access 6/6/22.
[9] L. Lavazza and G. Liu, "An empirical evaluation of simplified function point measurement processes," Journal on Advances in Software, vol. 6, no. 1& 2, 2013.
[10] L. Lavazza and R. Meli, "An evaluation of simple function point as a replacement of IFPUG function point," in IWSM–MENSURA 2014. IEEE, 2014, pp. 196–206.
[11] F. Ferrucci, C. Gravino, and L. Lavazza, "Simple function points for effort estimation: a further assessment," in 31st Annual ACM Symposium on Applied Computing. ACM, 2016, pp. 1428–1433.
[12] International Software Benchmarking Standards Group, ""Worldwide Software Development: The Benchmark, release 11," ISBSG, 2009.
[13] C. Jones, "A new business model for function point metrics," 2008, http://concepts.gilb.com/dl185 last access 6/6/22.
[14] Total Metrics, "Methods for Software Sizing – How to Decide which Method to Use," 2007 last access 6/6/22, https://www.totalmetrics.com/function-point-resources/downloads/R185_Why-use-Function-Points.pdf.
[15] W. S. Cleveland, "Robust locally weighted regression and smoothing scatterplots," Journal of the American statistical association, vol. 74, no. 368, 1979, pp. 829–836.
[16] R core team, "R: a language and environment for statistical computing," 2015.
[17] B. Kitchenham, L. Pickard, S. MacDonell, and M. Shepperd, "What accuracy statistics really measure [software estimation]," in Software, IEE Proceedings-, vol. 148, no. 3. IET, 2001, pp. 81–85.
[18] D. Chicco, M. J. Warrens, and G. Jurman, "The coefficient of determination R-squared is more informative than SMAPE, MAE, MAPE, MSE and RMSE in regression analysis evaluation," PeerJ Computer Science, vol. 7, 2021, p. e623.
[19] J. Cohen, "Statistical power analysis for the behavioral sciences Lawrence Earlbaum Associates," Hillsdale, NJ, 1988, pp. 20–26.
[20] A. Vargha and H. D. Delaney, "A critique and improvement of the cl common language effect size statistics of mcgraw and wong," Journal of Educational and Behavioral Statistics, vol. 25, no. 2, 2000, pp. 101–132.
[21] M. Torchiano et al., "effsize: Efficient effect size computation," R package version 0.7, vol. 1, 2017.
[22] G. Liu and L. Lavazza, "Early and quick function points analysis: Evaluations and proposals," Journal of Systems and Software, vol. 174, 2021, p. 110888.
[23] D. B. Bock and R. Klepper, "FP-S: a simplified function point counting method," Journal of Systems and Software, vol. 18, no. 3, 1992, pp. 245–254.
[24] G. Horgan, S. Khaddaj, and P. Forte, "Construction of an FPA-type metric for early lifecycle estimation," Information and Software Technology, vol. 40, no. 8, 1998, pp. 409–415.
[25] L. Santillo, M. Conte, and R. Meli, "Early & Quick Function Point: sizing more with less," in 11th IEEE International Software Metrics Symposium (METRICS'05). IEEE, 2005, pp. 41–41.
[26] DPO, "Early & Quick Function Points Reference Manual - IFPUG version," DPO, Roma, Italy, Tech. Rep. EQ&FP-IFPUG-31-RM-11-EN-P, April 2012.
[27] L. Santillo, "Easy Function Points – 'Smart' Approximation Technique for the IFPUG and COSMIC Methods," in IWSM–MENSURA, 2012.
[28] L. Lavazza, S. Morasca, and G. Robiolo, "Towards a simplified definition of function points," Information and Software Technology, vol. 55, no. 10, 2013, pp. 1796–1809.
[29] NESMA–the Netherlands Software Metrics Association, "Definitions and counting guidelines for the application of function point analysis. NESMA Functional Size Measurement method compliant to ISO/IEC 24570 version 2.1," 2004.
[30] International Standards Organisation, "ISO/IEC 24570:2005 – Software Engineering – NESMA functional size measurement method version 2.1 – definitions and counting guidelines for the application of Function Point Analysis," 2005.
[31] F. G. Wilkie, I. R. McChesney, P. Morrow, C. Tuxworth, and N. Lester, "The value of software sizing," Information and Software Technology, vol. 53, no. 11, 2011, pp. 1236–1249.
[32] J. Popović and D. Bojić, "A comparative evaluation of effort estimation methods in the software life cycle," Computer Science and Information Systems, vol. 9, no. 1, 2012, pp. 455–484.
[33] P. Morrow, F. G. Wilkie, and I. McChesney, "Function point analysis using nesma: simplifying the sizing without simplifying the size," Software Quality Journal, vol. 22, no. 4, 2014, pp. 611–660.
[34] L. Lavazza and G. Liu, "An Empirical Evaluation of the Accuracy of NESMA Function Points Estimates," in ICSEA, 2019, pp. 24–29.
[35] S. Di Martino, F. Ferrucci, C. Gravino, and F. Sarro, "Assessing the effectiveness of approximate functional sizing approaches for effort estimation," Information and Software Technology, vol. 123, July 2020.
[36] T. Iorio, R. Meli, and F. Perna, "Early&quick function points® v3. 0: enhancements for a publicly available method," in SMEF, 2007, pp. 179–198.
[37] R. Meli, "Early & quick function point method-an empirical validation experiment," in Int. Conf. on Advances and Trends in Software Engineering, Barcelona, Spain, 2015.
[38] C. Tichenor, "The IRS development and application of the internal logical file model to estimate function point counts," in IFPUG Fall Conf., 1997.
[39] L. Bernstein and C. M. Yuhas, Trustworthy systems through quantitative software engineering. John Wiley & Sons, 2005, vol. 1.
[40] R. Meli and L. Santillo, "Function point estimation methods: A comparative overview," in FESMA, vol. 99. Citeseer, 1999, pp. 6–8.

Detecting Novel Variants of Application Layer (D)DoS Attacks using Supervised Learning

Etienne van de Bijl
Centrum Wiskunde & Informatica
Amsterdam, the Netherlands
Email: evdb@cwi.nl

Jan Klein
Centrum Wiskunde & Informatica
Amsterdam, the Netherlands
Email: j.g.klein@cwi.nl

Joris Pries
Centrum Wiskunde & Informatica
Amsterdam, the Netherlands
Email: joris.pries@cwi.nl

Rob van der Mei
Centrum Wiskunde & Informatica
Amsterdam, the Netherlands
Email: mei@cwi.nl

Sandjai Bhulai
Vrije Universiteit Amsterdam
Amsterdam, the Netherlands
Email: s.bhulai@vu.nl

***Abstract*—Denial of Service (DoS) attacks and their distributed variant (DDoS) are major digital threats in today's cyberspace. Defense mechanisms such as *Intrusion Detection Systems* aim at finding these and other malicious activities in network traffic. They predominantly use *signature-based* approaches to effectively detect intrusions. Unfortunately, constructing a database with signatures is very time-consuming and this approach can only find previously seen variants. Machine learning algorithms are known to be effective tools in detecting intrusions, but it has not been studied if they are also able to detect unseen variants. In this research, we study to what extent supervised learning algorithms are able to detect novel variants of *application layer* (D)DoS attacks. To be more precise, we focus on detecting *HTTP* attacks targeting a web server. The contributions of this research are as follows: we provide a procedure to create intrusion detection datasets combining information from the transport, network, and application layer to be directly used for machine learning purposes. We show that specific (D)DoS variants are successfully detected by binary classifiers learned to distinguish benign entries from another (D)DoS attack. Despite this result, we demonstrate that the performance of a classifier trained on detecting variant A and tested on finding variant B is not necessarily similar to its performance when trained on B and tested on A. At last, we show that using more types of (D)DoS attacks in the training set does not necessarily lead to a higher detection rate of unseen variants. Thus, selecting the right combination of a machine learning model with a (small) set of intrusions included in the training data can result in a higher novel intrusion detection rate.**

Keywords*—*Machine learning; intrusion detection; anomaly detection; closed-world assumption.

I. INTRODUCTION

In our increasingly digitized world, network security has become more challenging as the Internet is used for virtually all information operations, such as storage and retrieval. The rat race between attackers and defenders is perpetual as new tools and techniques are continuously developed to attack web servers containing this information. Significant threat types for these servers are *Denial-of-Service* (DoS) attacks and their distributed variant (DDoS). Tremendous problems for organizations and individuals arise when legitimate users cannot access data due to these attacks. Modern (D)DoS attacks are designed to mimic legitimate user behavior and target vulnerabilities in *application-layer* protocols, such as the *Hypertext Transfer Protocol* (HTTP). This mix makes detecting them a challenging and complex task.

Defenders often use an *Intrusion Detection System* (IDS) to perform the task of detecting intrusions. An IDS can be viewed as the burglar alarm of the cybersecurity field [1]. It monitors network traffic and aims to detect malicious activities. Generally speaking, the two mainly used methodology classes by these systems are *signature-based* and *anomaly-based* [2]. A signature-based detector compares observed network events against patterns that correspond to known threats. In contrast, anomaly-based detectors search for malicious traffic by constructing a notion of normal behavior and flags activities which do not conform to this notion. Where signature-based is time-consuming but effective, anomaly-based often suffers from a high false-positive rate. Within anomaly detection methods, *Machine Learning* (ML) algorithms are getting more attention as they might overcome this problem.

The thought of using ML algorithms to detect intrusions is not new. Various studies are performed on using ML for detecting intrusions. Unfortunately, there is a striking imbalance between the extensive amount of research on ML-based anomaly detection techniques for intrusion detection and the rather clear lack of operational deployments [3]. ML algorithms are highly flexible and adaptive methods to find patterns in big stacks of data [4], but they seemed better at this task rather than discovering meaningful outliers [3]. Modern (D)DoS attacks are often occurring in large quantities and thus do not entirely conform to the premise that patterns cannot be found for these outliers. Therefore, using ML for the task of detecting these attacks should be appropriate.

There appear two issues when looking at anomaly-based ML research in intrusion detection [5][6]. Firstly, the performance of most of these methods is measured on outdated datasets [7]. This makes it hard to estimate the performance of these methods on modern network traffic. A major issue is that the composition of benign and malicious traffic in these datasets does not represent modern real-time environments. Also, there used to be a lack of representative publicly available intrusion detection datasets, but this lack was noticed by the cyberdefense community and recently they have generated more intrusion datasets [8]. Still, the available datasets are often limited to features extracted from the transport and network layer, but lack application layer features. Thus, not all attainable features are extracted in these datasets. Secondly, it is not examined how supervised learning methods perform in detecting novel variants of known attacks. The performance of these methods is measured in either a *closed-world assumption*, training, and test classes are the same, or an *open-world assumption* with unrelated attacks. However, it is not tested how the methods perform in an open-world setting with novel variants.

The aim of this paper is to study to what extent ML models are accurately able to detect novel variants of known cyberattacks. To be more precise, we use supervised binary classifiers to learn from a dataset containing benign and a set of (D)DoS attacks and we evaluate them on their ability to detect unseen variants of these attacks. We examine how the selected classifiers perform when using only a single (D)DoS variant in the training dataset on this task. Afterward, we study the effect of combining (D)DoS variants in the training phase on the performance of classifiers detecting unseen variants. Furthermore, we give a procedure to transform raw network traffic data into ML usable datasets containing information from the network, transport, and application layer. The code of this procedure is publicly available [9].

The main contributions can be summarized as follows: Firstly, we show that ML classifiers are to a great extent able to detect known (D)DoS attacks in a closed world setting. Secondly, we show that there are situations where these classifiers are able to detect a novel variant when they are trained to detect a different variant. This is however not a two-way street: learning to detect attack A and being able to also detect attack B does not imply that it is vice versa. Thirdly, we show that training on imbalanced data has an adverse effect on the evaluation performance of some ML classifiers. Finally, we demonstrate that it is not necessary to use many (D)DoS variants to detect a novel attack. Sometimes a few known attacks can already lead to the highest detection rate.

The organization of this paper is as follows. Section II gives a literature overview regarding detecting novel intrusions with ML. Section III states which datasets are selected for this research. Section IV describes how these datasets are modified into ML applicable datasets and states metadata about them. In addition, a set of ML models used for conducting the experiments are given in this section. Section V outlines the conducted experiments. Section VI shows the results of the conducted experiments. Finally, we conclude and summarize in Section VII.

II. Related Work

Detection of novel attacks with supervised learning techniques has been studied before in the context of *Transfer Learning* (TL). TL is an ML paradigm where a model trained on one task is used as a starting point for another task. [10] introduces a feature-based TL approach to find novel cyberattacks by mapping source and target dataset in an optimized feature representation. This approach is however very dependent on a similarity parameter and the dimensions of the new feature space. Therefore, [11] extended this method by proposing another approach to automatically find a relationship between the novel and known attacks. Both of these approaches are tested on an outdated dataset and it does not contain variants of a single cyberattack. In our research, we are interested in the detection of novel variants rather than novel variants. In [12], a Convolutional Neural Network is used to detect novel attacks also in a TL setup, but it is not studied if learning one specific attack affects the detection of another novel variant. The experiments conducted in our research resemble the experiments performed in [13]. In their research, an intrusion detection method is introduced which transfers knowledge between networks by combining unrelated attacks to train on. More recent work focuses on applying Deep Neural Networks in the context of TL for intrusion detection tasks [14].

III. Datasets

It is stated that a perfect intrusion detection dataset should at least be up-to-date, correctly labeled, publicly available, contain real network traffic with all kinds of attacks and normal user behavior, and spans over a long time [8]. The main reasons for a lack of appropriate datasets satisfying these properties are privacy concerns regarding recording real-world network traffic and labeling being very time-consuming. However, researchers have been able to generate synthetic or anonymized datasets which satisfy some of these ideal properties. It is therefore recommended to test methodologies on multiple datasets instead of only one [3]. In this research, we focus on the detection of (D)DoS attacks and for that reason have selected the CIC-IDS-2017 [15] and the CIC-IDS-2018 [16] datasets created by the Canadian Institute for Cybersecurity (CIC). These popular datasets fulfill properties such as being correctly labeled, publicly available, up-to-date, and containing (D)DoS variants.

IV. Methodology

We discuss the procedure to convert raw network traffic into usable intrusion detection datasets containing information from the network, transport, and application layer for ML purposes. The converted and extracted features are described in detail so it is clear which features are included. Furthermore, we provide metadata describing the final datasets. At last, the classification models and their set of considered hyperparameters are given for detecting novel variants.

A. Feature Extraction

The selected datasets are provided by the CIC in two formats: a set of raw network traffic (`pcap`) files and a set of files containing extracted features by a network analysis tool called CICFlowMeter [17]. These features mainly describe network and transport protocol activities, but there are no features describing application activities. As this study focuses on detecting application layer (D)DoS variants, it is desirable to have a dataset also containing application layer features. Therefore, we start with the raw internet traffic format and have selected a feature extraction tool matching this requirement.

The feature extraction tool used in this study is the open-source network traffic analyzer called Zeek (formerly Bro) [18]. Zeek is a passive standalone IDS and derives an extensive set of logs describing network activity. These logs include an exhaustive record for all sessions seen on the wire, but also application layer documentation. Zeek was also used as a feature extraction tool for the creation of other popular network intrusion detection datasets, e.g., DARPA98 [19] from the Defense Advanced Research Projects Agency (DARPA) and the UNSW-NB15 [20] from the University of New South Wales (UNSW). It has a good track record in creating intrusion detection datasets and therefore an appropriate tool.

Zeek generates by default a large set of log files, but not all of them are required for this research. We limit ourselves to the *Transmission Control Protocol* (TCP) entries given in the connection logs (`conn.log`), describing network and transport layer activity, and HTTP interactions given in HTTP logs (`http.log`). These log files include entries showing malicious (D)DoS activities. The entries in the connection log files are transport-layer sessions, while the HTTP log file consists of entry logs showing conversations between a client and a web server. Entries between these logs are unilaterally linked as each HTTP entry is assigned to a single connection entry. Malicious activities that are not (D)DoS attacks are excluded as we only focus on these attacks.

B. Feature Engineering

We describe how the extracted features are converted into ML admissible features. This section states the additional created features, which features are replaced for better extraction of patterns, and how categorical features are smartly one-hot-encoded. We start with describing the feature engineering steps in the connection log file and afterward do the same for the HTTP log file.

a) Connection log: Zeek counts the number of packets and bytes transferred in each connection. Table I shows additional created features from these counters. A higher level statistic called the *Producer-Consumer Ratio* (PCR) [21] shows the ratio between sending and receiving packets between the hosts. In a TCP connection, an originator host is an uploader if a PCR is close to 1.0 and purely a downloader if it is close to -1.0.

The feature `conn_state` constructed by Zeek refers to the state with which a TCP connection was ended. This state is determined by registering flags exchanged during the communication between hosts. Looking only at the end of a connection implies that the establishment and termination of the connection are merged. Preliminary results showed

TABLE I. NETWORK LAYER ENGINEERED FEATURES.

Feature	Description	Type
orig_bpp	$\frac{\text{orig\_bytes}}{\text{orig\_packets}}$	Float
resp_bpp	$\frac{\text{resp\_bytes}}{\text{resp\_packets}}$	Float
PCR	$\frac{\text{orig\_bytes}-\text{resp\_bytes}}{\text{orig\_bytes}+\text{resp\_bytes}}$	Float

that classifiers were more able to find patterns in (D)DoS traffic when differentiating between the establishment of a connection and the termination of it. On this note, we replaced the `conn_state` feature with features describing both ends of a connection. The *3-Way Handshake* is the correct way to establish a TCP connection before data is allowed to be sent. This procedure is however not always correctly executed and incorrect establishments can indicate misuse. Hosts can terminate TCP connections gracefully, or not. A graceful termination occurs when both hosts send a packet with a *final* (FIN) flag. When a host sends a packet containing a *reset* (RST) flag, it will abruptly end a TCP connection, which is very common in practice. If neither is the case, connections are in theory still open. In Table II, we distinguish different establishment and termination scenarios by looking at the exchanged flags between the hosts. Each of these scenarios is included in the data as a binary feature. Other Zeek connection log flags ([d, t, g, w]) are one-hot-encoded for both originator and responder.

TABLE II. TCP CONNECTION ESTABLISHMENT AND TERMINATION SCENARIOS.

Feature	Description
S0	No SYN packet is observed
S1	Merely a connection attempt (SYN), but no reply
REJ1	A connection attempt but replied with a RST packet.
S2	A connection attempt followed by SYN-ACK, but no final ACK
REJ2O	Scenario S2 but originator sends RST packet
REJ2R	Scenario S2 but responder sends RST packet
S3	Connection is established according to the 3-way handshake
WEIRD	A connection attempt but none of the above cases were observed
OPEN	A connection was established, but no FIN or RST flag is observed
TERM	Connection gracefully terminated by originator and receive
CLSO	Originator sends a FIN flag but receiver did not respond
CLSR	Receiver sends a FIN flag but originator did not respond
RSTO	Originator abruptly ends connection by sending an RST flag
RSTR	Receiver abruptly ends connection by sending an RST flag

b) HTTP log: Communication in this protocol starts with a client sending a request message to a web server and this server will, hopefully, reply with a response message. Both message types consist of a start-line, zero or more header fields, an empty line indicating the end of the header fields, and possibly a message-body. The start-line of a request message, called the request-line, contains three components: a method (command), a path on which to apply this command, and an HTTP version indicating the version a client wants to use. Hosts must agree on the HTTP version to use before they continue talking. If they did not agree on the HTTP version, a "-1" is imputed to distinguish it from other versions.

The feature `method`, showing the command given in the

request message, is a feature showing the one-word command given in the request-line. Common used commands are {GET, HEAD, POST, PUT, DELETE, CONNECT, OPTIONS, TRACE, PATCH}, but other commands also exist. This categorical feature is one-hot-encoded to one of those common commands to limit the number of options. In case an uncommon command is given, it will be assigned to a feature called `method_other`, while if no command is given at all, it is assigned to `method_-`.

A web server applies a `method` on the `URI` (Uniform Resource Identifier) stated in a request line. This `URI` can be parsed in different components by a library called urllib [22]. Figure 1 gives an example of how this tool splits a *URL* (Uniform Resource Locator) into four components. We extracted descriptive statistics from each component by counting the number of special characters (not letters or digits), the number of characters, and the number of unique characters. A typical `URI` constitutes three components: a path, a query, and a fragment. Statistics are extracted for each of those components. For example, one extracted feature called `URI_path_len` describes the length of the path of a URI. In addition, Zeek extracts `host` (only netloc) and the `referrer` (all components) and these descriptive statistics are also extracted for these features.

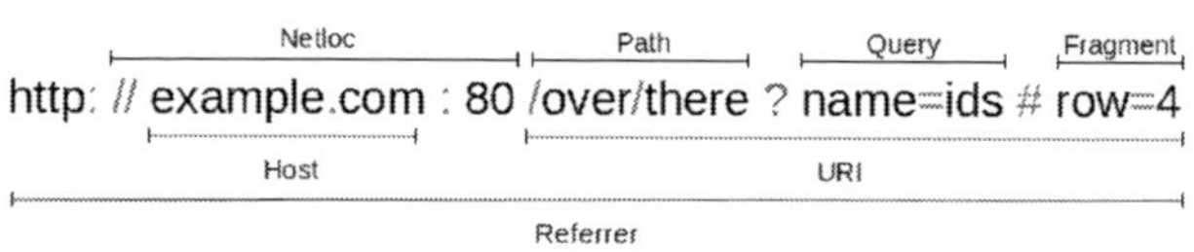

Figure 1. Example URL showing the four components parsed by urllib and the component coverage of extracted features by Zeek.

Web servers process received request messages and reply to them with a response message. In the status line of this message is the agreed HTTP version stated and a response code if the web server is able to process the request. The response codes are grouped by their first digit. So, for example, the error code 404 is assigned to the `4xx` code. Furthermore, it is registered what type of data ({application, audio, example, font, image, model, text, video}) is sent by the web server to the client or vice versa. This info is one-hot-encoded in a similar manner as the `method` for both directions.

C. Final Dataset

The log files are merged into a single dataset after feature engineering them. The resulting dataset consists of HTTP interactions, while in contrast, the datasets provided by the CIC consist of connection flows. Connection log features are added to the HTTP entry features to combine application, network, and transport layer features. This merge gives a dataset with a total of 103 features. The CIC-IDS-2017 consists of 524,698 instances and the CIC-IDS-2018 has 9,595,037 instances. Table III shows the distribution of the labels of the entries. The benign/malicious ratio is approximately balanced for both datasets. However, if we differentiate between (D)DoS attacks, we observe that there is a clear imbalance between the malicious classes. For example, the *Hulk* (HTTP Unbearable Load King) attack generated a lot more HTTP entries in comparison to a *Slowloris* or *GoldenEye*.

TABLE III. CLASS DISTRIBUTION OVER THE HTTP ENTRIES.

		CIC-IDS-2017		CIC-IDS-2018	
Class	**(D)DoS**	**Amount**	**Percentage**	**Amount**	**Percentage**
Benign	-	258,197	49.209%	6,252,950	65.169%
Botnet	DDoS	736	00.140%	142,925	01.490%
GoldenEye	DoS	7,908	01.507%	27,345	00.285%
HOIC	DDoS	0	00.000%	1,074,379	11.197%
Hulk	DoS	158,513	30.210%	1,803,160	18.793%
LOIC	DDoS	95,683	18.236%	289,328	03.015%
SlowHTTPTest	DoS	1,416	00.270%	0	00.000%
Slowloris	DoS	2,245	00.428%	4,950	00.052%

D. Models

Four ML algorithms are selected for our classification problem: Decision Tree (DT), Random Forest (RF), K-Nearest Neighbors (KNN), and Gaussian Naive Bayes (GNB). A grid search approach is performed to find the optimal hyperparameters for these algorithms. Table IV shows the considered parameters for each model. The optimal set of parameters for each model will be used on the test dataset by selecting the highest F_1 score achieved on a validation set. As there was a limited amount of computational time, the hyperparameter space of computationally expensive models like KNN is smaller than simpler models like DT.

TABLE IV. HYPERPARAMETERS OPTIONS FOR THE SELECTED CLASSIFIERS.

Model	Scikit Parameter	Options
GNB	var_smoothing	1e-200
DT	criterion	[Gini , Entropy]
	splitter	[Best, Random]
	class_weight	[None, Balanced]
	max_features	[Auto, None, Sqrt, log2]
RF	criterion	[Gini, Entropy]
	class_weight	[None, Balanced]
	max_features	Auto
	n_estimators	[10, 50, 100, 250]
KNN	n_neighbors	5
	algorithm	[Ball Tree, KD Tree]

V. EXPERIMENTAL SETUP

In this section, we describe the experiments conducted in this research. First, the three experiments to tackle the research aim are described. Afterward, the evaluation metric to measure the performance of an ML classifier is given.

A. Proposed approach

It is common practice in ML to split a dataset into two non-overlapping sets: a training set and a test set. To get a proper estimation of the performance of a classifier on the task at hand, the train-test split should be performed multiple times. In our experiments, we have performed multiple hold-out-cross validation splits with each split an 80/20 split in a random manner. Before splitting the data, all redundant features (features with only 0 values) are removed as these features do not contain any new information. Each split is performed in a stratified manner to maintain the class distribution (Table III). In the training set, a validation set (20%) is randomly selected to obtain the best hyperparameters for each model. The classifiers are tested on these datasets in three different experimental setups:

1) Detecting Known Attacks: Firstly, we study to what extent the selected classifiers are able to detect known attacks in a closed-world assumption. To test this, the training data and the evaluation data will contain the same two classes: *Benign* and one attack. For example, in one setup we train on *Benign* against *Hulk* and test on the same two classes. This gives insights into the upper bound to what extent our models could achieve if we would have known about the attack.

2) Detecting Novel Variants: Secondly, we examine to what degree classifiers are able to detect a novel variant when the training dataset only contains benign traffic and one different variant. For example, we train on *Benign* against *Hulk* entries and evaluate the trained model on a test set containing *Benign* and *LOIC* (Low Orbit Ion Cannon). The labels of the attacks in the train and test set are both converted to a new label named *Malicious* so that the task is still a binary classification problem. This experiment shows how similar the training attack is to the test attack.

3) Class Importance to Detect Novel Variants: Finally, we study what we call *class importance*: does learning on a combination of multiple attacks help identify novel variants. We look at combinations of (D)DoS attacks in the training set and test the trained model on detecting a novel attack. For example, we train on *Benign* and a combination of attacks such as *LOIC* and *Hulk* entries and test on a dataset containing *Benign* and a different novel attack such as *SlowHTTPTest*. To make this a binary classification problem, the attacks are again mapped to the *Malicious* class. This experiment shows if combining cyberattacks in the training set helps to detect novel variants. Also, it can be tested if adding certain classes in the training set impacts the detection of novel variants.

B. Evaluation Metrics

In our classification task, the positive class represents malicious instances while the negative class represents benign entries. The considered evaluation metric to test the selected classifiers is the F_1 score, which is the harmonic mean between *recall* and *precision*. Recall shows the ratio intrusions the classifiers were successfully able to detect, while precision gives the ratio between the *true positives* and the number of positively predicted instances. For (D)DoS attacks aiming to exhaust a resource, it is better to have a low false alarm rate than a high recall as it is not necessary to block all malicious traffic. We simply want to prevent the resource from being overloaded and prevent blocking legit HTTP requests. This makes the task at hand different in contrast to detecting intrusions in general as there the cost of a false negative is higher. Still, optimizing only precision is not desirable. Therefore, the F_1 score is an appropriate middle ground as it optimizes the harmonic mean of those metrics. When data is imbalanced, this score is more suitable than accuracy as it corrects for this imbalance.

VI. Experimental Results

In this section, we show the results of the three experiments performed in this research. First, we discuss the results of a dataset with a closed-world assumption. Secondly, this assumption is relaxed and we look at the performance of models in detecting known and novel attacks. At last, we discuss the results of classifiers trained on a set of attacks to detect a novel attack. The results of the experiments are gathered by testing the classifiers on 20 different train-test sets for the CIC-IDS-2017 and 10 different for the CIC-IDS-2018. Furthermore, as the CIC-IDS-2018 is very large and there was limited computational time, a subset of the data was used for parameter tuning. We have selected randomly 10% of the training data for hyperparameter search for the DT and RF model for the CIC-IDS-2018. Randomly 1% was selected for hyperparameter search of the KNN model and the same percentage was randomly selected from the training data to evaluate the model. For the CIC-IDS-2017, no subset sampling was required.

A. Detecting Known Attacks

In this experiment, the classes included in the learning dataset are the same as the test dataset. Table V shows the average F_1 scores if classifiers are tested on the task of detecting known attacks. Each row in this table shows the attack used in the training, as well as in the testing set. It can be observed that in almost all scenarios the considered models are able to learn the relevant characteristics of the considered attacks. One exemption is the GNB model learning and testing on the *SlowHTTPTest* attack. This model obtained a sufficient recall (0.997), but an inferior score on its precision (0.154). Even though the model is able to detect most malicious instances, there are many false positives leading to a lower precision.

TABLE V. F_1 SCORES OF CLASSIFIERS DETECTING KNOWN INTRUSIONS.

CIC-IDS-2017	**GNB**		**DT**		**RF**		**KNN**	
Attack	**Mean**	**Std**	**Mean**	**Std**	**Mean**	**Std**	**Mean**	**Std**
Botnet	1.0000	0.0000	0.9971	0.0046	0.9998	0.0008	0.9909	0.0076
GoldenEye	0.9972	0.0010	0.9997	0.0002	1.0000	0.0000	0.9983	0.0006
Hulk	0.9990	0.0002	0.9999	0.0000	1.0000	0.0000	0.9999	0.0000
LOIC	0.9999	0.0000	1.0000	0.0000	1.0000	0.0000	1.0000	0.0000
SlowHTTPTest	0.2339	0.2065	0.9955	0.0042	0.9956	0.0031	0.9874	0.0046
Slowloris	0.9013	0.0078	0.9976	0.0016	0.9969	0.0023	0.9929	0.0035
CIC-IDS-2018								
Botnet	0.9998	0.0001	1.0000	0.0000	1.0000	0.0000	0.9974	0.0011
GoldenEye	0.9919	0.0006	0.9843	0.0010	0.9914	0.0004	0.9536	0.0051
HOIC	0.9964	0.0001	0.9964	0.0001	0.9964	0.0001	0.9961	0.0002
Hulk	0.9999	0.0000	1.0000	0.0000	1.0000	0.0000	0.9997	0.0000
LOIC - HTTP	1.0000	0.0000	1.0000	0.0000	1.0000	0.0000	1.0000	0.0000
Slowloris	0.9876	0.0018	0.9982	0.0012	0.9986	0.0007	0.9586	0.0054

B. Detecting Novel Attacks with One Attack Learned

Let us relax the closed-world assumption: What if our trained algorithm sees a variant of the learned attack? Figure 2 shows the average F_1 scores achieved by the classifiers in this experiment. The diagonal of this matrix shows the F_1

scores of the closed-world assumption, also obtainable from Table V, while numbers outside this diagonal are the scores of detecting novel attacks. It can be observed in the open-world setting that *Botnet* attacks are hard to detect in this setting, neither can it easily be used to detect other variants. However, there are situations where classifiers are able to detect novel variants. This is, however, not symmetrical: learning attack A and finding attack B does not mean it works also the other way around.

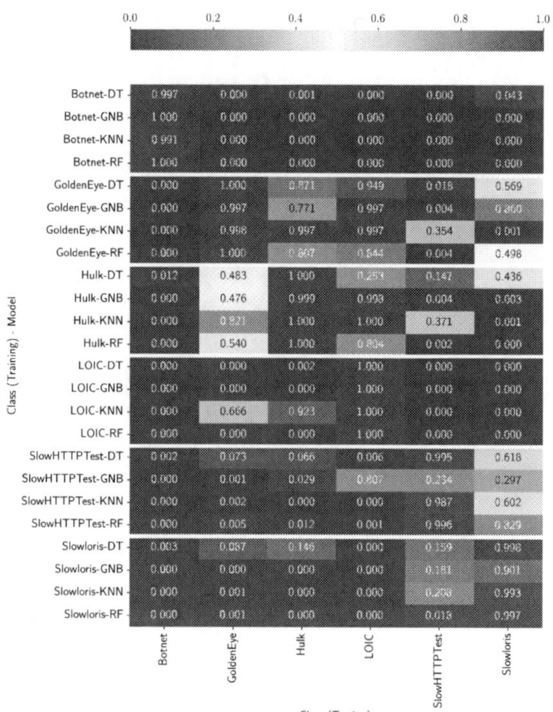

Figure 2. Average F_1 scores for the CIC-IDS-2017 dataset tested using 20 different train-test settings.

The same approach is applied to the CIC-IDS-2018 dataset. Figure 3 shows the results of the same experimental setup performed on the CIC-IDS-2018. Similar results are observable on the diagonal: ML algorithms are indeed able to detect attacks it has trained on. In these results, it is less apparent that learning one (D)DoS attack leads to the model being able to detect another attack. Only a few combinations of train and test attacks are successful. For example, learning the *HOIC* (High Orbit Ion Cannon) with the KNN model results in high scores for testing on the *LOIC* and the *Hulk*. Results showed that classifiers such as DT and RF were not able to learn sufficiently from the training data as a striking class imbalance between benign and the attack led to low performance. Still, the same observation as in the CIC-IDS-2017 is apparent: when training on attack A and being able to detect B, it does not imply it works the other way around.

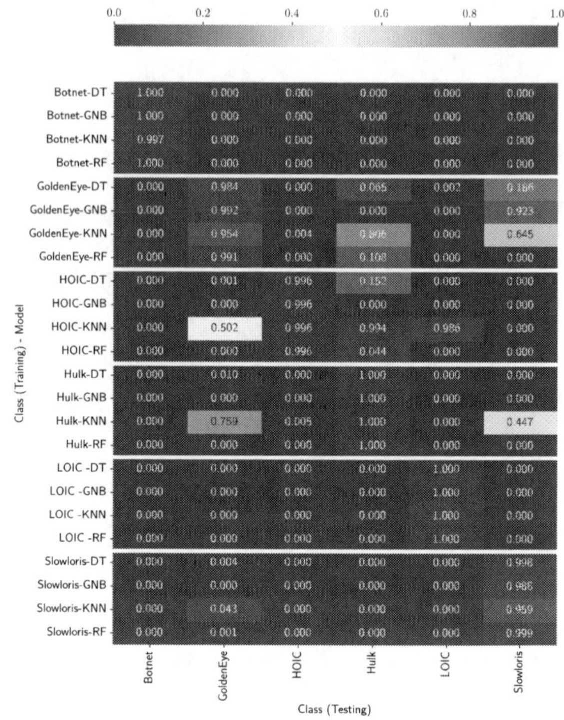

Figure 3. Average F_1 scores for the CIC-IDS-2018 dataset tested using 10 different train-test settings.

C. Learning on a Set of Variants to Detect a Novel Variant

In our last experiment, we look at combining attacks in the learning phase to detect a novel variant. The objective here is to find a set of attacks leading to the highest novel attack detection performance. Table VI shows the results of the classifiers using a set of attacks to learn from on and the corresponding combination of attacks that led to the highest performance. Despite the fact that models can use more attacks to detect a novel variant, it is not necessarily the case that this yields the highest detection rate: even a few attacks are enough to obtain the highest performance. It can be observed that for the CIC-IDS-2017 the KNN model is dominantly getting the highest average F_1 scores, while for the CIC-IDS-2018 it is the GNB model. In neither case does the RF model outperform other models, as bold indicated performances show the highest, which is unexpected as this model outperforms other models in detecting known attacks. For the CIC-IDS-2017 dataset, the *Hulk* attack is almost always used to obtain the highest scores with the least number of attacks required. The strong imbalance affects the learning process of the DT and the RF, similar as in experiment 2. These models could have been improved by downsampling benign entries so that the training classes are balanced.

TABLE VI. HIGHEST OBTAINED F_1 SCORE FOR EACH MODEL BY TRAINING THEM ON MULTIPLE INTRUSIONS TO DETECT A NOVEL ATTACK.

CIC-IDS-2017	DT	GNB	KNN	RF	Train Set Opt Model
Botnet	**0.460**	0.291	0.000	0.000	{Hulk, LOIC, Slowloris}
GoldenEye	0.664	0.476	**0.821**	0.782	{Hulk}
Hulk	0.870	0.986	**0.997**	0.833	{GoldenEye, LOIC}
LOIC	0.949	0.998	**0.999**	0.999	{Hulk}
SlowHTTPTest	0.240	0.181	**0.399**	0.100	{Hulk, Slowloris}
Slowloris	**0.878**	0.860	0.601	0.874	{Bot, Eye, Hulk, HTTP}
CIC-IDS-2018	**DT**	**GNB**	**KNN**	**RF**	**Train Set Opt Model**
Botnet	0.000	0.000	0.000	0.000	-
GoldenEye	0.290	**0.862**	0.773	0.100	{LOIC, Hulk, Slowloris}
HOIC	0.000	**0.853**	0.500	0.000	{LOIC, Hulk}
Hulk	0.899	**0.999**	0.997	0.986	{GoldenEye, Slowloris}
LOIC	0.100	0.288	**0.985**	0.000	{HOIC}
Slowloris	0.539	**0.922**	0.837	0.000	{GoldenEye}

VII. CONCLUSION

This research provides a procedure to construct intrusion detection datasets combining multiple layers with the tool Zeek. Zeek generates a bunch of extensive log files and two of them are selected to create a machine learning admissible dataset for the detection of (D)DoS attacks. This procedure to create such a dataset is not limited to only these protocols but can be extended to also combining other protocols, such as TCP with the *File Transfer Protocol* (FTP). The aim of this research was to test to what extent ML classifiers are able to detect novel variants of known intrusions. A set of classifiers were applied in three different experimental setups and we studied their ability to detect (D)DoS variants. The focus of this research was to study the detection of variants of (D)DoS intrusions, but the same analysis can be performed on variants of another cyberattack. It has been shown in the first experiment that ML classifiers are to a great extent able to detect known (D)DoS attacks in a closed world setting. Finding patterns in large datasets is a typical task for ML algorithms. In the second experiment, it is observed that there are scenarios in which classifiers are able to detect a novel variant when trained on a different (D)DoS variant. Detecting novel variants is however not a two-way street: learning to detect attack A and being able to also detect attack B does not have the property that it is vice versa. The third experiment showed that it is not necessary to use many (D)DoS variants to detect a novel attack. Sometimes a few known attacks can already lead to the highest detection rate. For the last two experiments, it is observed that when the training data is very imbalanced, DT and RF are inferior in detecting novel attacks in an open-world assumption. GNB seems better at detecting novel attacks when this is the case.

To sum up, this research shows that ML algorithms can detect (D)DoS cyberattacks almost as well as signature-based approaches, but also have the capability to detect novel variants. Selecting the right combination of an ML model with a (small) set of intrusions included in the training data can result in a higher novel intrusion detection rate.

REFERENCES

[1] S. Axelsson, *Intrusion detection systems: A survey and taxonomy*, 2000, unpublished, http://www.cse.msu.edu/~cse960/Papers/security/axelsson00intrusion.pdf, retrieved: May, 2022.

[2] H.-J. Liao, C.-H. R. Lin, Y.-C. Lin, and K.-Y. Tung, "Intrusion detection system: A comprehensive review," *Journal of Network and Computer Applications*, vol. 36, no. 1, pp. 16–24, 2013.

[3] R. Sommer and V. Paxson, "Outside the closed world: On using machine learning for network intrusion detection," in *2010 IEEE Symposium on Security and Privacy*. IEEE, 2010, pp. 305–316.

[4] P. García-Teodoro, J. Díaz-Verdejo, G. Maciá-Fernández, and E. Vázquez, "Anomaly-based network intrusion detection: Techniques, systems and challenges," *Computers & Security*, vol. 28, no. 1–2, pp. 18–28, 2009.

[5] A. L. Buczak and E. Guven, "A survey of data mining and machine learning methods for cyber security intrusion detection," *IEEE Communications Surveys & Tutorials*, vol. 18, no. 2, pp. 1153–1176, 2016.

[6] Y. Xin et al., "Machine learning and deep learning methods for cybersecurity," *IEEE Access*, vol. 6, pp. 35365–35381, 2018.

[7] Z. Ahmad, A. Shahid Khan, C. Wai Shiang, J. Abdullah, and F. Ahmad, "Network intrusion detection system: A systematic study of machine learning and deep learning approaches," *Transactions on Emerging Telecommunications Technologies*, vol. 32, no. 1, pp. 1–29, 2020.

[8] M. Ring, S. Wunderlich, D. Scheuring, D. Landes, and A. Hotho, "A survey of network-based intrusion detection data sets," *Computers & Security*, vol. 86, pp. 147–167, 2019.

[9] *NIDS*. (2022). [Online]. Available: https://github.com/etiennevandebijl/NIDS

[10] J. Zhao, S. Shetty, and J. W. Pan, "Feature-based transfer learning for network security," in *MILCOM 2017 - 2017 IEEE Military Communications Conference (MILCOM)*. IEEE, 2017, pp. 17–22.

[11] J. Zhao, S. Shetty, J. W. Pan, C. Kamhoua, and K. Kwiat, "Transfer learning for detecting unknown network attacks," *EURASIP Journal on Information Security*, vol. 2019, no. 1, pp. 1–13, 2019.

[12] P. Wu, H. Guo, and R. Buckland, "A transfer learning approach for network intrusion detection," in *2019 IEEE 4th International Conference on Big Data Analytics (ICBDA)*. IEEE, 2019, pp. 281–285.

[13] Z. Taghiyarrenani, A. Fanian, E. Mahdavi, A. Mirzaei, and H. Farsi, "Transfer learning based intrusion detection," in *2018 8th International Conference on Computer and Knowledge Engineering (ICCKE)*. IEEE, 2018, pp. 92–97.

[14] M. Masum and H. Shahriar, "TL-NID: Deep neural network with transfer learning for network intrusion detection," in *2020 15th International Conference for Internet Technology and Secured Transactions (ICITST)*. IEEE, 2020, pp. 1–7.

[15] I. Sharafaldin, A. H. Lashkari, and A. A. Ghorbani, "Toward generating a new intrusion detection dataset and intrusion traffic characterization," in *Proceedings of the 4th International Conference on Information Systems Security and Privacy (ICISSP 2018)*. SCITEPRESS, 2018, pp. 108–116.

[16] *A realistic cyber defense dataset*, Canadian Institute for Cybersecurity, May. 2021. [Online]. Available: https://registry.opendata.aws/cse-cic-ids2018

[17] A. H. Lashkari, G. D. Gil, M. S. I. Mamun and A. A. Ghorbani, "Characterization of tor traffic using time based features," in *Proceedings of the 3rd International Conference on Information Systems Security and Privacy (ICISSP 2017)*. SCITEPRESS, 2017, pp. 253–262.

[18] V. Paxson, "Bro: A system for detecting network intruders in real-time," *Computer Networks*, vol. 31, no. 23-24, pp. 2435–2463, 1999.

[19] M. Bijone, "A survey on secure network: Intrusion detection & prevention approaches," *American Journal of Information Systems*, vol. 4, no. 3, pp. 69–88, 2016.

[20] N. Moustafa and J. Slay, "UNSW-NB15: A comprehensive data set for network intrusion detection systems (UNSW-NB15 network data set)," in *2015 Military Communications and Information Systems Conference (MilCIS)*. IEEE, 2015, pp. 1–6.

[21] J. Klein, S. Bhulai, M. Hoogendoorn, R. Van Der Mei, and R. Hinfelaar, "Detecting network intrusion beyond 1999: Applying machine learning techniques to a partially labeled cybersecurity dataset," in *2018 IEEE/WIC/ACM International Conference on Web Intelligence (WI)*. IEEE, 2018, pp. 784–787.

[22] *urllib* (3.9) [Online]. Available: https://docs.python.org/3/library/urllib.html

Identification of Tropical Dry Forest Transformation in the Colombian Caribbean Region Using Acoustic Recordings through Unsupervised Learning

Nestor Rendon
SISTEMIC, Engineering Faculty
Universidad de Antioquia
Calle 70 No. 52-21
Medellín, Colombia
email: nestor.rendon@udea.edu.co

Susana Rodríguez-Buritica
Alexander Von Humbolt institute,
Avenida Circunvalar 16 - 20, Bogotá, D.C.
Bogota, Colombia
email: drodriguez@humboldt.org.co

Claudia Isaza
SISTEMIC, Engineering Faculty
Universidad de Antioquia
Calle 70 No. 52-21
Medellín, Colombia
email: victoria.isaza@udea.edu.co

***Abstract*—Passive Acoustic Monitoring (PAM) is one of the alternatives to monitoring endangered ecosystems. PAM uses acoustic recordings of monitored sites to understand the dynamics of communities, and landscape transformation, among other ecological indicators. PAM studies of landscape transformation have applied machine learning techniques using discrete labels for transformation states (i.e., high, medium, low). However, a site does not necessarily belong to a discrete label but can be between two transformation states. Thus, discretely labeling a degraded site while ignoring intermediate states is biased. Due to the natural variability of soundscape, multiple groups that describe different patterns are a requirement for clustering recordings that can belong to specific transformations. This paper proposes an unsupervised methodology based on clustering to identify the ecological transformation. Our proposal does not use transformation labels, either selecting the variables or training the models. This allows to find sites with intermediate states and associate different clusters to a specific level of ecological transformation. Similar groups of recordings were found and linked with ecological transformation using Gaussian Mixture Models (GMMs) in three periods of the day: morning (5-8), day (8-17), and night (17-5). We evaluated 13 Clustering Internal Validation Indices (CIVI) to know which one establishes the number of clusters associated with ecological transformation. Acoustic Indices (AIs) operated as variables to provide information on the acoustic complexity of the sites. We use the Dependence Guided Unsupervised Feature Selection (DGUFS) method to select the most relevant AIs. With data collected from 2015 to 2017, we tested the proposal in a Tropical Dry Forest ecosystem located in the Bolivar region of northern Colombia. Results showed that it is possible to identify the ecological transformation with an F1 score of 0.86 using the Scattering Distance (SD) index as CIVI. In the paper, we evidenced that it is possible to identify the ecological transformation not limited to known a-priori discrete labels.**

Index Terms*—Machine learning, Ecoacoustics, Soundscape, Clustering.

I. Introduction

One of the emerging ways to complement ecosystem monitoring studies is Passive Acoustic Monitoring (PAM) [1]. PAM involves acoustic soundscape recordings that incorporate information from geophony (earth-related sounds such as rain and thunder), biophony (animal sounds), and anthrophony (human and machine sounds). The acoustic data are used in Machine learning algorithms taking advantage of the rich information from soundscape estimating species richness [2], occupancy models [3], temporal trends of species [4], among others.

In particular, an emerging field in PAM is the study of the acoustic signature of ecosystem transformation [1]. The understanding of ecological transformation can help with conservation policies and restoration strategies, especially for endangered ecosystems [5]. Previous studies have demonstrated the effectiveness of Acoustic Indices (AIs) to determine the transformation of sites [6] and cover types [7]. So far, PAM works that have analyzed the transformation [8] and changes in habitats [9] have used supervised machine learning methods.

Ecological transformation labels used by supervised PAM methodologies are based on discrete pre-classification of health states by satellite imagery [5]. These transformation labels do not take into account community dynamics [10] and do not consider intra-class variability and the intermediate states in which sites could be. Then, supervised methodologies do not let data provide new information on site-specific variability associated with acoustic community dynamics. Some PAM methodologies have used clustering to give information about disturbances [11], geophonic, anthrophonic, biophonic activities [12], temporal patterns and cover types [5]. However, no studies have analyzed the soundscape to identify ecological transformation with unsupervised methodologies. Therefore, we propose a fully unsupervised methodology to identify ecological transformation and analyze acoustic gradients in each site using acoustic patterns.

Given that fine-tuning of parameters (number of clusters) under an unsupervised approach is a complex task, clustering validation indices have emerged to evaluate the resulting partitions [13]. There are two types of criteria in the cluster validation indices: The external, which compares results with existing classes (expected labels), and the internal, which compares results with similarity metrics (no labels usage) [14]. As in our proposal, we need to find information on the ecological transformation gradients, we use the Clustering Internal Validation Indices (CIVIs). However, these indices have drawbacks such as sensitivity to noisy datasets or overlapping classes, where each index gives different results regarding the recommended number of clusters [15]. Moreover, internal validation indices' performance is context-dependent [15], which implies that evaluations should be conducted at each application to select the index with the best performance. Nevertheless, to our knowledge, all clustering PAM studies have only considered one cluster validity index, and they did not implement an evaluation to select the adequate validity index for the particular study case. We integrate into our proposal an unsupervised feature selection of AIs, and an evaluation of 13 CIVIs to determine partitions that give complementary information to the ecological transformation models. Therefore, we propose a fully unsupervised automatic methodology to analyze the acoustic patterns related to ecological transformation gradients in a tropical dry forest.

The structure of the article is as follows. In Section II , we describe the proposed methodology and the used data. Results are given in Section III, and discussed in Section IV. Finally, conclusions are drawn in Section V.

II. Materials and Methods

A. Study site

The data used in this work were provided by the Alexander Von Humbold Institute. The acoustic recordings were acquired from 2015 to 2017 in the Colombian Caribbean region, in the department of Bolivar through a Global Environment Facility (GEF) project. The study sites correspond to a tropical dry forest ecosystem, which is an ecosystem distributed below 1000 m.a.s.l. highly seasonal in its rainfall with dry periods of at least three months. In the locality of Arroyo Grande (Bolivar), twelve sites were sampled along a landscape transformation gradient for over 1 week to reach a total of 2476 recordings. The recordings were obtained using Wildlife Acoustics' SM2 and SM3 recorders which were programmed to record 5-min every 10 minutes during 5 continuous days and stopping to record 5 days periodically. Prior to field campaigns and after a landscape transformation analysis was conducted, each site was classified as high, medium and low transformation. High transformation are sites with a low proportion of retained forest and high proportion of lost forest between 2000 and 2016.Low transformation are sites with a high proportion of retained forest and a low proportion of lost forest. The medium transformation are sites between theses two extremes. These labels were used to compare results of unsupervised algorithms and internal validation indices through the external validation index F1 score (explained in Table III).

B. Unsupervised methodology for transformation identification

For the unsupervised identification of ecological transformation, we propose the methodology presented in Figure 1. Our methodology follow these steps: First, calculate the AIs and select the most representative indices through the DGUFS method explained in section II-B2. With the selected AIs, train a GMM for each day period varying the number of clusters (see subsection II-B3). We tested 13 CIVIs (see Table I) to set the number of clusters. We found that the CIVI SD gives more information related to ecological transformation (see section III). We explain each step in the next subsections:

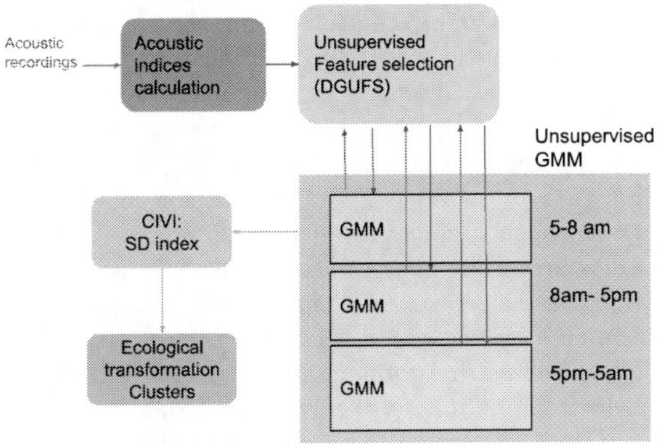

Fig. 1. Automatic unsupervised identification of ecological transformation through acoustic recordings Methodology.

1) Soundscape metrics : Acoustic Indices (AIs) are mathematical functions designed to estimate the acoustic complexity from communities to soundscapes. As equivalent to biodiversity indices in ecology, acoustic indices are indices that emphasize diversity of acoustic elements (similar to species) in a community (alpha (α) diversity), or indices that emphasize the similarity between two areas in terms of shared acoustic elements (beta (β) diversity) [16].

In this work, we focused on the α AIs to characterize the sound of each study site. We used the most popular AIs: Acoustic Complexity Index (frequency- time): 'ACIft' [17], Acoustic Diversity Index: 'ADI' [18], Acoustic Complexity Index (time- frequency): 'ACItf' [17], Bioacoustic index:'B' [19], Temporal Entropy: 'TE' [16], Entropy of spectral maxima: 'ESM' [20], Normalized Difference Soundscape Index: 'NDSI' [21], Ratio of biophony to anthrophony: 'P' [22], Median of amplitude envelope: 'M' [23], Number of peaks: 'NP' [23], Mid-band activity: 'MID' [20], Frequency Background Noise: 'BNF' [24], Temporal Background Noise: 'BNT' [24], Musicality Degree: 'MD' [25], Frequency Modulation: 'FM' [26], Spectral Flatness 'SF', Root Mean Square 'RMS', Crest Factor 'CF', Spectral Centroid 'SC', Spectral Bandwith 'SB', 'Tonnets', Signal Noise Ratio 'SNR' [27]. Also, we calculate the ADI index in each of the 1-11 frequency bands. These indices measure characteristics of the audios related to acoustic complexity. All these AIs were implemented in a user interface application available in [28] . Some of these indices have been used to classify in a supervised way sites by ecological transformation [6], cover types [7], quantify ecosystem changes over time [29] and study the ecological integrity [30].

The behaviors of the soundscape could vary in the hours of the day. Sanchez [30] showed that the relationship between AIs and ecological integrity can vary between different periods of the day. Rendon Hurtado [31] proposed three periods with different patterns of the sound: morning (5-8), day (8-17) and night (17-5). We used these periods to create three clustering models, one for each period.

2) Unsupervised feature selection method: Usually, feature selection in PAM studies has been done based on expert knowledge [29], [30], [32]. However, there are feature selection methods such as the wrapper methods that do not use the data labels. Wrapper methods help to improve the quality of clustering algorithms results based on unsupervised criteria [33]. The Dependence Guided Unsupervised Feature Selection (DGUFS) [34] is a wrapper method that enhances the interdependence among original data, cluster labels and selected features using the L_2 norm [34]. In this work, we use the DGUFS to select the most informative AIs. As a result, we obtain an $\boldsymbol{x}$ vector with the selected features.

3) Unsupervised transformation level model: To determine the transformation level of a site, we use the Gaussian Mixture Models (GMM) algorithm in an unsupervised way. As input features for the clustering, we use the selected AIs. GMM establishes a $P(x)$ distribution of nc clusters for the $\boldsymbol{x}$ feature vector;

$$P(\boldsymbol{x}) = \sum_{i=1}^{nc} \frac{1}{(2\pi)^{\frac{D}{2}} |\boldsymbol{\Sigma}_i|^{\frac{1}{2}}} exp[-\frac{1}{2} * (\boldsymbol{x} - \boldsymbol{\mu_G i})' * \boldsymbol{\Sigma_i}^{-1} (\boldsymbol{x} - \boldsymbol{\mu_G i})] \tag{1}$$

where $\boldsymbol{\mu_{Gi}}$ and $\boldsymbol{\Sigma}_i$ are GMM mean and covariance matrices of the data, respectively. The data is the matrix containing all estimated vector AIs for all training audios. D is the number of features (i.e., number of selected AIs). The algorithm parameters are denoted as $\lambda = (\boldsymbol{\mu_{Gi}}, \boldsymbol{\Sigma_i})$. To determine these parameters, we used the Expectation-Maximization (EM) algorithm refining the parameters using the log-likelihood in the data distribution. One of the characteristics of the GMM is that it requires the number of clusters. If we choose a number of clusters larger than the number of original transformation labels, then several clusters could belong to one transformation state (i.e. high, medium, low) providing information on intra-transformation patterns. We determine the number of clusters evaluating 13 CIVIs presented in the sub-section II-B4. The F1 score results were used as a benchmark to compare the unsupervised approach using CIVIs. We also tested other clustering algorithms (K-means, Gkmeans, DBscan, Fuzzy-Cmeans, Hidden Markov Model with Gaussian Mixture Model emissions (GMMHMM)) to contrast the results.

4) Cluster validation indices (CVIs): The task of finding clusters using unsupervised algorithms depends on the relative nature of the data [15]. CIVIs are proposed to select the best clustering according to a specific criteria [13]. However, CIVIs have certain drawbacks such as low performance due to noise and outliers in data [13], validating the clustering result for large data-sets involves a high computational cost [35], lack of stability and sensitivity to data-set size, and a number of features [14]. Furthermore, different clustering validation indices often recommend different partitions for the same data-set (with a different number of clusters) [36]. Performing comparisons between cluster validation indices would increase the robustness of the application using unsupervised learning. CIVIs are useful to compare solutions up to a limit that depends on the nature of the data. Therefore, the best solution must be found, according to each application. Comparing several CIVIs is relevant because each index can give information about clusters with different soundscape properties. Then, as we searched for partitions related to ecological transformation, we included a comparison of 13 CIVIs. We compared the behaviors of the CIVI presented in Table I with the external validation index F1, also presented in the table.

III. RESULTS

The 35 AIs mentioned above were calculated for each recording and standardized (0 to 1 values). We obtain the following AIs using the DGUFS method: 'ACIft', 'ACItf', 'BETA', 'NDSI', 'P', 'M', 'NP', 'MID', 'BNF', 'MD', 'FM', 'SF', 'RMS', ' SC', 'Tonnets'. Six clustering algorithms were tested by performing a grid search by tuning each algorithm with a different number of clusters (grid search from 2 to 80 clusters). Table II presents a comparison of clustering algorithms using the F1 score. The results show that GMM has the best performance for transformation identification. Then, we selected GMM as the proposed clustering algorithm in our methodology.

TABLE II
CLUSTERING ALGORITHMS COMPARISON USING THE F1 SCORE EXTERNAL CLUSTERING VALIDATION INDEX.

	Kmeans	Gkmeans	Dbscan	**GMM**	Fuzzy cmeans	GMM HMM
Maximum F1 score test data	0.8	0.79	0.5	**0.84**	0.79	0.74

GMM was used to cluster audios in each period (morning, day, and night). Figure 2 shows the F1 score varying the number of clusters from 2 to 80 for each period of the day. Stabilization of the F1 score was achieved at cluster numbers 53, 55 and 57 in the morning, daytime and evening periods.

TABLE I
COMPARED VALIDATION INDICES

Name	Equation	Principle	Reference
F1 score	$F1 = \frac{tp}{tp+\frac{1}{2}(fp+fn)}$	External validation index F1 score corresponds to the harmonic mean. tp represents the true positive, fp the false positives and fn the false negatives	[37]
Silhouette	$S = \sum_1^M (s(\boldsymbol{x_i}))$, $a(\boldsymbol{x_i}) = \frac{1}{\lvert A\rvert} \sum_{\boldsymbol{x_j}} d(\boldsymbol{x_i}, \boldsymbol{x_j})$ $b(\boldsymbol{x_i}) = \underset{B \epsilon K, B \neq A}{min} \frac{1}{\lvert B\rvert} \sum_{\boldsymbol{y_j} \epsilon B} d(\boldsymbol{x_i}, \boldsymbol{y_j})$ s($\boldsymbol{x_i}$)= b($\boldsymbol{x_i}$)-a($\boldsymbol{x_i}$)/max(b($\boldsymbol{x_i}$),a($\boldsymbol{x_i}$))	Silhoette (S) computes which data points fall properly withing the cluster. K is the number of centroids and M is the total number of data. A and B are clusters, $\boldsymbol{x_i}$ and $\boldsymbol{y_j}$ are points in A and B, respectively. $a(\boldsymbol{x_i})$ is the average dissimilarity of the object x_i. $b(\boldsymbol{x_i})$ is the minimum average dissimilarity of the point $\boldsymbol{x_i}$	[35]
Calinksy	$CH = \frac{M-k}{k-1} \frac{\sum_{A \epsilon K} d(\boldsymbol{c_A}, \bar{X})}{\sum_{A \epsilon K} d(\boldsymbol{x_i}, \boldsymbol{c_A})}$	The ratio between clusters variance and within clusters variance, where M is the number of data, d is the distance and **c_*A*** is the centroid of cluster A and $\bar{X}$ is the mean of all data.	[38]
SD	Scat= (1/$\boldsymbol{nc}$) $\sum_{i=1}^{K} \frac{\lVert\sigma(\boldsymbol{c_i})\rVert}{\lVert\sigma(\boldsymbol{X})\rVert}$ $Dis = \frac{(max\lVert\boldsymbol{c_a}-\boldsymbol{c_b}\rVert)}{(min\lVert\boldsymbol{c_a}-\boldsymbol{c_b}\rVert)} * \sum_{k=1}^{K} \left(\sum_{z=1}^{nc} \lvert\lvert\boldsymbol{c_a} - \boldsymbol{c_b}\rvert\rvert\right)^{-1}$ $SD = Scat + Dis$	Sum of the average scattering ($Scat$) and average separation between clusters (Dis).	[39]
S_Dbw	$\sigma = \frac{1}{K}\sqrt{\sum_{k=1}^{nc} \lvert\lvert\boldsymbol{v}(k)\rvert\rvert}$ $R_{kk'} = \frac{\gamma_{kk'}(\boldsymbol{H}_{kk'})}{max(\gamma_{kk'}(\boldsymbol{G}^k), \gamma_{kk'}(\boldsymbol{G}^{k'}))}$ $\varsigma = \frac{2}{K(K-1)} \sum_{k<k'} R_{kk'}$ $\delta = \frac{\frac{1}{K}\sum_{k=1}^{k} \lvert\lvert\boldsymbol{v}(k)\rvert\rvert}{\lvert\lvert\boldsymbol{v}\rvert\rvert}$ $S_{Dbw} = \varsigma + \delta$	The S_Dbw relies on the notion of density belonging to two clusters. $\boldsymbol{v}$ is the vector of clusters variances . $\gamma_{kk'}$ is the number of points of clusters C_k and $C_{k'}$, $\boldsymbol{G^k}$ and $\boldsymbol{G^{k'}}$ are the clusters barycenters, $\boldsymbol{H_{kk'}}$ are the midpoints, and ς is the between cluster density.	[35]
PC	$PC = \frac{1}{M} \sum_{A \epsilon K} \sum_{l}^{M} \boldsymbol{w}^{\mathbf{2}}_{\mathbf{A},\boldsymbol{l}}$	The Partition Coefficient (PC) is the sum of the squared individual fuzzy membership $\boldsymbol{w_{i,j}}$ by the number of total data.	[40]
GStr	$oi_{rex,A} = min_{j=1,\ldots,k,j\neq A}(\tau_{Aj} - \Lambda_{corr,A} - \Lambda_{corr,j})$ $oi_{str,A} = min_{j=1,\ldots,k,j\neq A}(\tau_{Aj} - \Lambda_{ext,A} - \Lambda_{ext,j})$ $G(oi, \Lambda) = \frac{\sum_{j=1}^{k} oi_{Aj} \lVert A_j \rVert}{\sum_{j=1}^{k} \Lambda_{Aj} \lVert A_j \rVert}$ $G_{str} = G(oi_{str}, \Lambda_{ext})$	G_{str} is the strict version of G (in the 50% of the points). τ is the distance between each pair of clusters. $\Lambda_{cor,A}$ is the median of distances of a point and its cluster that embraces exactly the 50% of the points. $\Lambda_{ext,j}$ ensures that, at least, 75 percent of the samples fall within the extended volume boundary. G uses the five determinant elements that are necessary to draw a summarized representation of the dataset geometry: number of spheres k , sphere center c_j , sphere separation oi_j, and sphere mass A_j.	[15]
Grex	$\mathrm{G}_{ext} = G(oi_{rex}, \Lambda_{cor})$	G_{ext} is the strict version of G (in the 75% of the points)	[15]
Gmin	$\mathrm{G}_{min} = min_{j \epsilon k}\left(\left\{\frac{oi_{str,j}}{\Lambda_{ext,j}}\right\}\right)$	G_{min} is the minimum relation of the strict overlap index $oi_{str,j}$ and the median of the external distances $\Lambda_{cor,A}$	[15]
CE	$CE = -\frac{1}{M} \sum_{A \epsilon K} \sum_{l}^{M} \boldsymbol{w}_{\boldsymbol{A},\boldsymbol{l}} log_{\alpha} \boldsymbol{w}_{\boldsymbol{A},\boldsymbol{l}}$	The Classification Entropy index (CE) is the sum of the entropies of $\boldsymbol{w_{i,j}}$ scores. Good partition is expected to show low entropy values. α is the base of the logarithm. In our work, we use the natural logarithm.	[15]
Xie Beni	$XB = \frac{\sum_{A \epsilon k} \sum_{M}^{l} \boldsymbol{w}_{\boldsymbol{A},\boldsymbol{l}}{}^{\beta} d(\boldsymbol{x_l}, \boldsymbol{c_A}{}^2)}{M min_{A,B \epsilon K}\{d(\boldsymbol{c_A}, \boldsymbol{c_B})^2\}}$	Xie Beni index is defined as the ratio of compactness and separation of a hard or fuzzy partition. $\beta = 2$ is used in our work.	[14]
DI	$\delta(A, B) = min_{x_i \epsilon A, y_j \epsilon B}\{d(\boldsymbol{x_i}, \boldsymbol{y_j})\}$ $\Delta(A) = max_{\boldsymbol{x_i}, \boldsymbol{x_j} \epsilon A} d(\boldsymbol{x_i}, \boldsymbol{x_j})$ $DI = \frac{min_{A \epsilon k}\{min_{B \epsilon, B \neq A} \delta(A,B)\}}{max_{A \epsilon K} \Delta(A)}$	Dunn Index (DI) is defined as the minimal ratio between the distance of the closest points between clusters, and largest clusters diameter (the most separated objects withing a cluster)	[41]

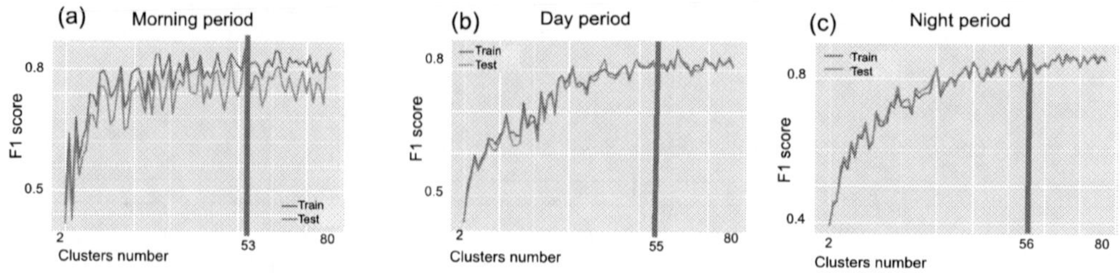

Fig. 2. F1 score varying the number of clusters with the GMM algorithm in each period (a) morning period (5-8), (b) day period (8-17), and (c) night (17-5). The results suggest that the stabilization (red line) is obtained with the cluster numbers of 53, 55 and 56 in each period

These results show that it is not enough to have only three discrete categories (high, medium, low). A large number of clusters is required to identify the transformation. Since our objective was the automatic and unsupervised identification of ecological transformation, we estimated the CIVIs explained in Table I, with the clustering obtained varying the number of the cluster in each GMM model. Table III shows the recommended number of clusters of the CIVIs in each day period.

TABLE III
RECOMMENDED NUMBER OF CLUSTERS FOR EACH CIVI VARYING THE NUMBER OF CLUSTERS FROM 2 TO 80 USING GMM AS CLUSTERING ALGORITHM

Indice	Daily periods		
	5-8 (morning)	8-17 (day)	17-5 (night)
F1 score (stabilization)	53	55	56
Silhouette	2	2	2
Calinksy	2	3	3
Davies	21	10	23
SD	61	62	44
S_Dbw	2	2	2
PC	2	2	2
GStr	7	7	2
Grex	1	1	2
Gmin	2	2	2
CE	2	2	2
Xie Beni	79	74	79
DI	2	2	2

We expected three groups representing the three transformation labels. However, the partitions found with a number of clusters of 3 did not correspond to the ecological transformation (see Calinksy index performance in Figure 3).

IV. DISCUSSION

In this work, it was proved that it is possible to build GMM models to identify the tropical dry forest transformation in a completely unsupervised way. Our proposal includes automatic feature selection and a selection of adequate partitions. Our proposal was tested in the Bolivar region in northern Colombia. Figure 3 presents a comparison of the best performance clustering validation indices.

The Calinksy index suggests a lower number of clusters in each period (morning:2, day:3, night:3). These are the number of labels of previously categorized transformations. The low

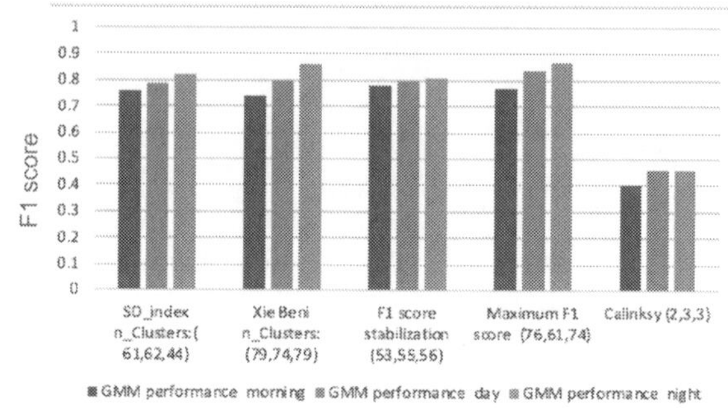

Fig. 3. F1 score using CIVIs: SD index, Xie Beni index, F1 score stabilization, and Calinksy. In each approach the parenthesis show the number of the recommended clusters for each day period

performance of Calinksy index (max F1=0.47) shows that there exist acoustic nuances that describe more variability than the preliminary discrete categories of the transformation.

Only the Xie Beni index and SD index recommended a number of clusters that correspond to ecological transformation using as a metric the external F1 score (F1<0.75). The Xie Beni index suggests 79 clusters for the morning model, 74 for the day model, and 79 for the night period. These number of clusters permit to identify the ecological transformation with a high f1 score (see Figure 3). The behavior of the Xie Beni index (see Figure 4) establishes that the adequate cluster number corresponds to the minimum value (0 in this case). Then, we tested the behavior of the index with different limits: 30, 80, and 200, obtaining the number of clusters 29, 79, and 197, respectively for each threshold. The Xie Beni value decreases when the number of clusters increases. These results suggest that Xie Beni values tend to grow when the number of clusters grows without reaching stabilization. This problem had already been mentioned in the literature by Rita de Franco et al. [42] and Singh et al. [43], who made a modification of the index. However, these CIVIs were proposed for fuzzy clustering algorithms. For this reason, we do not use them in our study.

The SD recommends cluster numbers 61, 62, and 44, which are much closer to the external performance stabilization (F1 score stabilization in Figure 2). Thus, using the unsupervised Gaussian mixtures approach and with the use of the SD,

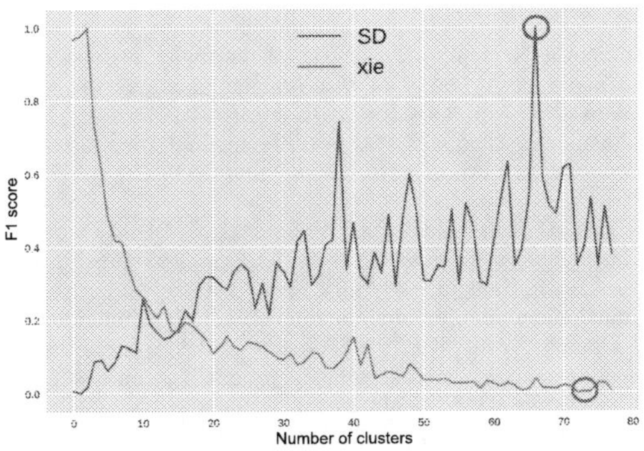

Fig. 4. Comparison of the SD (blue) and Xie Beni (green) behaviors in the morning period, varying the number of clusters in the GMM algorithm. Where the recommended partitions are the maximum value for the SD and the minimum value Xie Beni index (red points in the graph).

it is possible to identify the ecological transformation of ecosystems through sound.

In order to identify the meaning of the intermediate clusters not included in the discrete labels, the behavior of AIs means in some found clusters are shown in Figure 5.

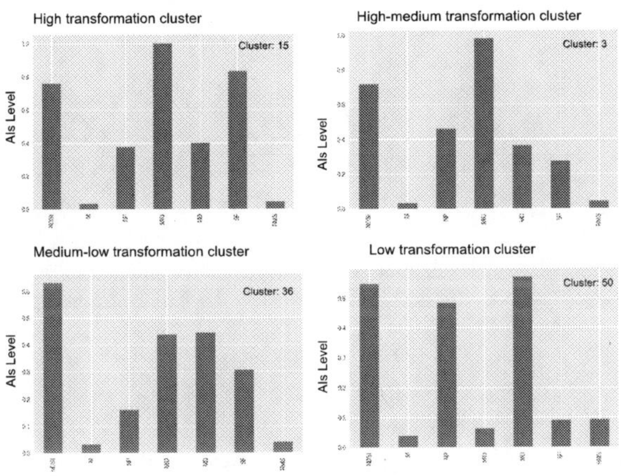

Fig. 5. AIs mean in different clusters that represents different ecological transformation levels. Clusters 13, 3, 36 and 50 represents high, high-medium, medium-low, and low transformation levels, respectively

Analyzing acoustic indices using machine learning techniques increases results interpretation regarding ecological aspects which cannot be achieved with other techniques such as deep learning. For example, in Figure 5, it is evident that the NP index increases as the transformation decreases. This behavior was expected since this index is related to the biodiversity of a site. On the other hand, the graph shows intermediate clusters (high-medium and medium-low transformation), which would not have been found using a supervised approach. These clusters show AIs with intermediate values between high and low transformation.

V. Conclusions

This paper shows a methodology to identify tropical dry forest transformation in a completely unsupervised way. Having an unsupervised approach allows not only to have an adequate identification of 3 discrete states (high, medium, low) but also to find intermediate states. Results show that it is possible to determine the ecological transformation by sound in an unsupervised manner in a tropical dry forest. In addition, in the field of clustering validation, more work should be done on the task of finding CIVIs specially designed for this type of application.

Acknowledgment

This work was supported by Universidad de Antioquia, Instituto Tecnológico Metropolitano de Medellín, Alexander von Humboldt Institute for Research on Biological Resources, Colombian National Fund for Science, Technology and Innovation, Francisco Jose de Caldas - MINCIENCIAS (Colombia) [Program No. 111585269779], and ECOSNord program: MESRI (France) et MINCIENCIAS (Colombia) [Cod. 83477. Cto.494-2021].

References

[1] R. Gibb, E. Browning, P. Glover-Kapfer, and K. E. Jones, "Emerging opportunities and challenges for passive acoustics in ecological assessment and monitoring," *Methods in Ecology and Evolution*, vol. 2019, pp. 169–185, 2018.

[2] K. Darras, P. Pütz, Fahrurrozi, K. Rembold, and T. Tscharntke, "Measuring sound detection spaces for acoustic animal sampling and monitoring," *Biological Conservation*, vol. 201, pp. 29–37, 9 2016.

[3] D. I. Rappaport, J. A. Royle, and D. C. Morton, "Acoustic space occupancy: Combining ecoacoustics and lidar to model biodiversity variation and detection bias across heterogeneous landscapes," *Ecological Indicators*, vol. 113, p. 106172, 2020.

[4] A. Gasc, J. Sueur, S. Pavoine, R. Pellens, and P. Grandcolas, "Biodiversity Sampling Using a Global Acoustic Approach: Contrasting Sites with Microendemics in New Caledonia," *PLoS ONE*, vol. 8, no. 5, pp. 279–287, 2013.

[5] Y. Deng, W. Qi, B. Fu, and K. Wang, "Geographical transformations of urban sprawl: Exploring the spatial heterogeneity across cities in china 1992–2015," *Cities*, vol. 105, pp. 123–144, 10 2020.

[6] D. C. Duque-Montoya and C. Isaza, "Automatic Ecosystem Identification Using Psychoacoustical Features," no. 52, pp. 1–4, 2018.

[7] W. E. Gómez, C. V. Isaza, and J. M. Daza, "Identifying disturbed habitats: A new method from acoustic indices," *Ecological Informatics*, vol. 45, no. March, pp. 16–25, 2018.

[8] R. Hurtado, Isaza-Narváez, and Rodrigueez-Buritica, "Automatic identification of transformation in the colombian tropical dry forest using gmm and ubm-gmm," *IEEE Transl. Revista Facultad de Ingeniería*, vol. 29, no. 54, pp. 1–19, 2020.

[9] D. Bormpoudakis, J. Sueur, and J. Pantis, "Spatial heterogeneity of ambient sound at the habitat type level: Ecological implications and applications," *Landscape Ecology*, vol. 28, pp. 495–506, 03 2013.

[10] B. Krause, "The niche hypothesis: A virtual symphony of animal sounds, the origins of musical expression and the health of habitats," *Soundscape Newsletter (World Forum for Acoustic Ecology)*, pp. 6–10, 06 1993.

[11] C. Flowers et al., "Looking for the -scape in the sound: Discriminating soundscapes categories in the sonoran desert using indices and clustering," *Ecological Indicators*, vol. 127, pp. 1–15, 8 2021.

[12] R. Benocci et al, "Eco-acoustic assessment of an urban park by statistical analysis," *Sustainability (Switzerland)*, vol. 13, pp. 110–125, 7 2021.

[13] S. H. Lee, Y. S. Jeong, J. Y. Kim, and M. K. Jeong, "A new clustering validity index for arbitrary shape of clusters," *Pattern Recognition Letters*, vol. 112, pp. 263–269, 2018.

[14] M. Muranishi, K. Honda, and A. Notsu, "Xie-beni-type fuzzy cluster validation in fuzzy co-clustering of documents and keywords,"

[15] F. Iglesias, T. Zseby, and A. Zimek, "Absolute cluster validity," *IEEE Transactions on Pattern Analysis and Machine Intelligence*, vol. 42, no. 9, pp. 2096–2112, 2020.
[16] J. Sueur, S. Pavoine, O. Hamerlynck, and S. Duvail, "Rapid acoustic survey for biodiversity appraisal," *PLoS ONE*, vol. 3, no. 12, pp. 1–14, 2008.
[17] A. Farina, N. Pieretti, P. Salutari, E. Tognari, and A. Lombardi, "The Application of the Acoustic Complexity Indices (ACI) to Ecoacoustic Event Detection and Identification (EEDI) Modeling," *Biosemiotics*, vol. 9, no. 2, pp. 227–246, 2016.
[18] J. Sueur and A. Farina, "Ecoacoustics: the Ecological Investigation and Interpretation of Environmental Sound," *Biosemiotics*, vol. 8, no. 3, pp. 493–502, 2015.
[19] N. T. Boelman, G. P. Asner, P. J. Hart, and R. E. Martin, "Multi-Trophic Invasion Resistance in Hawaii: Bioacoustics, Field Surveys, and Airborne Remote Sensing," *Ecological Applications*, vol. 17, no. 8, pp. 2137–2144, 2007.
[20] M. Towsey, J. Wimmer, I. Williamson, and P. Roe, "The use of acoustic indices to determine avian species richness in audio-recordings of the environment," *Ecological Informatics*, vol. 21, no. 100, pp. 110–119, 2014.
[21] E. P. Kasten, S. H. Gage, J. Fox, and W. Joo, "The remote environmental assessment laboratory's acoustic library: An archive for studying soundscape ecology," *Ecological Informatics*, vol. 12, pp. 50–67, 2012.
[22] R. Planqué and H. Slabbekoorn, "Spectral overlap in songs and temporal avoidance in a peruvian bird assemblage," *Ethology*, vol. 114, pp. 262 – 271, 02 2008.
[23] M. Depraetere et al., "Monitoring animal diversity using acoustic indices: Implementation in a temperate woodland," *Ecological Indicators*, vol. 13, no. 1, pp. 1–10, 2012.
[24] M. Towsey, "Noise removal from waveforms and spectrograms derived from natural recordings of the environment.," pp. 1–4, 2013.
[25] B. De Coensel, *Introducing the temporal aspect in environmental soundscape research.* PhD thesis, Ghent University, 2007.
[26] M. Towsey, L. Zhang, M. Cottman-Fields, J. Wimmer, J. Zhang, and P. Roe, "Visualization of long-duration acoustic recordings of the environment," *Procedia Computer Science*, vol. 29, no. Krause 2008, pp. 703–712, 2014.
[27] D. Ellis et al., "librosa: Audio and Music Signal Analysis in Python," *Proceedings of the 14th Python in Science Conference*, no. Scipy, pp. 18–24, 2015.
[28] C. Isaza, D. Duque, and R. E. Rendon, N, "Acoustic indices application." https://udeaeduco-my.sharepoint.com/:u:/g/personal/nestor_rendon_udea_edu_co/Eb_g2fJbQKBLmRHliwXsp5wB7MhSbE8msTvIJ1V1sVEZOg?e=4B7MzX, 2022. [Online; accessed 10-July-2022].
[29] J. Doser, A. Finley, E. Kasten, and S. Gage, "Assessing soundscape disturbance through hierarchical models and acoustic indices: A case study on a shelterwood logged northern michigan forest," *Ecological Indicators*, vol. 113, p. 106244, 06 2020.
[30] C. Sánchez-Giraldo, C. C. Ayram, and J. M. Daza, "Environmental sound as a mirror of landscape ecological integrity in monitoring programs," *Perspectives in Ecology and Conservation*, vol. 19, pp. 319–328, 7 2021.
[31] N. Rendon Hurtado, "Automatic acoustic heterogeneity identification in transformed landscapes from Colombian tropical dry forests," Master's thesis, Universidad de Antioquia, Medellin, Colombia. pp 1-57, 2020.
[32] A. Rodriguez, A. Gasc, S. Pavoine, P. Grandcolas, P. Gaucher, and J. Sueur, "Temporal and spatial variability of animal sound within a neotropical forest," *Ecological Informatics*, vol. 21, pp. 133–143, 2014.
[33] S. Solorio-Fernández, J. A. Carrasco-Ochoa, and J. F. Martínez-Trinidad, "A review of unsupervised feature selection methods," *Artificial Intelligence Review*, vol. 53, pp. 907–948, 2 2020.
[34] J. Guo and W. Zhu, "Dependence guided unsupervised feature selection," *Proceedings of the AAAI Conference on Artificial Intelligence*, vol. 32, pp. 0–18, Apr. 2018.
[35] A. Dudek, "Silhouette index as clustering evaluation tool, classification and data analysis., springer international publishing," in *Classification and Data Analysis* (K. Jajuga, J. Batóg, and M. Walesiak, eds.), (Cham), pp. 19–33, Springer International Publishing, 2020.
[36] M. Kim and R. S. Ramakrishna, "New indices for cluster validity assessment," *Pattern Recognition Letters*, vol. 26, pp. 2353–2363, 11 2005.
[37] M. Sokolova, N. Japkowicz, and S. Szpakowicz, "Beyond accuracy, f-score and roc: A family of discriminant measures for performance evaluation," vol. Vol. 4304, pp. 1015–1021, 01 2006.
[38] T. Caliński and Harabasz, "A dendrite method for cluster analysis," *Communications in Statistics - Theory and Methods*, vol. 3, pp. 1–27, 01 1974.
[39] M. Halkidi, M. Vazirgiannis, and Y. Batistakis, "Quality scheme assessment in the clustering process," vol. 1910, pp. 265–276, 01 2000.
[40] J. Bezdek, R. Ehrlich, and W. Full, "Fcm—the fuzzy c-means clustering-algorithm," *Computers Geosciences*, vol. 10, pp. 191–203, 12 1984.
[41] J. C. Dunn, "A fuzzy relative of the isodata process and its use in detecting compact well-separated clusters," *Journal of Cybernetics*, vol. 3, no. 3, pp. 32–57, 1973.
[42] C. Rita de Franco, L. Silva Vidal, and A. Joaquim de Oliveira Cruz, "A validity measure for hard and fuzzy clustering derived from fisher's linear discriminant," in *2002 IEEE World Congress on Computational Intelligence. 2002 IEEE International Conference on Fuzzy Systems. FUZZ-IEEE'02. Proceedings (Cat. No.02CH37291)*, vol. 2, pp. 1493–1498, 02 2002.
[43] M. Singh, R. Bhattacharjee, N. Sharma, and A. Verma, "An improved xie-beni index for cluster validity measure," in *2017 Fourth International Conference on Image Information Processing (ICIIP)*, pp. 1–5, 2017.

An Epidemiological Approach for Mobile Ad-Hoc Networks Monitoring

Christophe Guyeux, Abdallah Makhoul, and Jacques Bahi
Femto-St Institute, UMR 6174 CNRS
Université de Bourgogne Franche-Comté, France
Email: {first}.{last}@femto-st.fr

***Abstract*—MANETS are vulnerable to many types of attacks. Moreover, many challenges arise in the MANET management, such as dynamic network topology, limited bandwidth, storage capacity, battery life and processing power. In order to ensure high network performance, an important function of network management is monitoring. It consists in observing the operational states of the connected mobile nodes and controlling the application quality of service and prevent attacks. Indeed, malicious participants may disrupt the system through altering the collected data, reporting false measurements, defining new management policies or flooding f alse a larms. I n t his paper, an epidemic model is developed to ensure an efficient MANET monitoring. It will be useful in various contexts, to provide for instance design parameters of the MANET such that the number of malicious nodes always remains under control. Theoretical modeling and analysis of various situations are then provided, and simulations results on real case scenario are proposed.**

***Keywords*—Mobile ad hoc networks; Epidemiological approach; Monitoring model; Security.**

I. Introduction

A Mobile Ad hoc NETwork (MANET) is defined a s an autonomous and infrastructure less system of mobile devices, such as laptop, mobile phones,Personal Digital Assistant (PDA), etc. [1] [2] which can be connected everywhere [3] [4] [5] [6]. These devices can cooperate to maintain this temporary network and to provide services like routing, service discovery, and other application services. Some of the challenges that face MANETs are dynamic network topology, undefined geographical coverage area, limited resources (battery power, bandwidth, central processing unit (CPU) and storage space), communication overhead, security, mobility, scalability, and so on [7] [8] [9] [10]. Considering these specific c onstraints, a mechanism of self monitoring must be implemented to control the network state.

Monitoring of MANET consists in observing the operational states of the connected mobile nodes, controlling the application quality of service and preventing attacks. Monitoring can further be concerned with malicious attacks prevention. This monitoring is achieved by a subset of mobile nodes (called monitors) which are elected according to several predefined parameters [11]. Each monitor performs its assigned tasks (collect and process data) and, at the same time, is responsible for controlling and monitoring a subset of mobile nodes in its area called the monitored nodes.

In this article, we propose to determine the optimal parameters of a the network monitoring by means of epidemiological models. The total number of sensors is divided by compartment, according to their intrinsic nature: monitored, monitoring, selfish, or malicious. Furthermore, various rates define the state modification of a sensor (e.g., from monitoring to malicious after a successful attack) [12] [13]. According to the complexity of the model, which can take under consideration the death rates, any scheduling process, or the discovery of new nodes, the resulted differential system can either be theoretically handled or it can only be observed through numerical simulations. All these situations are presented in this article, whose aim is to illustrate the power of epidemiological modeling in the study of MANET monitoring.

The remainder of the paper is organized as follows. A brief state of the art is presented in the next section. Then, an example of study of a MANET at short timescales is proposed in Section III. Section IV presents some numerical simulations in the most complex situation where monitored, monitoring, selfish, and malicious nodes are present in the network. This article ends by a conclusion section, where the contribution is summarized and intended future work is outlined.

II. Related Work

In the literature, we can find several approaches for MANET monitoring. The aim of these works is to guarantee an efficient quality of service of the network in spite of the presence of some anomalies and in the presence of malicious or selfish nodes [14].

Liu et al. [15] propose an epidemic model for rechargeable wireless sensor networks. This model is based on pulse charging and aims to model the low and normal energy in each periodic pulse point. In [16], the authors propose a secure multi-casting in order to ensure data secret transmission between the manager, the cluster heads, and the agents. Thus, the exchanged data must be encrypted with timeliness information and with a digital signature. Moreover, a level-based access control model is implemented to protect the monitoring data from unauthorized access. However, the authors do not specify how the manager generates the security level of each node. In [17], the authors propose a probabilistic scheme in order to enhance the reliability of monitoring by excluding the dishonest managed nodes that provide unreal data management from the data collection. Nevertheless, the scheme effectiveness depends on the exchanged measurements correctness [18]. Furthermore, the authors do not take into account the managers malicious behavior.

A survivable monitoring that allows a set of nodes called domain nodes to monitor the behavior of visitors when they join their domains, is presented in [19]. It supposes that the supervisor is reliable and trusted and that the domain nodes are too. In [20], the authors propose to assess the selfish behaviors of each monitored node regarding its co-operations in forwarding others packets. However, it is a passive monitoring. In addition, they do not take into account the monitoring units malicious and selfish behaviors.

The authors of [21] propose to authenticate mobile nodes in order to detect intrusion. Thus, they use a non-interactive zero knowledge technique to determine a set of nodes having access to specific applications or services in MANET. Among these authorized nodes, only those with the highest battery life can play the role of monitors. However, the authors do not take into account the monitors malicious or selfish behaviors. Finally, in [22], the authors aim to detect the inappropriate behaviors of mobile nodes for ensuring efficient routing. In fact, they propose to add three components: a monitor, a reputation system, and a path manager, to the DSR (Dynamic Source Routing) routing protocol functionality.

All these limitations in the related works provide us with the motivation to propose a new monitoring scheme based on epidemiological modeling [23] [24]. Indeed, in this paper, we consider a monitoring approach as efficient if it aims to perform correctly and legally the monitoring tasks in spite of the presence of some anomalies (mobility or the failure of a monitor, unavailability of routes between monitors and some monitored nodes, etc.) and in the presence of malicious and selfish nodes as well. The theoretical study will encompass short and large timescales, while a more complete model will be investigated by means of numerical simulations.

III. Studying the MANET at short timescales

Let us firstly consider 3 types of sensors:

- monitored $S(t)$,
- monitoring $I(t)$,
- malicious $R(t)$.

Malicious nodes attack the monitors and make them unable to do their work. These monitors, once attacked, become in turn malicious. The adversary goal is to corrupt all the monitor nodes ($I(t) \longrightarrow 0$ when $t \rightarrow +\infty$). Conversely, the user wants the guarantee that, at each time, at least one of these monitors is available for network surveillance ($\forall t, I(t) > 0$).

We suppose in this article that attacks need contacts to be performed (*i.e.*, a monitor must be within the transmission range of a malicious node), and we denote by β the rate of successful attacks per contact. It is therefore, a rate of "effective contacts" between monitor and malicious nodes, in terms of epidemiological models. When such an effective contact occurs, the considered sensor moves from the I compartment (monitoring) to the R (malicious) one.

Furthermore, let us denote by α the rate, constant over time, of sensors moving from the "monitored" state to the "monitoring" one. In practice, this rate depends on numerous parameters: node reputation, their capacity, and their ability (CPU, memory, mobility, energy, etc.). Let us remark that, if the number of neighbors (that is, the degree of the node in the connectivity graph) can be part of these parameters, most of the times it is only a secondary factor according to the literature.

We denote by $N = S(t) + I(t) + R(t)$ the total number of sensors. It will firstly be supposed to be constant, as we will consider first the evolution of the network on small timescales: the energy consumption (and the node failure due to an empty battery) is negligible under such assumption. Indeed, the objective at the beginning of this study is to evaluate if it is possible to avoid, on small timescales, that $I(t)$ becomes equal to 0.

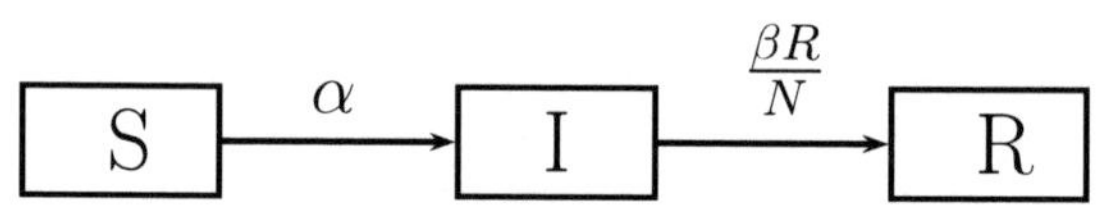

Figure 1: Our first compartmental model

Having the definitions of S, I, and R on the one hand, and the rates α and β on the other hand, we are then left to study the compartmental model depicted in Figure 1. To begin with, let us remark that, in the literature of epidemiological models, susceptible individuals become infected proportionally to their contacts with infected individuals, while infected people become recovered at a rate independent from any contact. In other words, the non-linearity is usually between S and I compartments, leading to the classical SIR model depicted in Figure 2.

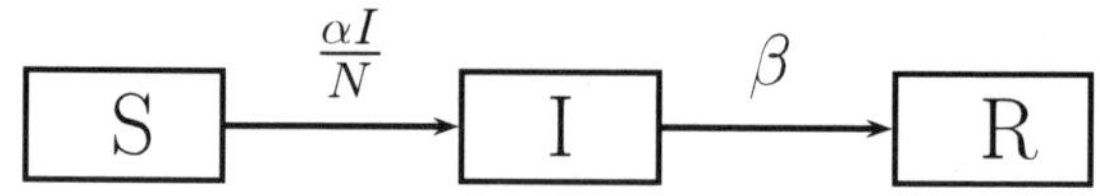

Figure 2: Usual SIR model

Our first model based on the MANETs study is not usual and, until now, it has never been studied in the literature. This remark still remains valid for the more refined models that will be presented later in this article. However, if the differential equations deduced from a compartmental modeling of MANET monitoring are different from the ones usually found with classical models (like the so-called SIR, SIS, SEIS, and so on), their shape is similar enough to consider that existing tools and methods may be applied to them too, in order to resolve them. The model in Figure 1 can be formulated using differential equations, as follows.

$$\begin{cases} \dot{S} = -\alpha S \\ \dot{I} = \alpha S - \frac{\beta}{N} IR \\ \dot{R} = \frac{\beta}{N} IR \end{cases} \quad (1)$$

As we suppose, in this section, that the total number of sensors is constant over time, then $S(t)$ can be deduced from $I(t)$ and $R(t)$, as follows:

$$S(t) = N - I(t) - R(t).$$

We can thus only consider the two last variables and the two last equations in Eq. (1):

$$\begin{cases} \dot{I} = \alpha(N - I - R) - \frac{\beta}{N} IR \\ \dot{R} = \frac{\beta}{N} IR \end{cases}$$

We can focus now on proportions $\frac{I}{N}$ and $\frac{R}{N}$, which are renamed as I and R, which leads to the normalized equation:

$$\begin{cases} \dot{I} = \alpha(1 - I - R) - \beta IR \\ \dot{R} = \beta IR. \end{cases} \quad (2)$$

Let us remark first that $\dot{R} \geqslant 0$. So, at short timescale such that the energy consumption is negligible, the number of malicious nodes necessarily increases (similarly, in the usual SIR model, the number of susceptible necessarily decreases).

The equilibrium solutions satisfying $\dot{I} = \dot{R} = 0$ are such that:

- either $R = 0$, and so $I = 1$,
- or $I = 0$, and so $R = 1$.

In other words, the two equilibrium solutions of the system are either when all the nodes are monitor ones, or when they all are malicious. Starting in such a configuration, the system will obviously not evolve.

Let us now study the behavior of the network at the neighborhood of these equilibrium points, *i.e.*, when the proportions of monitor I and malicious R nodes are either close to $(1, 0)$ (almost all nodes are monitors) or $(0, 1)$ (almost all nodes are malicious). In order to do so, the system can be linearized. Its Jacobian matrix is equal to:

$$\begin{pmatrix} -\alpha - \beta R & -\alpha - \beta I \\ \beta R & \beta I \end{pmatrix}.$$

At the equilibrium $(1, 0)$, this latter is equal to:

$$\begin{pmatrix} -\alpha & -\alpha - \beta \\ 0 & \beta \end{pmatrix}.$$

This matrix being triangular, its eigenvalues are on the main diagonal: $-\alpha$ and β. α and β being positive, we thus find non null eigenvalues with opposite signs. So, the equilibrium point $(1, 0)$ is a saddle point in the phase diagram of (I, R).

Let us consider now the neighborhood of the point $(0, 1)$. The Jacobian matrix on this equilibrium point is equal to:

$$\begin{pmatrix} -\alpha - \beta & -\alpha \\ \beta & 0 \end{pmatrix}.$$

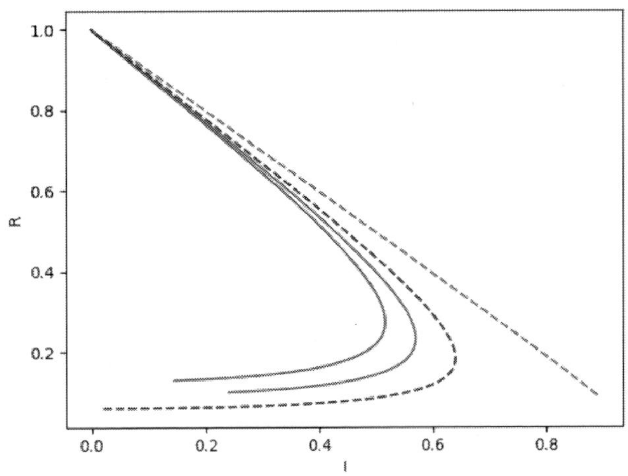

Figure 3: Network behavior (I and R rates) close to the equilibrium position (0,1).

The characteristic polynomial being $X^2 + (\alpha + \beta)X + \alpha\beta$, its two eigenvalues are $-\alpha$ and $-\beta$. Being of the same negative sign, we can conclude that this equilibrium position $(0, 1)$ is stable, see Figure 3. Note that, as $\dot{R} = \beta IR$, we have $\dot{R} \geqslant 0$. So, R can only increase, which explains the shape of the curves in Figure 3.

To sum up, either there is no malicious node at initial time, and so in the absence of energetic considerations, all the monitored nodes eventually become monitoring ones. Or there is at least one malicious node and, over time, all nodes become malicious. Such a description of the MANET behavior is only valid when operations between nodes are negligible when compared to the sensors lifetime.

After having investigated some capabilities of a theoretical study of a MANET described in terms of epidemiological models, we now numerically illustrate various evolutions of the numbers of nodes according to the parameters of the system.

IV. Numerical Simulations

We now consider the existence of selfish nodes, that for instance become inactive for the monitoring when their battery is below a given threshold. We consider too the possibility that a monitoring node switches to the monitored state, for example if its battery is below a critical value. Such considerations evoked in the literature lead to the compartment model depicted in Figure 4. This model contains now four compartments, corresponding to the inactive (compartment A), monitored (B), monitoring (C), and malicious (D) nodes. Various parameters can be defined between these four compartments.

- Λ is the rate used to define the integration of new mobile devices within the area, which will populate the

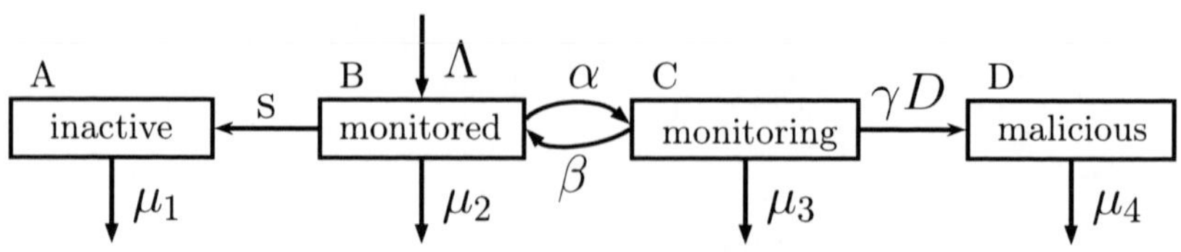

Figure 4: A more global compartmental model for MANET

B compartment (as new devices are first set to monitored mode).

- s is the rate under which some monitored nodes become selfish, and thus stop to participate to the network. This rate can be defined as a proportion of monitored devices that, under a given energy threshold, prefer to preserve themselves instead of the network.
- α is the rate at which monitored nodes start to monitor the network. By doing so, they become more useful for the network, but their activity increases accordingly, leading to a reduced lifetime.
- Conversely, β is the rate on which a monitoring device stops its monitor activity. According to the literature, this may be for a large variety of reasons, encompassing a coverage issue (too many monitors in a given area, or a too small number of devices to monitor), battery level, etc.
- Between C and D compartments, the rate is γD, which is proportional to the number of malicious devices. γ measures the probability of success that a malicious node achieves to convert a monitoring node. Indeed, we consider in this simulation that, in case of a successful attack, the attacked monitoring device becomes a malicious one (but other configurations are possible). As such an attack needs a contact with a malicious node, this rate is proportional to D.
- μ_1, μ_2, μ_3, and μ_4 are the "death" rates associated with the four aforementioned compartments. They are the rates that correspond to the depopulation of each compartment: mobiles that have emptied their batteries or that become deficient stop to be considered in their associated compartment, as they cannot participate anymore to the network life.
- Finally, the activity and the strength of malicious devices are associated to μ_4 and γ, respectively.

Such a compartment model leads to the following nonlinear system of ordinary differential equations:

$$\begin{cases} \dot{A} = sB - \mu_1 A, \\ \dot{B} = \Lambda - sB - \alpha B + \beta C - \mu_2 B, \\ \dot{C} = \alpha B - \beta C - \frac{\gamma}{N} DC - \mu_3 C, \\ \dot{D} = \frac{\gamma}{N} DC - \mu_4 D. \end{cases}$$

This system can be investigated theoretically, by following an approach similar to what has been introduced in the previous section. However, its larger number of variables and parameters make it harder to study, theoretically speaking. Furthermore, our objective in this article is to show the usefulness of compartment models for MANET studies, and such models can be investigated either theoretically or through numerical simulations. We are then left, in this section, to provide an illustration of the usefulness of numerically simulated compartment models for decision-making aids in complex MANETs.

To reach this goal, we have fully designed a mobile ad-hoc network by using the Python language [25]. Each simulated mobile device belongs initially to one of the four compartments considered in this section, and they change compartments according to the model depicted in Figure 4. For cross validation, the system of ordinary differential equations has been numerically solved too, by using lsoda from the FORTRAN library odepack [26], as it is embedded in SciPy [27]. The obtained results are convergent, and various situations can be emphasized, according to the parameters of the system and to the initial population.

Let us first discuss about the worst case scenarios that are depicted in Figure 5 (for the MANET designer, not for the attackers). First of all, a disastrous situation can be seen in Simulation 1 of Figure 5: the number of malicious devices, which initially were quite low, has increased until reaching the three-quarters of the network. Monitoring and monitored nodes have decreased accordingly. This behavior is mainly due to a very aggressive behavior of the malicious devices, that most of the times achieve their attacks (see the value of the γ parameter). The arrival of new devices, modeled by Λ, is not high enough to counteract the node defections within the MANET. Even though the death rate μ_4 of malicious devices is large here, as such attack performances lead to a large battery consumption, the inactivation of some malicious nodes is totally compensated by the new conversion of monitoring devices to the malicious node.

This behavior is independent from the initial size of the compartment, as can be seen in Simulation 2 of Figure 5. In this simulation, the initial condition is different, but we recover a pronounced increase of malicious nodes over time. This increase is still preserved even if we consider that the malicious device activity has a very important impact on its morbidity (μ_4 is now equal to 0.95).

V. Conclusion and Future Work

In this article, a short state of the art in the field of MANET monitoring has firstly been presented. This study has then been completed by regarding intermediate timescales, and the evolution of sensor number per compartment has been

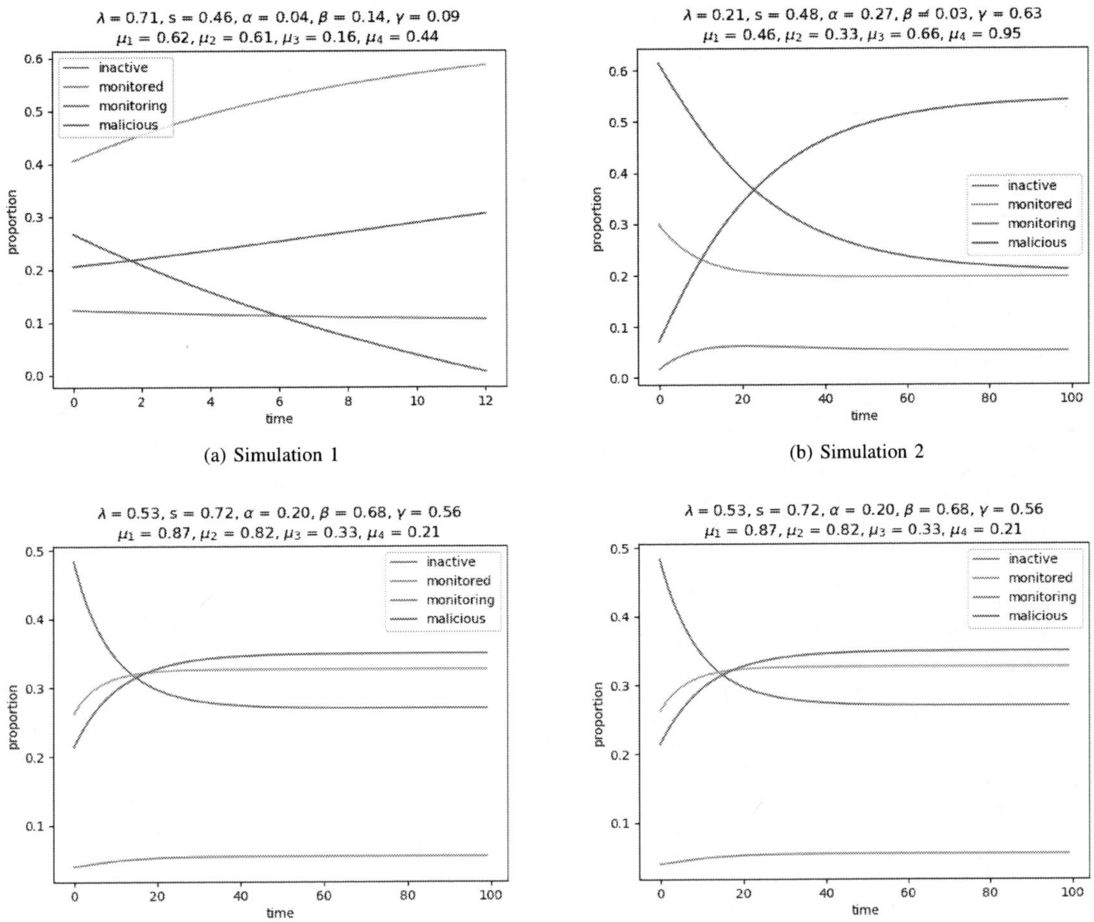

(a) Simulation 1

(b) Simulation 2

(c) Simulation 3

(d) Simulation 4

Figure 5: Worst case scenarios

theoretically detailed. Some numerical simulations have finally been presented, in a more complex situation where monitored, monitoring, selfish, and malicious nodes are present in the network.

Other theoretical results can be produced by using this theoretical formulation, using compartments, on the monitoring of a MANET in an hostile environment. For instance, it is possible to compute the maximal number of monitors or of malicious nodes that can be reached for a given set of parameters, and the time needed to reach such an optimum, etc. The results, and the difficulties that can be faced to obtain them, depend both on the compartment model and on parameters. Their exhaustive study, which cannot be completed in an article of limited number of pages, is not the objective of this work. Our intention was just to illustrate the relevance of such a modeling to study the monitoring of MANETs. However, this exhaustive study will be initiated in a couple of forthcoming articles we intend to propose in the future.

ACKNOWLEDGMENT

This work is partially funded by the EIPHI Graduate School (contract "ANR-17-EURE-0002").

REFERENCES

[1] J. P. Hubaux, L. Buttyan, and S. Capkun, The quest for security in mobile ad hoc networks. In *Proceedings of the 2nd ACM international symposium on Mobile ad hoc networking & computing*, pp. 146–155, 2001.

[2] M. Ghonge, S. Pramanik, and A. D. Potgantwar, Software defined networking for ad hoc networks, publisher: Springer, 2022.

[3] P. Satyanarayana, M. Vani Pujitha, G. Venkata Subbaiah, and Mugada Srivani. Enhancement of performance parameters in wireless mobile adhoc networks using dsr and cache-modified dsr routing protocols. In *Smart and Intelligent Systems*, pp. 257–267. Springer, 2022.

[4] D. Kanellopoulos and F. Cuomo, Recent developments on mobile adhoc networks and vehicular ad-hoc networks. electronics 2021, 10, 364. *Recent Developments on Mobile Ad-Hoc Networks and Vehicular Ad-Hoc Networks*, p. 1, 2021.

[5] J. Azar, A. Makhoul, R. Couturier, and J. Demerjian, Robust IoT time series classification with data compression and deep learning. *Neurocomputing*, 398:222–234, 2020.

[6] A. Makhoul and C. Pham, Dynamic scheduling of cover-sets in randomly deployed wireless video sensor networks for surveillance applications. In *2009 2nd IFIP Wireless Days (WD)*, pp. 1–6, 2009.

[7] M. Chatzidakis and S. Hadjiefthymiades, A trust change detection mechanism in mobile ad-hoc networks. *Computer Communications*, 187:155–163, 2022.

[8] M. Fayaz, G. Mehmood, A. Khan, S. Abbas, and J. Gwak, Counteracting selfish nodes using reputation based system in mobile ad hoc networks. *Electronics*, 11(2):185, 2022.

[9] H. Harb, A. Makhoul, and C. Abou Jaoude, A real-time massive data processing technique for densely distributed sensor networks. *IEEE Access*, 6:56551–56561, 2018.

[10] H. Harb, A. Makhoul, R. Couturier, and M. Medlej, Atp: An aggregation and transmission protocol for conserving energy in periodic sensor networks. In *2015 IEEE 24th International Conference on Enabling Technologies: Infrastructure for Collaborative Enterprises*, pp. 134–139, 2015.

[11] N. Battat, H. Seba, and H. Kheddouci, Monitoring in mobile ad hoc networks: A survey. *Computer Networks*, 69:82–100, 2014.

[12] J. Bahi, C. Guyeux, and A. Makhoul, Secure data aggregation in wireless sensor networks: Homomorphism versus watermarking approach. In Jun Zheng, David Simplot-Ryl, and Victor C. M. Leung, editors, *Ad Hoc Networks*, pp. 344–358, Berlin, Heidelberg, 2010. Springer Berlin Heidelberg.

[13] A. Makhoul, R. Saadi, and C. Pham, Risk management in intrusion detection applications with wireless video sensor networks. In *IEEE WCNC*, vol. 182, p. 10. Sydney, Australia, 2010.

[14] J. Bahi, C. Guyeux, A. Makhoul, and C. Pham. Low cost monitoring and intruders detection using wireless video sensor networks. *International Journal of Distributed Sensor Networks*, 2012, November 2012.

[15] G. Liu, K. Su, F. Hong, X. Zhong, Z. Liang, X. Wu, and Z. Huang, A novel epidemic model base on pulse charging in wireless rechargeable sensor networks. *Entropy*, 24(2), 2022.

[16] W. Chen, N. Jain, and S. Singh, Anmp: Ad hoc network man-agement protocol. *IEEE Journal on selected areas in communications*, 17(8):1506–1531, 1999.

[17] R. Badonnel, R. State, and O. Festor, Probabilistic Management of Ad-Hoc Networks. In *NOMS*, pages 339–350, Vancouver, Canada, 2006.

[18] Remi Badonnel, Radu State, and Olivier Festor. Management of ad-hoc networks. In *Handbook of Network and System Administration*, pages 331–360. Elsevier, 2008.

[19] G. Ateniese, C. Riley, and C. Scheideler, Survivable Monitoring in Dynamic Networks. *IEEE Transactions on Mobile Computing*, 5:33–47, Sept. 2006.

[20] H. Kazemi, G. C. Hadjichristofi, and L. A. Dasilva. MMAN - a monitor for mobile ad hoc networks: design, implementation, and experimental evaluation. In *Mobile Computing and Networking*, pp. 57–64, 2008.

[21] M. K. Rafsanjani and A. Movaghar, Identifying Monitoring Nodes with Selection of Authorized Nodes in MANET. *World Applied Sciences Journal*, 4, 2008.

[22] K. Gopalakrishnan and V. R. Uthariaraj, Neighborhood Monitoring Based Collaborative Alert Mechanism to Thwart the Misbehaving Nodes in Mobile Ad Hoc Networks. *European Journal of Scientific Research*, 57(3):411–425, 2011.

[23] A. Makhoul, C. Guyeux, M. Hakem, and J. Bahi, Using an epidemiological approach to maximize data survival in the internet of things. *ACM Transactions on Internet Technology (TOIT)*, 16(1), February 2016.

[24] J. Bahi, C. Guyeux, M. Hakem, and A. Makhoul, Epidemiological approach for data survivability in unattended wireless sensor networks. *Journal of Network and Computer Applications*, 46, November 2014.

[25] G. Rossum, Python reference manual. Technical report, Amsterdam, The Netherlands, 1995.

[26] A. C. Hindmarsh, ODEPACK, a systematized collection of ODE solvers. In R. S. Stepleman, editor, *Scientific Computing*, pp. 55–64, Amsterdam, 1983. North-Holland.

[27] E. Jones et al., SciPy: Open source scientific tools for Python, 2001–. [Online; accessed July 2022].

A Camera-Vision-based Indoor Navigation and Obstacle Avoidance Wearable Assistive Device for Visually Impaired People

Wei-Jun Lin, Mu-Chun Su, Chun-Hsiang Cheng, Cheng-Yu Tsai, Yi-Hsin Chen
Department of Computer Science & Information Engineering
National Central University, Taoyuan City, Taiwan
emails: {weijen, muchun.su}@g.ncu.edu.tw, {jerrysmoove3, roy1997860328}@gmail.com, yihsinchen@g.ncu.edu.tw

***Abstract*—In the past, if visually impaired people needed to go to an unknown/unfamiliar environment they had never been before, they had to rely on the assistance of relatives or friends and unavoidably caused trouble for both visually impaired people and their helpers. In this paper, we present a wearable assistive device to aid the visually impaired people. We use YOLOv5 to detect signages and Convolutional Recurrent Neural Network (CRNN) to recognize texts embedded in the detected signages. Via a stereo camera, our system can help visually impaired people independently move in unknown environments. In addition, MobileNet was used to detect uneven pavements in front of visually impaired people to alert them whenever dangerous conditions exist on the road.**

Keywords-visually impaired people; indoor navigation; object detection.

I. INTRODUCTION

Mobility is essential for blind and visually impaired people to move safely and efficiently as independently as possible through all environments. The white cane is the most popular navigation tool used by visually impaired people to scan their surroundings for obstacles or orientation marks. However, the detection range of white cane is restricted to about 1.5 meters from the user and the white cane must always be used to tap the surface of the road while walking, which is still limited.

Another well-known method is to adopt a guide dog. A well-trained guide dog will actively look out for hazards and obstacles that the visually impaired person cannot detect, such as a blocked path or an overhead obstruction. However, it takes a long time and cost to train a qualified guide dog. It also takes a long time to match a new handler after training. On average, a guide dog can only serve for six to seven years, which leads to another problem is their retirement.

Although visually impaired people tend to have a better sense of space than ordinary people, they still cannot reach an unknown environment without assistance from others and will resist going out for fear of disturbing others.

For the reasons outlined above, it would be helpful for visually impaired people to develop a wearable assistive device to inform the visually impaired user of any type of danger and help them navigate while moving in unfamiliar environments. In this paper, we present a wearable assistive device that can detect obstacles and different levels of heights. The device can also analyze the information of signages as well as help visually impaired people to navigate indoors.

In Section II, we introduce the related works on indoor navigation and obstacle avoidance and their shortcomings. In Section III, we introduce the hardware system for our work. In Section IV, we describe the system architecture which includes the algorithms and experiments of both obstacle detection and indoor navigation for visually impaired people. Finally, Section V is the conclusion of this paper.

II. RELATED WORK

In the last couple of years, various technologies focusing on helping visually impaired people have been introduced. They aim at increasing mobility of visually impaired users and providing additional information about nearby surroundings.

For obstacle avoidance, [1] introduced a method using infrared sensors to detect the position of obstacles. [2] uses depth cameras to build an indoor map to detect obstacles, and [3][4] build maps based on Device and Application Programming Interface (API) from Google's Tango project to help visually impaired people avoid obstacles.

For indoor navigation, the easiest way to guide a visually impaired person to walk indoors is to use a car-like navigation device. Global Positioning System (GPS) does not work well indoors and walls, ceilings, insulation etc., can absorb the signals making it harder or even impossible for a GPS device to determine its location. Many researchers have proposed various methods for indoor positioning. Yang [5] used the Round-Trip Time (RTT) of WiFi to calculate the distance by sending messages to multiple WiFi access points and using Angle of Arrival (AoA) technology to calculate the angle to the user itself in order to achieve indoor positioning. [6] and [7] presented methods which are based on the Received Signal Strength Indication (RSSI) of Bluetooth to determine the user's location. There are methods based on Radio Frequency Identification (RFID) location tracking system [8] or methods based on Ultra-Wideband (UWB) [9]. All these methods are using signal strength, angle of signal and arrival time to achieve indoor positioning. However, these methods consume a large amount of manpower and resources to pre-built maps in each public place, or the visually impaired people have to walk through these areas once to record the maps. It does not help visually impaired people to visit those places that have not been visited before. Instead of using indoor positioning, we provide a method using signage detection to parse the information on signage and help visually impaired people to navigate indoors.

III. THE HARDWARE SYSTEM

The wearable assistive device made in this paper includes a ZED Stereo Camera and NVIDIA AGX Jetson Xavier.

The ZED Stereo Camera is a depth camera made of two-color lenses with up to 20 meters effective distance. We use ZED for acquiring the depth information of the surroundings and the signages.

We use NVIDIA AGX Jetson Xavier as a wearable computer that computes all the deep learning networks. Although NVIDIA provides other lighter-weight devices, Xavier is one of the few embedded systems that meets the requirements of memory and computing performance.

IV. SYSTEM ARCHITECTURE

For the system architecture, our system provides two major features:

1. Obstacles Detection and Avoidance: To warn the visually impaired people whether there is uneven pavement ahead, so as to avoid kicking or missing their foot. We will discuss the detailed algorithm in Section 4. A.
2. Signage Detection and Navigation: To help visually impaired people navigate to find their destination in an unknown public place by analyzing the information of the signages and parsing the text on these signages. We will discuss the detailed algorithm in Section 4. B.

A. Obstacles Detection and Avoidance

We use MoblieNet to detect obstacles. However, because there are some obstacles and uneven pavements cannot be detected by specific shape or color, we use (1) Edge information (2) Depth image (3) Grayscale image as the input of MobileNet (see Figure 1).

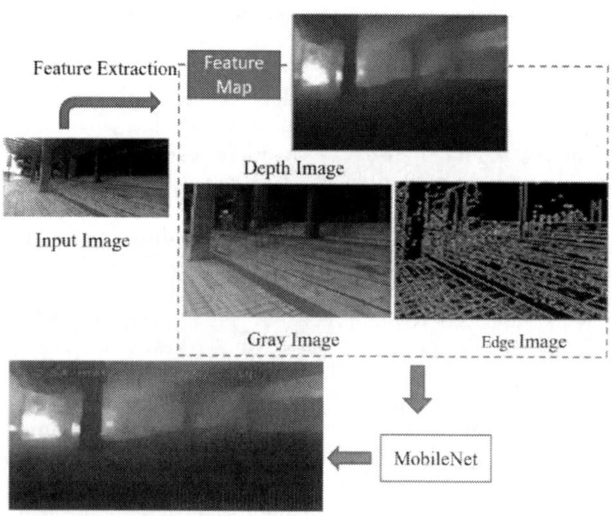

Figure 1. The process of obstacle detection

We use the Canny Edge Detection as the detector to find the edges in the images. It uses changes in color or brightness to find depth discontinuities, texture changes and differences in an image.

However, edge information is not only obtained by the different levels of height of the pavement. It can be more likely obtained by the texture of the pavement. Therefore, we use the depth image as the second input.

Finally, the color image itself is also important information. But, in order to reduce the memory load of the model, we compressed the color image into a grayscale image.

We divide our predicted output as four types: (1) Flat (2) Upstairs (3) Downstairs (4) Obstacles. We use MoblieNet and DenseNet121 to test the results, respectively. The results are shown in Table 1 and Table 2.

TABLE 1. CONFUSION MATRIX FOR OBSTACLE RECOGNITION USING MOBILENET

		Target				
Predicted		Flat	Upstairs	Downstairs	Obstacles	Precision
	Flat	1,502	0	0	0	100%
	Upstairs	0	1,016	34	1	96.67%
	Downstairs	59	11	518	0	88.01%
	Obstacles	133	88	0	1,678	88.36%
	Recall	88.67 %	91.12%	93.84%	99.94%	Accuracy =93.53%

TABLE 2. CONFUSION MATRIX FOR OBSTACLE RECOGNITION USING DENSENET121

		Target				
Predicted		Flat	Upstairs	Downstairs	Obstacles	Precision
	Flat	1,563	54	0	0	96.66%
	Upstairs	0	1,004	14	10	97.67%
	Downstairs	131	0	538	7	79.59%
	Obstacles	0	57	0	1,662	96.68%
	Recall	92.27 %	90.05 %	97.46%	98.99%	Accuracy =94.58%

B. Signage Detection and Navigation

We use object detection and text recognition to analyze the information on the signage. We use the distance information detected by the stereo camera to guide the visually impaired people to their destination. The whole process of signage detection is shown in Figure 2.

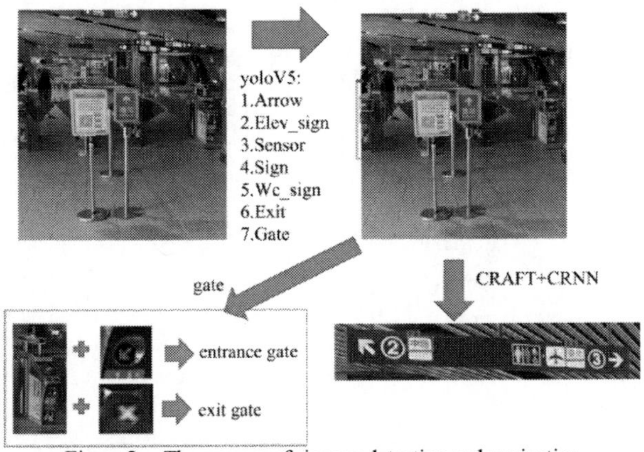

Figure 2. The process of signage detection and navigation

First, we use YOLOv5 to detect the objects (signages, gates, arrow symbols, toilet signs, elevator signs, sensors, no-passing signs etc.) in indoor public places.

Second, because there are a lot of arrow symbols on signages, entry gates and the elevator signs themselves (up and down arrows), some of them do not actually tell the users directions. We want to exclude those arrow symbols that do not follow the signage. For entry gates, both entry and exit gates are detected. We want only entry gates to be shown in our result. We use the following rules to delete the irrelevant arrow symbols and gates:

- If a "no-passing sign" is inside the detection area of an entry gate, the model would label this as a gate users cannot pass. We avoid combining International System of Units (SI) and Centimeter–Gram–Second (CGS) units, such as current in amperes and magnetic field in oersteds. This often leads to confusion because equations do not balance dimensionally. If mixed units need to be used, the units need to be clearly states for each quantity that is used in an equation.
- If an "arrow symbol" is inside the detection area of an entry gate, the model would label this as a gate users can pass.
- If an "arrow symbol" is inside the detection area of an elevator sign, it is represented as part of an elevator sign. The model would not label this arrow symbol as a valid input.
- If an "arrow symbol" is followed by a signage, the arrow indicates the orientation of the place. The model would mark its orientation.
- We would exclude all arrow symbols not listed above.

In addition to the graphic signages detected, text signages recognition would also be included in our solution. We take the image of signages detected by YOLOv5 as input. We use CRAFT [10] to detect the text position on the detected image. Then, we use CRNN [11] to extract the text (location) from the images.

Finally, we take the bounded box of the detected signage on the color image to correspond to the same position of the depth image captured by ZED as the estimation of the distance. In order to improve the accuracy of the distance, we shrunk each side of the bounded box inward by 25% to reduce the distance deviation when the detected signage is sloped.

V. CONCLUSION

In this paper, we present a wearable assistive device to aid the visually impaired people. We have asked visually impaired people to test our system to prove the feasibility of the system. The signage detection and navigation algorithm designed in this paper does not accurately locate the visually impaired people's position, but it can help the visually impaired people navigate to a specific location by analyzing the information on the signage. With our obstacles detection and avoidance, visually impaired people can be warned by our system that there may be bumps or depressions ahead. When the visually impaired people are climbing stairs, the detection system can warn that the user is approaching a flat surface or not. Our system would improve the mobility and ability for visually impaired people to walk in an unfamiliar environment and improve their safety during walking.

ACKNOWLEDGMENT

This paper was partly supported by the Ministry of Science and Technology, Taiwan, R.O.C, under 109-2221-E-008 -059 -MY3 and 110-2634-F-008 -005 -.

REFERENCES

[1] D. A. Ross and A. Lightman, "Talking braille: a wireless ubiquitous computing network for orientation and wayfinding," in Assets '05: Proceedings of the 7th international ACM SIGACCESS conference on Computers and accessibility. New York, NY, USA: ACM, 2005, pp. 98–105.

[2] Y. Lee and G. Medioni, "Wearable RGBD indoor navigation system for the blind", Proc. Eur. Conf. Comput. Vis., pp. 493-508, 2014.

[3] B. Li et al., "Vision-Based Mobile Indoor Assistive Navigation Aid for Blind People," in IEEE Transactions on Mobile Computing, vol. 18, no. 3, pp. 702-714, 1 March 2019, doi: 10.1109/TMC.2018.2842751.

[4] R. Jafri and M. M. Khan, "Obstacle detection and avoidance for the visually impaired in indoors environments using googles project tango device" in Computers Helping People with Special Needs ser. Lecture Notes in Computer Science, Springer International Publishing, pp. 179-185, Jul. 2016.

[5] C. Yang and H. Shao, "WiFi-based indoor positioning," in IEEE Communications Magazine, vol. 53, no. 3, pp. 150-157, March 2015, doi: 10.1109/MCOM.2015.7060497.

[6] N. Pakanon, M. Chamchoy and P. Supanakoon, "Study on Accuracy of Trilateration Method for Indoor Positioning with BLE Beacons," 2020 6th International Conference on Engineering, Applied Sciences and Technology (ICEAST), 2020, pp. 1-4, doi: 10.1109/ICEAST50382.2020.9165464.

[7] E. Essa, B. A. Abdullah and A. Wahba, "Improve Performance of Indoor Positioning System using BLE," 2019 14th International Conference on Computer Engineering and Systems (ICCES), 2019, pp. 234-237, doi: 10.1109/ICCES48960.2019.9068142.

[8] S. Willis and S. Helal, "RFID information grid for blind navigation and wayfinding," Ninth IEEE International Symposium on Wearable Computers (ISWC'05), 2005, pp. 34-37, doi: 10.1109/ISWC.2005.46.

[9] J. Fu, Y. Fu and D. Xu, "Application of an Adaptive UKF in UWB Indoor Positioning," 2019 Chinese Automation Congress (CAC), 2019, pp. 544-549, doi: 10.1109/CAC48633.2019.8996692.

[10] Y. Baek, B. Lee, D. Han, S. Yun and H. Lee, "Character Region Awareness for Text Detection," 2019 IEEE/CVF Conference on Computer Vision and Pattern Recognition (CVPR), 2019, pp. 9357-9366, doi: 10.1109/CVPR.2019.00959.

[11] B. Shi, X. Bai and C. Yao, "An End-to-End Trainable Neural Network for Image-Based Sequence Recognition and Its Application to Scene Text Recognition," in IEEE Transactions on Pattern Analysis and Machine Intelligence, vol. 39, no. 11, pp. 2298-2304, 1 Nov. 2017, doi: 10.1109/TPAMI.2016.2646371.

Digital Twin Based Industrial Services - Just Hype or Real Business?

Jukka Hemilä
Data based asset management and business models
VTT Technical Research Centre of Finland Ltd.
Espoo, Finland
e-mail: jukka.hemila@vtt.fi

Abstract - **The paradigm change towards digitalization in industries has been a huge hype for years. The Internet of Things, Industry 4.0, and recently Digital Twins, are the buzzwords that every practitioner notices in the manufacturing industry. However, how to make real business after the hype? The ongoing international research is developing the utilization of machine operations data as a basis for Digital Twins. Digital Twins are the digital replications of real industrial machines. New industrial services and new earning logics can be created, but it takes time to get a real business going with digitalization. This study presents the findings from multiple case studies in Europe and discusses the business opportunities related the Digital Twin concept.**

Keywords-Digital Twin; Data; Industry4.0; Industrial Services.

I. INTRODUCTION

Data based industrial services are still hard to realize in practice, despite the fact that there is plenty of hype around Industry 4.0 and related concepts [1]. However, in the future of the industrial service systems, value creation will be data driven, as there has now been many digitalization initiatives and development activities in manufacturing industries globally [2]. In some sectors, individual companies already generate more than 50% of their revenue and 100% of their profit with their service businesses [3]. The servitization trend is still today continuing in manufacturing industries and will become the norm across the industry over the next few years [3]. By 2030, companies will sell most equipment as part of bundled solutions including software and services, reducing the hardware's share of total profits [3].

A Digital Twin (DT) is a virtual representation of a physical object, product or process, or even factory [4]. The level of data integration marks the difference of DT compared to the concept of Digital Model (DM), sometimes called a Virtual Model (VM), and the concept of Digital Shadow (DS) [4]. These mentioned concepts are often used synonymously. The digital representation can be modeled manually, without connection to a real physical counterpart. Alternatively, digital representation can be done fully automated way. DM is realized manually, with a manual data exchange flow. DS has an automatic data flow from the physical object towards the digital object, but the reverse data flow is manual. The data flow between an existing physical object and a digital object fully integrated in both directions is referred to as DT [4]. Multiple DTs are a real-time integrated combination of many physical objects and their digital objects. This paper uses the DT concept to refer to fully automated data exchange between real physical object and its digital replication. Therefore, because of real-time and automated data exchange, DTs can be the basis of new kinds of industrial services with entirely new value offerings. Often digitalization helps the machine manufacturer themselves, but the added customer value is just a nice to know or a nice to have type of benefit. The real benefit, which a customer is willing to pay for is hardly achieved. The purpose of this paper is to explore DT-based industrial service opportunities and examine how to develop and commercialize DT-based services successfully. The nature of the study is conceptualization. However, it does not focus on technologies for realizing DT, data analytics or data connection technologies. Today Artificial Intelligence (AI) can be used for data analytics, machine operation simulations and maintenance optimization. The rest of the paper is structured as follows. Section II defines the used research approach and methodologies. Section III presents the study findings. We conclude our work in Section IV.

II. DESIGN/METHODOLOGY/APPROACH

This study is a part of an international project focused on researching the new service opportunities provided by the DT concept in several industrial use cases. The project includes three machine manufacturing companies, one automotive supplier with an operative production line, seven software development partners, three universities and two research institutes that represent three different business ecosystems in three countries. The empirical data is gathered by semi-structured interviews with company practitioners, which research organization facilitated workshops developed further. The findings of company interviews were used as a basis for understanding the current stage and the future business potential of digital twin enabled services. Next, several workshops were conducted to map the service processes of the use cases in three ecosystems in Finland, Turkey and the Netherlands. The ecosystem partners are listed in Table I below, and more detailed information is available at the project website [5].

TABLE I. ECOSYSTEM PARTNERS ROLES AND SIZES

Ecosystem	*Company role in the ecosystem*
Ecosystem in Turkey	Company 1: Manufacturing company innovating and offering new digital twin enabled services for their customers, large-scale company.

	Company 2: Service development partner, Software (SW) provider, Small and medium sized (SME).
Ecosystem in Netherlands	Company 1: Manufacturing company innovating and offering new digital twin enabled services for their customers, SME Company 2: Manufacturing company innovating and offering new digital twin enabled services for their customers, SME Company 3: Service development partner, SW provider, SME. Company 4: Service development partner, SW provider, SME. Research institute 1: Software Research and Development (SW R&D) partner University 1: SW R&D partner
Ecosystem in Finland	Company 1: Manufacturing company innovating and offering new digital twin enabled services for their customers, large-scale company Company 2: Manufacturing company innovating and offering new digital twin enabled services for their customers, SME Company 3: Service development partner, SW provider, SME Company 4: Service development partner, SW provider, SME Company 5: Service development partner, SW provider, Large University 1: SW R&D partner Research institute 1: Service development partner

The workshops were held remotely using Microsoft Teams due to the ongoing COVID-19 situation and the limitations to travel. The methods for conducting the workshops in each ecosystem were customized to correspond the specific background of the consortiums. Customer Journey Mapping was used for identifying the actual customer view of DT services within the ecosystems [6] and the Service Blueprinting method for understanding the roles and responsibilities within the service ecosystems [7]. A total number of ten interviews and workshops were organized within the ecosystems. The details of data collection interviews and workshops are in following Table II below.

TABLE II. DATA COLLECTION INTERVIEWS AND WORKSHOPS

Interviews / workshops			
Country	***Date***	***Workshop theme***	***Participants***
Turkey	October 12th, 2021	Mapping the DT enabled service process by service business blueprinting	2 R&D engineers, large manufacturing company; 4 SW developers, SME SW provider
The Netherlands	January 25th, 2022	Mapping the current state of DT enabled services and service business blueprinting	1 SW developer, research institute; 1 Research and Development (R&D) engineer, SW provider; 1 SW engineer, University; 1 SW engineer, SME SW provider
The Netherlands	January 25th, 2022	Mapping the current state of DT enabled services and service business blueprinting	2 R&D engineers, SME machine manufacturer
The Netherlands	January 26th, 2022	Mapping the current state of DT enabled services and service business blueprinting	1 R&D engineer, SME machine manufacturer
The Netherlands	March 22nd, 2022	Future vision of DT enabled services	1 R&D engineer, SME machine manufacturer
The Netherlands	March 22nd, 2022	Future vision of DT enabled services	1 R&D engineer, SME machine manufacturer
Finland	June 11th, 2021	DT solutions in the Smart Factory domain	3 researchers, 1 professor, university; 3 SW engineers, SME SW provider 4 Engineers, large machine manufacturer; 1 engineer, SME machine manufacturer; 1 SW engineer, SME SW provider; 4 research scientists, research institute
Finland	February 4th, 2022	DT solutions in the Smart factory ecosystem and roles	3 researchers, 1 professor, university; 1 SW engineer, SME SW provider; 4 Engineers, large machine manufacturer; 1 engineer, SME machine manufacturer; 1 SW engineer, SME SW provider; 4 research scientists, research institute
Finland	March 8th, 2022	DT solutions in the Smart factory ecosystem and roles	3 researchers, 1 professor, university; 2 SW engineers, SME SW provider; 3 Engineers, large machine manufacturer; 1 SW engineer, SME SW provider; 4 research scientists, research institute
Finland	March 23rd, 2022	DT solutions in the Smart factory ecosystem and roles	3 researchers, 1 professor, university; 2 SW engineers, SME SW provider; 3 Engineers, Large machine manufacturer; 1 SW engineer, SME SW provider; 4 research scientists, research rnstitute

A literature study and benchmarking studies enriched the empirical findings [8][9]. Two research questions were formulated: 1) How can the Digital Twins boost value creation in the industrial product-service lifecycle, and 2) Which kinds of business models are needed in the future digitalized industrial contexts. The research questions are related to the main theme of this paper, namely are the DT services real business or just hype? The study discusses the business potential and business development challenges related to the DT concept.

III. Findings

Digitalization has reached a mature level in industries, as the companies have modern Information and Communication Technology (ICT) tools for supporting operations. Enterprise Resource Planning (ERP) solutions are today cloud based software, available everywhere and support many kinds of industrial operations, not only production. Customer Relationship Management (CRM) software supports every kind of customer interaction from marketing, to sales and aftersales. For service operations, like installation and maintenance, markets offer dedicated solutions. Every kind of documentation can be managed in the digital format. The latest trend of Industry 4.0 brings the Internet of Things (IoT) to manufacturing industry. Cheap sensors and connectivity solutions create many opportunities to collect real-time data from machines which supports decision making related operations and maintenance. Data itself is not valuable, but the information gathered from the data using analytics and visualization is. Artificial Intelligence (AI) and machine learning can be utilized for data analytics, operative predictions and maintenance optimization. Generally, today all industrial operations can be digitalized. However, these mentioned solutions mostly support manufacturing companies internally, and the value of the software solutions is clear for the manufacturers themselves. The customer value is questionable, as it is not clear how digitalization helps the customers who are using the machines. Customer understanding is the key for success. Which kind of information does the customer need? Do they need information at all or are they just interested in operational efficiency or the minimized downtime of the machines? In many cases, the answer is yes. The data collected by the machine manufacturer, when the customer operates with the machine, should be turned to a customer value proposition. The value proposition is dependent on the case and customer [10]. The data can be used for DT, the digital replication of the machine. Then, the DT can be used as a basis for a value proposition for customers. According to our case studies, typically, value is created in the selling, installation and operations, and maintenance phases of the machine lifecycle. The following subsections describe the main findings from the case studies in the different lifecycle stages.

A. The selling stage

The selling stage includes machine ordering and planning of the service delivery. The main actions in this stage demand a lot of interaction between the customer and the manufacturing company. In the selling stage, the identification of potential customers for DT enabled services, arguing the value propositions of DT enabled services to the customers and helping them to make a positive purchasing decision take place. Based on the machine design data, DT visualizes the machine for the customer. Surely, DT is not a sellable or monetized service in the selling stage, but DT can have positive enabler role for buying decision.

B. The installation and operation stage

At this stage, collecting and processing data plays a pivotal role. In the installation and operation stage, the main activity is ensuring Overall Equipment Effectiveness (OEE) by making sure that all necessary software is functioning as expected and that is updated accordingly. DT can support installation when all requested documentations can be achieved via DT, and machine operational setup can be simulated with DT to ensure operations at the customer site. Training at the customer site can utilize virtual replication of the real world by using Virtual Reality glasses and 3D models of the machine and the surrounding factory environment. In this stage, all actors (the customer, the manufacturing company offering digital twin enabled services and the service development partners) have a great role and seamless cooperation and communication between the actors is very important. Our case studies have identified the following operation phase benefits where the DT has a strong supporting or enabling role (in random order):

- Machine works as expected (availability guarantee, e.g., 98%)
- Formally proves what is wrong and proves what has been fixed
- Detailed view from each component on what has gone wrong
- Time savings, money savings
- Just in time delivery support
- New business model opportunities for the machine manufacturer because of a detailed view of how the machine operates
- Simplifies the job of the machine users: Less time needed on the daily work activities and more time available on the non-daily activities, e.g., "operator being more a manager". Operator work content can be moved towards operations planning, production scheduling and other activities than they do today. The DT can support organizational changes in the future.
- For moving robots, DT supports route planning, as well as management of unexpected situations in operations
- Higher quality and traceability of the final products
- Easier for the customer to know what happens inside the machines
- Improved interaction with the customer
- The customer is able to have customized views (control room/ Human-Machine Interface (HMI) solutions) of the factory and machine situation for different users (production managers, machine operators, service personnel).
- The customer is able to visualize in a real-time what the machine is doing
- Reduced waiting time and faster time to market by generating new operation schedules (optimized operations based on the DT) for the system

Generally, the digital twin is used as a communication tool to enable the interaction at the machine, line, factory, or ecosystem level. The customer benefits include improvements in safety (e.g., product safety and occupational safety), improvement in product delivery efficiency, improvement in the reliability of operations, improvement in product quality, and financial factors, such as savings in operative costs.

C. The maintenance stage

In the maintenance stage, the main focus is on predictive maintenance activities enabled by the digital twin. On a general level, the key customer benefit is maintenance downtime optimization. Prediction, in general, tends to be highlighted as one of the key benefits of the digital twin-enabled service across the service process stages. Communication and data exchange within the diverse levels of digital twin implementation play an important role. If the machine is a critical part of the customer's operation or production line, DT is even more important for ensuring successful maintenance operations. The main activities of the software partners are to make sure that the software works as it should and that it provides accurate information related to the machine, machine fleet or the entire factory. The main activities of the manufacturing companies offering DT-based services are to make sure that the preventive activities based on the information enabled by the digital twin are done accordingly. The main activity of the customers is to let the maintenance activities take place in order for their downtime to be minimized and their operations to run with full operational rate. Below is a summary of preventive maintenance and modernization possibilities with the DT:

- Easiness for the customer when service operations are well planned and predicted
- Time savings in service operations
- Fewer ad hoc situations
- Added revenue for the customer can be collected from the end-users by providing updates
- Make sure that the software system is without any errors (simulations with DT)
- New business model for services/maintenance: Make a model that provides constant updates for end-users

IV. CONCLUSIONS

Because of the growing volume, complexity, and strategic importance of data in industry, manufacturers need to create DT-based services together with selected strategic partners. The participants of future digital twin-enabled service operations are forming an industrial ecosystem with multiple actors and roles. Actors are needed to fulfil dedicated tasks when delivering digital twin solutions with and to different stakeholders. The realization of DT requires new kinds of competencies, because of the need for data analytics, visualization, simulations and other functionalities that might be new for manufacturers. Therefore, collaboration is needed between manufacturers and SW providers to consolidate data collection, aggregation and analytics for making data and insights available across different business functions and units. These mentioned tasks need many kinds of individual roles from the employees. Roles can be considered as action-oriented tasks, like connectors, identity verifiers or service provides. As part of a customer's personnel, there are, e.g., persons responsible for production, different levels of managers, procurement personnel and service engineers. The most apparent roles in a manufacturing company are e.g., sales, maintenance, training and engineering staff taking part in the DT enabled service operations. The ecosystem orchestrator role is also something that is currently being discussed to determine whether, in the future, there should or could be one actor that is responsible for selling the total DT enabled service solution to the customer with one-stop-shop principle. So far, there is no such actors in the manufacturing industry.

Unique and new value propositions can be formulated with DT. However, while sellable services are not easily done, there are many commercialization opportunities in DT-based services. Business strategies should be updated when investing in DT-based service offerings. In the end, an entire new business model is needed for the manufacturers. As the value proposition change, new outsourced SW elements are needed and the customer base needs to be segmented differently, since traditional customers might not be interested in DT offerings.

A. Practical implications

This paper highlights the DT-based service opportunities and challenges. A new understanding is needed on how to develop economically sustainable service offerings with the data and with multiple DTs of products. The study presented promising results, but realization in each case is dependent on the DT level of detail. With systematic development steps, a successful DT-based service business can be realized. Practitioners need to think about existing competencies within the company, and make or buy decisions are needed for realizing DT-based services in practice.

B. Research limitations

The present study has limitations that need to be taken into account. The phenomenon of utilizing DTs in industrial service development is very extensive and complex and this study approached this phenomenon from a rather narrow empirical perspective with three manufacturing ecosystems in three different countries. However, by understanding these particular cases in more depth, we eventually learned about the greater phenomenon of DT-based service development in the industrial context. Practical evidence of multiple DTs is still limited, as multiple DTs were not in an operative environment within the case examples.

C. Future research

Future research will focus on the development of a new frame of reference for the service business innovations based on DT and future business models in manufacturing industries. The service business development model will be updated, i.e., by Service Development Phases [11]. With the updated step-by-step service development phases, an entire business model can be made more competitive. A very promising concept spinning out from this research project is the Digital Twin Web (DTW). The DTW is a network of digital twins formed by DT documents that describe the contents of DTs and the relationships between the DTs. The DTW concept can support multiple DT realizations in practice. Factory DT and Ecosystem DT can benefit from DTW, but so far, the DTW's relation to industrial services is unclear and, therefore, needs to be studied in the future.

REFERENCES

[1] J. Hemilä, M. Salo and P. Petänen, "Utilization of Digital Twins in Industrial Service Supply Chains", The 17th International research symposium on service excellence in management (QUIS17), Jan 2022, pp. 326-335 DOI: http://dx.doi.org/10.4995/QUIS17.2022.15169

[2] M. E. Porter and J. E. Heppelmann, "How smart, connected products are transforming companies", Harvard Business Review, October 2015.

[3] P. Roth, K. Strempel, O. Straehle and H. Liu, "Machinery as a Service: A Radical Shift Is Underway", [online]. Available from: https://www.bain.com/insights/machinery-as-a-service-global-machinery-and-equipment-report-2022/ [Retrieved: 06, 2022]

[4] W. Kritzinger, M. Karner, G. Traar, J. Henjes and W. Sihn, "Digital Twin in manufacturing: A categorical literature review and classification". IFAC-PapersOnLine, Volume 51, Issue 11, pp. 1016-1022, 2018.

[5] Machinaide. Knowledge-based services for and optimisation of machines, Machinaide project website [Online]. Available from: https://www.machinaide.eu/ [Retrieved: 07/2022]

[6] A. Richardson, "Using Customer Journey Maps to Improve Customer Experience", Harvard Business Review, November 2010.

[7] L. Patrício, R. P. Fisk, J. Falcão e Cunha and L. Constantine, "Multilevel service design: from customer value constellation to service experience blueprinting". Journal of Service Research, 14(2), pp. 180–200, 2011.

[8] K. M. Eisenhardt, "Building theories from case study research", The Academy of Management Review, Vol. 14, No. 4, pp. 532–550, 1989.

[9] R. Yin, "Case Study Research – Design and Methods", 3rd ed., Applied Social Research Methods Series, Vol. 5, Sage Publications Inc., Thousand Oaks, CA, 2003.

[10] T. Rintamäki and H. Saarijärvi, "An integrative framework for managing customer value propositions". Journal of Business Research, 134, pp. 754–764, 2021.

[11] J. Hemilä and J. Vilko, "The development of a service supply chain model for a manufacturing SME", The International Journal of Logistics Management, Vol. 26 No. 3, pp. 517-542, Nov 2015, https://doi.org/10.1108/IJLM-01-2014-0001

Explainable Kinship: The Importance of Facial Features in Kinship Recognition

Britt van Leeuwen[a], Arwin Gansekoele[b], Joris Pries[c], Etienne van de Bijl[d] and Jan Klein[e]

Centrum Wiskunde & Informatica, Stochastics group
Science Park 123, Amsterdam, the Netherlands
Email: [a]britt.van.leeuwen@cwi.nl, [b]arwin.gansekoele@cwi.nl,
[c]joris.pries@cwi.nl, [d]etienne.van.de.bijl@cwi.nl, [e]jan.klein@cwi.nl

***Abstract*—Kinship Recognition, the ability to distinguish between close genetic kin and non-kin, could be of great help in society and safety matters. Previous studies on *human* kinship recognition found an interesting insight when looking for the most important features. Results showed that analyzing only the top half of a face gives equal or even better performance compared to analyzing the whole face. In this paper, we aim to find the important features for *automated* kinship recognition based on the theory of *human* kinship recognition; this set of features was researched using features from pre-trained metrics from the StyleGAN2 model. We found that the most important facial features from the selection of 40 features are mostly focused on the facial hair traits. Furthermore, age-related features were found to be very important. This set of features does not entirely comply with the set of features important in *human* kinship recognition. Previous research has shown *human* kinship recognition performance does not decrease when removing the bottom half of the image of the face. In contrast, our results show that for *automated* kinship recognition, removing either the bottom or the top half of a face results in a decrease in the performance of our classifiers.**

***Keywords*—kinship recognition; StyleGAN2; Families-in-the-Wild; feature importance; transfer learning.**

I. INTRODUCTION

A. Kinship Recognition

Kinship Recognition (KR) is the ability to distinguish between close genetic kin and non-kin. The distinction involves people who are directly related and people who are not. One example of the usage of KR is on families who are spread throughout multiple refugee camps. One of these cases involved a father and his daughter being in one camp, while his wife and other children were in another camp. It took them over a year to get reunited by the Red Cross Restoring Family Links [1]. If a KR system is able to pick such family members out as a possible match for a kinship relation, a family could be reunited almost instantly. Issues with communication and limited manpower could be reduced with the discussed automation.

The main contribution of this paper is to make a first step towards understanding automated KR and the importance of facial features in it. In the field of KR, there is a lot of room for improvement, especially on the importance of facial features. This is what we tackled in our research by researching whether kinship is recognizable by using a set of extracted facial features with the use of machine learning. Specifically, we focus on what specific set of features is important for automated kinship recognition and if this set of features complies with the set of features important in human kinship recognition. First presented in this paper is a literature discussion on human as well as automated kinship recognition. Then, in Section II, the data is discussed. In Section III, an overview of the used models is presented. Next, the results of different experiments are discussed in Section IV. Lastly, a discussion and conclusion of the presented experiments is given in Sections V and VI.

B. Related work

Studies on human KR contribute to our search for the set of important features in automated KR. Several studies [2]–[4] have been conducted on human KR, which showed that kinship is indeed recognizable by humans. Robinson et al. [5] used the Families-In-the-Wild (FIW) data set for their human performance measurement. This data set contains images of people's faces that are extracted from family pictures. Robinson et al. state that humans scored an overall average of 56.6% accuracy. Other research on KR [3], [6], [7] shows similar results. One of the interesting results is that the average accuracy of human KR is higher when face, hair color and background are taken into account compared to when the focus is purely on the face.

We take a look at the Feature Importance (FI) in some of these studies on human kinship detection. The reason behind this specific set of features for human KR might be of help in automated KR. One of the studies is by Martello and Maloney [2], [3], who raised the question which parts of a face are most important for human KR. In [2], they conducted a study in which humans were tested on their KR skills based on three separate conditions: (1) the right hemi-face masked, (2) the left hemi-face masked, and (3) the face fully visible. Most interestingly, the results showed that there is no significant difference in results for recognizing kinship by humans when the left or right part of the face is covered. On the contrary, a similar study [3] showed that the covering of the top or bottom part of a face does give a significant difference. The effect on kin recognition performance of masks that covered the upper half or the lower half of the face (experiment 1) and the eye region or the mouth region (experiment 2) were measured. An example of the covering up of facial parts for experiment 1 and 2 can be seen in Figure 1a and 1b below. In these experiments, it was found that masking the eye region led to a 20% reduction in performance, whereas masking the mouth region led to a non-significant, although fascinating increase in performance. This leads us to consider the insight that the performance in KR is heavily dependent on only the upper half of a person's face.

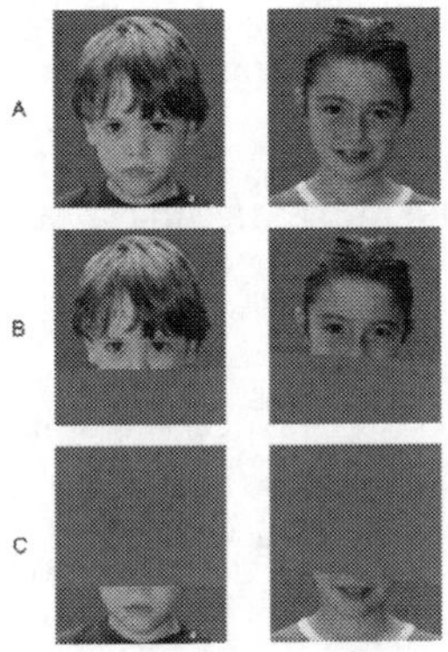

(a) Experiment 1: Masking the bottom and top half of the face

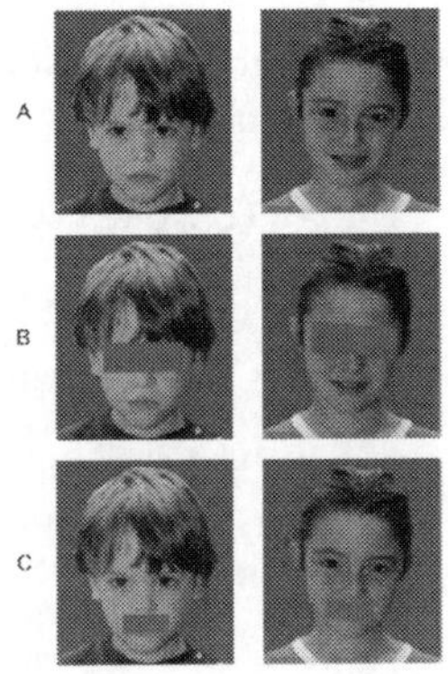

(b) Experiment 2: Masking the eye area and lip area of the face

Figure 1. Illustration of the masking of faces in [3].

Overall, the theory that we researched is based on the possible change in performance when using a specific set of facial features compared to facial features from the whole face. This could lead to only requiring specific parts of faces to identify kinship relations, thus to more accessible data and a decrease of the computational costs of KR models.

For *automated* KR, several approaches have been proposed. Most approaches are not only focused on machine learning models, but also on feature selection. Feature-based methods aim to preserve facial, genetically determined characteristics in the feature descriptors used for the model. These methods identify local facial features such as inconsistencies of an individual's eyes, mouth, nose and skin from the individual's image. Feature-based methods can decrease computational cost and improve the model's performance. Most of the proposed models and algorithms were trained on only small data sets.

These data sets demonstrated to be insufficient for the task at hand. Most of the proposed classifiers are lower-level models and algorithms, which use handcrafted feature extraction (features using information presented in the image itself), Support Vector Machines (SVMs) or K-Nearest Neighbor classifiers.

Since 2016, a more extensive data set has been constructed in [4]: Families-in-the-Wild (FIW). This data set has been produced to verify kinship and classify relations [8]. The creators of this data set specify promising results in detecting kinship. Robinson et al. [5] state the best results were obtained when using the SphereFace model with an average accuracy of 69.18% and standard deviation of 3.68. All models performed well compared to previous work, although much improvement could still be made.

After publishing this FIW data set, more research in the field of KR models was done. Many models in KR include the use of FaceNet or other small feature selections for their models' input [9]. FaceNet is a neural network that extracts features of an image. The model provides a mapping from a picture of a face to the Euclidean space. The distances in this space correlate to the amplitude of face resemblance [10]. It produces an output vector to be used as input for a classification model. FaceNet creates embeddings by learning the mapping from images. A disadvantage of using FaceNet is that especially when looking at FI, information gets lost due to lack of feature interpretation [11].

FaceNet could help improve KR models, although we are interested in the similarities between faces by using facial features instead of the faces as a whole. Hence, we use a different approach than FaceNet. Fang et al. [12] proposed different feature extractions. One of the extractions is based on different colors of different parts of the face. Other extractions are based on image coordinates of certain parts of the face, facial distances and gradient histograms. Together, these feature extraction methods constructed 44 facial features. The top selected features are right eye RGB color, skin gray value, left eye RGB color, nose-to-mouth vertical distance, eye-to-nose horizontal distance and left eye gray value. The results show a high importance for eye related features. 10 out of the 14 top features include the eye area. While this study does include specific facial features like eye color, it only included 22 low-level features. It is indeed shown that most of the selected features are in the upper face area, which complies with the insight.

Most studies on the subject focus on either the overall similarities between faces, or on pre-determined facial feature sets. These studies treat KR tasks similar to the task of a standard facial recognition. Guo et al. [13] argue that kinship classification should be treated differently, since trait similarities are measured across age and gender. Additionally, kinship has a combination of traits and familial traits are special for each family pair.

Models proposed by researchers in this field are based on an input of just the images with little to no alterations. Although, some research focus on specific facial features by using for example a weighted graph embedding-based metric learning framework [14] or by using sparsity to model the genetic visible features of a face [15].

Another group of researchers thought of combining the StyleGAN2 algorithm with KR [16]. In the task at hand, there is a restriction that family members should be recognized on the basis of physical facial features. However, several mentioned attempts neglect this constraint and do not employ any facial landmark before using a classification model. For this reason, Nguyen et al. [16] experimented with KR models using StyleGAN2 as an encoder to incorporate a facial landmark map. This method resulted in an average accuracy of 0.548 for recognizing kinship. Against expectations, no improvement was shown in the results from using StyleGAN2 in this manner, which is presumed to be due to the lack of a proper classification and thus it is argued to need more investigation. An algorithm proposed by Guo et al. [13] uses familial traits extraction and kinship measurement based on a stochastic combination of the familial traits. The authors use a similarity score based on a Bayes decision for each pair of facial parts. However, facial features used by the algorithm are limited to the eyes, nose and mouth and, in line with the observations by Guo et al. [13], more parts of the face could be explored. Existing data sets use faces from the same family picture, so models learn about the background similarity. This causes the models to get a higher performance, but when tested on real life pictures, not taken from a family picture, the performance could be lower. When using pre-determined features, this does not present a problem.

II. DATA

We used the Families in The Wild data set. The data is split up into training and test data using hold-out cross validation. The data is split up in a 70/30 split, respectively. The training set consists of information on families, persons and relations between persons including images of the persons. The data is distributed as follows: an average of about 12 images per family, each with at least 3 and as many as 38 members. Each family is assigned a unique id, each person is assigned an id and each image collected is assigned a unique id. The data set includes good quality images of a person's face, but also blurry images of faces, as shown in Figures 2a and 2b, respectively.

(a) Image from training data

(b) Blurry image from training data

Figure 2. Example data from the Families-in-the-Wild data set

A file containing all matches in the training data set is available. However, this does not include data on combinations of persons that do not have a familial relationship. So, these pairs have been constructed by taking random pairs of images from the set of training images of the FIW data set. This is excluding existing related pairs and each pair is unique. This resulted in 205,285 related and 205,285 unrelated pairs of images.

StyleGAN2 metric: linear separability

This research is focused on FI in KR. To be able to understand the FI of a model, the features extracted from a model should be interpretable. To collect a bunch of features and to avoid having to do manual annotation, we decide to use a feature description method from the StyleGAN2 model. With this, it can be easily deducted which of the features of a face are seen as most important by a model for detecting kinship. The pictures in the data are of size 108x124, while the StyleGAN2 description method expects pictures of size 256x256 as input. Interpolation of the pictures in the data is used to overcome this problem. The StyleGAN2 model contains a certain metric called linear separability. StyleGAN2's linear separability metric can be used to steer a generated picture in a certain direction by specifying 40 facial features which are shown in Table I. For example, the models can be used to make the generated face have blond hair and high cheekbones. What we are most interested in for this research are the pre-trained models used in StyleGAN2 which produce probabilities of the 40 features to be true for an image of a person.

TABLE I. FACIAL FEATURES OF LINEAR SEPARABILITY METRIC

1) 5-o-clock-shadow,	15) double chin,	28) pointy nose,
2) arched eyebrows,	16) eyeglasses,	29) receding hairline,
3) attractive,	17) goatee,	30) rosy cheeks,
4) bags under eyes,	18) gray hair,	31) sideburns,
5) bald,	19) heavy make up,	32) smiling,
6) bangs,	20) high cheekbones,	33) straight hair,
7) big lips,	21) male,	34) wavy hair,
8) big nose,	22) mouth slightly open,	35) wearing earrings,
9) black hair,	23) mustache,	36) wearing hat,
10) blond hair,	24) narrow eyes,	37) wearing lipstick,
11) blurry,	25) no beard,	38) wearing necklace,
12) brown hair,	26) oval face,	39) wearing necktie,
13) bushy eyebrows,	27) pale skin,	40) young.
14) chubby,		

The metric was trained using the CelebA Data set (CelebFaces Attributes Data set). This is a face attributes data set with 202,599 celebrity images, each with five landmark locations and 40 attribute annotations. StyleGAN2's linear separability metric is meant to be used for the StyleGAN2 model and its corresponding data. We are interested in using the metric on the data from FIW. The information gathered from the linear separability metric (the facial features) is used as a starting point for the kinship classification models. Transfer learning does not only save time, but it also has the possibility of making a learning process more efficient [17].

Consequently, some adjustments to the data were necessary to apply the metric. This resulted in an output of 40 features for all images in the data set, which then could be used to train the chosen automated KR models. As data points for the models, we chose a list of length 40 and a list of length 80, composed of the metric values for the features per two pictures. Two input types were experimented with: (1) a list of 80 features, consisting of 40 features per image, and (2) a list of 40 features, taking the absolute difference of the feature values between the images per feature.

III. MODEL DESCRIPTION

We implemented and tested several models to see how well the models work on our data and to find a recurring pattern in FI. For all models, the FI is investigated. The results of this are then used to understand whether the theory of human KR will hold for automated KR as well. Various machine learning models were selected for this task. For each model, the accomplished accuracy is obtained by K-fold cross validation. The number of folds is set to 10 and the data is shuffled before splitting into batches.

Machine learning methods

Using StyleGAN2's linear separability metric on our data results in an output of 40 features for all images in the data set, which then are used to train the models. As data points for the models, we chose a list of length either 40 or 80, composed of the metric values for the features per two pictures. The models we decided to experiment with are the following:

First, we have the decision tree algorithm with maximum depth set to 10, where we obtain the FI by using the Gini importance. Second, we have the random forest consisting of 100 trees, where the FI is obtained by using the impurity importance. Then, we have the Gaussian Naive Bayes, which obtains FI by using the permutation importance. Next is the linear SVM, where the weights of the model are used to determine FI. Lastly, we have logistic regression, where the FI is determined by using the coefficients of the decision function.

IV. Results

Two different approaches have been researched, the original StyleGAN2 description method and the bottom and top masked method. The results of these approaches are discussed and an overview of the results is provided.

A. Original StyleGAN2 descriptor experiment

The initial approach is taking the results of the StyleGAN2 model and using them as input for the different algorithms. Over all images, we calculated the probabilities of the image complying with the given 40 features. Extracting 40 features per picture resulted in 80 different values since we were working with two images per data point. The FI was determined per model. For the 80 feature input, we took the sum of each feature per picture. An overview of all the results from the StyleGAN2 descriptor experiment can be found in Table II and Table III.

Decision Tree: The accuracy of the decision tree with 40 features as input has mean 0.61 with a standard deviation of 0.003. The 80 features input gives a mean accuracy of 0.66 with a standard deviation of 0.005. The model is more leaning towards giving a positive (related) classification. For the decision tree model with input of 40 features, *arched eyebrows*, *no beard* and *heavy makeup* are the most important features. For the input of 80 features, the top three of important features is *young*, *no beard* and *wearing necklace*.

Random Forest: The accuracy of the random forest with 40 features as input has mean 0.74 with a standard deviation of 0.003. The 80 features input gives a mean accuracy of 0.80 with a standard deviation of 0.004. The model does not have a clear preference for either a positive or a negative classification. With the model giving 51.39% and 50.63% positive classifications for 40 and 80 features respectively, the even distribution of the data in half positive and half negative data points is represented well with a slight deviation towards positive classifications. For the random forest model with input of 40 features, *arched eyebrows*, *mustache* and *heavy make up* are the most important features. For the input of 80 features, the top three of important features is *young*, *no beard* and *mustache*.

Gaussian Naive Bayes: The accuracy of the Gaussian naive Bayes with 40 features as input has mean 0.60 with a standard deviation of 0.004. The 80 features input gives a mean accuracy of 0.59 with a standard deviation of 0.005. The model has a preference for a positive classification. With the model giving 59.56% and 64.21% positive classifications for 40 and 80 features respectively, most errors are false positives. For the Gaussian naive Bayes model with input of 40 features, *eyeglasses*, *mustache* and *arched eyebrows* are the most important features. For the input of 80 features, the top three of important features is *eyeglasses*, *rosy cheeks* and *no beard*.

Linear Support Vector Machine: The accuracy of the linear SVM with 40 features as input has mean 0.59 with a standard deviation of 0.004. The 80 features input gives a mean accuracy of 0.63 with a standard deviation of 0.005. The model does not have a clear preference for a positive or negative classification. With the model giving 47.08% and 52.92% positive classifications for 40 and 80 features respectively, we see a slight effect of the different input values. The 40 values input gives the model a bit more lenience towards negative classification and the 80 values input gives the model slightly more lenience towards positive classification. For the LSVM model with input of 40 features, *arched eyebrows*, *no beard* and *heavy make up* are the most important features. *no beard* and *arched eyebrows* are also among the most important features for the input of 80 features. Here the top three of features is *arched eyebrows*, *narrow eyes* and *no beard*.

Logistic Regression: The accuracy of the logistic regression with 40 features as input has mean 0.60 with a standard deviation of 0.003. The 80 features input gives a mean accuracy of 0.63 with a standard deviation of 0.005. The model does not have a clear preference for a positive or negative classification. The model gives 50.40% and 51.61% positive classifications for 40 and 80 features respectively, which shows the balance of the data with a slight deviation towards positive classification. For the logistic regression model with input of 40 features, *arched eyebrows*, *no beard* and *eyeglasses* are the most important features. These are also among the important features for the input of 80 features. Here the top three of important features is *no beard*, *arched eyebrows* and *pale skin*.

B. Masked StyleGAN2 descriptor experiment

To support the theory we found, all of StyleGAN2's linear separability features were taken of not the original image, but over an image with the bottom part of the face masked black like shown in Figure 3. The same was done with the top part of the face masked black, comparable to the experiments performed by Martello et al. [2], [3]. All the models are exactly the same as for the original StyleGAN2 description method. Only the input changed.

Bottom half masked: This experiment was done with all models previously used in the original StyleGAN2 descriptor

(a) (b)

Figure 3. Example data from the Families in the Wild data set with bottom masked (a) and top masked (b)

experiment. The accuracy and FI were obtained for the decision tree, random forest, Gaussian naive Bayes, LSVM and logistic regression models. An overview of the accuracy and important features for all the models from the bottom masked StyleGAN2 descriptor experiment can be found in Table II and Table III. Again, the results show that the 80 value input gives and overall better performance than the 40 value input and the best performing model is random forest for both inputs. Some of the most important features for the bottom masked approach are related to the nose (*pointy nose* and *big nose*) and the hair (*grey hair*, *blond hair* and *waivy hair*).

Top half masked: This experiment was done with all models previously used in the original StyleGAN2 descriptor experiment. The accuracy and FI were obtained for the decision tree, random forest, Gaussian naive Bayes, SVM and logistic regression models. An overview of the accuracy and important features for all the models from the bottom masked StyleGAN2 descriptor experiment can be found in Table II and Table III. Again, the results show the 80 value input to give overall better performance than the 40 value input and the best performing model is random forest for both inputs.

TABLE II. ACCURACY FOR THE 40 AND 80 VALUE INPUT PER EXPERIMENT: COMPLETE, BOTTOM MASKED AND TOP MASKED

	40 Compl.	**40 Bottom**	**40 Top**	**80 Compl.**	**80 Bottom**	**80 Top**
Decision Tree	0.61 ± 0.003	0.57 ± 0.004	0.57 ± 0.003	0.66 ± 0.005	0.64 ± 0.004	0.65 ± 0.003
Random Forest	0.74 ± 0.003	0.62 ± 0.003	0.63 ± 0.002	**0.83 ± 0.004**	0.81 ± 0.001	0.82 ± 0.001
Gaussian Naive Bayes	0.60 ± 0.004	0.53 ± 0.003	0.55 ± 0.002	0.59 ± 0.005	0.55 ± 0.003	0.57 ± 0.002
Support Vector Machine	0.59 ± 0.004	0.55 ± 0.002	0.57 ± 0.002	0.63 ± 0.005	0.60 ± 0.002	0.61 ± 0.002
Logistic Regression	0.60 ± 0.003	0.55 ± 0.003	0.57 ± 0.002	0.63 ± 0.005	0.59 ± 0.003	0.61 ± 0.002

V. Discussion

Multiple models have been tested on FI. Some approaches were based on the human KR experiments from [2], [3]. These experiments showed a certain area of the face to contain the important facial traits needed for KR. We researched the set of features that is most important for automated KR. Pre-trained metrics from the StyleGAN2 model that are meant to be used for synthesizing artificial examples of faces were

TABLE III. MOST IMPORTANT FEATURES PER EXPERIMENT

	Complete	**Bottom Masked**	**Top Masked**
Decision Tree	young, no beard, arched eyebrows, eyeglasses	attractive, blond hair, pointy nose, grey hair	young, no beard, arched eyebrows, eyeglasses
Gaussian Naive Bayes	eyeglasses, no beard, young, arched eyebrows	wavy hair, blond hair, pale skin, heavy makeup	eyeglasses, no beard, young, arched eyebrows
Support Vector Machine	young, no beard, pointy nose, arched eyebrows	grey hair, pale skin, wavy hair, big nose	young, no beard, pointy nose, arched eyebrows
Logistic Regression	blurry, no beard, wearing necklace, pointy nose	wavy hair, young, grey hair, big nose	blurry, no beard, wearing necklace, pointy nose
Random Forest	young, no beard, mustache, arched eyebrows	pointy nose, grey hair, smiling, attractive	young, no beard, mustache, arched eyebrows

used. The pre-trained models give 40 values for specific facial features. These 40 values can also be taken from pictures using the pre-trained models. These values were used as input for our machine learning models: decision tree, random forest, Gaussian naive Bayes, support vector machine and logistic regression. These models were trained and evaluated to show which of the features were seen as most important by the models. More experiments were conducted with the top and bottom parts of a face masked black to also test the theory of human KR.

Major findings: Interesting results were found when comparing the different models using the original StyleGAN2 description method. Four out of five models had a higher accuracy score when all features for both pictures were kept separate. The models are able to learn about combinations of different features between the two pictures, which has a positive influence on the accuracy score of the models.

The best performing model seems to be the random forest. Since this model has a very high accuracy compared to the other models, we are specifically interested in its corresponding FI scores. Accordingly, we mainly focus on the results of the random forest model. This model gives high importance values to the features *young*, *no beard*, *mustache* and *arched eyebrows*. It is also noticeable that in two of the five models, the feature *young* is found to be very important and in the other three models, the FI increases when using 80 features instead of 40 features as input. On top of that, in all models, the features *arched eyebrows* and *no beard* are in the top four of the most important features for the model. There is a clear pattern in the importance of facial hair. Beards, mustaches and arched eyebrows are found to be important features for most of the models. Another pattern is the age difference. This gives us reason to believe that the combination of facial hair and the age of a person is strongly correlated to the classification.

While the correlation scores do not show a correlation between the two features, the combination of the features do matter when comparing two pictures. A reason for these features to be found important is that most of the kinship relations (75%) in the data set are zero generation and first generation relations. Young people are not able to grow facial hair, if they have the genes, it comes with age. This would explain why both facial hair and age are found to be more important.

This set of features that are found to be the most important in our research do not comply with the selection of features proposed by Fang et al. [12]. The set of features used in their research is different, although it is clear that the eye area was found to be the most important by them. Contrasting, the set of important features we found is not particularly focused on the eye area.

For the masked experiment, all five models had a higher accuracy score when all features for both pictures were kept separate. When looking at the bottom masked method results, a clear decrease in the performance is found compared to the original StyleGAN2 description method. Remarkable is that the feature *young* and the features on facial hair are not found in the top features of almost all models. The original StyleGAN2 approach showed these features to be very important. This leads to the believe that the bottom part of a face is essential for extracting the feature *age*. This would also explain why the feature *grey hair* is found to be important in three out of five models. Grey hair is usually a sign of a higher age. When looking at the top masked method results, a decrease in the accuracy is found, although this decrease is not as excessive as with the bottom masked method. Above is mentioned that the feature young is likely to be extracted from mostly the bottom of a face. However, this is not shown in the results of the top masked method. It is curious that the feature *young* is still not found to be one of the most important. Like the original approach, the top masked method shows the feature *arched eyebrows* to be important. Although a pattern is difficult to find in the top masked method results.

For the bottom masked approaches the difference with the original approach is clear. Where humans showed equal or even better performance when masking the top half of a picture, the algorithms showed the opposite effect.

Limitations: The data set might not be very compatible with the StyleGAN2 metrics, which is an uncertainty. However, as for now, there are no other data sets that contain enough images which are of adequate quality. So for now, we have to accept this limitation. An issue was also encountered when using the linear separability metric for a different purpose than StyleGAN2. The results for the top masked method showed one very noteworthy important feature, namely the *arched eyebrows* feature. This feature should be focused on the top part of a face. However, it is found to be important when the top part of a face is masked. More features which show unusual behavior are *smiling* and *pointy nose*, since these are found to be important when masking the bottom half of the face. This is one of the problems that is encountered when combining StyleGAN2 metrics with other models. The models that are trained for the linear separability metric behave different than intuitively expected. Using the metric in tasks for which it is not initially intended can cause limitations to the models.

Unexpected findings: A surprising matter is the difference in performance between the top masked and bottom masked StyleGAN2 description method. Masking the bottom half of the face decreased the performance. As masking the top half of the face decreased the performance as well, it still performed better than the bottom masked method. This is against expectations and raises the question whether the bottom part of a face contains more information than the top part of a face does for KR.

VI. Conclusion

We researched the set of features that is most important for automated KR. For this, multiple models have been tested on FI. The results showed that the most important facial features from the selection of 40 features are mostly focused on the facial hair traits and age related features.

One of the issues we ran into is on transfer learning. The question rises whether StyleGAN2 is compatible enough for transfer learning combined with our data set. It could be more effective to write a new metric that focuses on more solid facial features. Despite that, the StyleGAN2 metrics are the most elaborate method in finding pre-determined facial features. Other models include not as many facial features or need manual annotation. It would be contributory to find a way to annotate all parts of the face for many more features as to train the models on.

In conclusion, this paper is an important first step towards understanding automated KR, but there are many challenges to be faced before it can be used in real-world applications. As it is now, a large set of clear pictures of complete faces are needed for a model to perform decently. Learning more about the most important parts of our face for automated KR is the next step to take to improve the field of KR.

VII. Acknowledgment

We thank Rob van der Mei and Sandjai Bhulai for their useful comments on drafts of this paper.

References

[1] E. Seselja, "How the Red Cross and a radio reconnected a family torn apart by conflict - ABC news", https://www.abc.net.au/news/2021-08-29/red-cross-reconnect-family-separated-by-conflict-after-16-years-/100413214, August 2021, (Accessed on 23/06/2022).

[2] M. F. Dal Martello and L. T. Maloney, "Lateralization of kin recognition signals in the human face", The Association for Research in Vision and Ophthalmology - Journal of vision, vol. 10(8), 2010.

[3] M. F. Dal Martello and L. T. Maloney, "Where are kin recognition signals in the human face?", The Association for Research in Vision and Ophthalmology - Journal of vision, vol. 6(12), 2006.

[4] J. P. Robinson, M. Shao, Y. Wu and Y. Fu, "Family in the Wild (FIW): A Large-scale Kinship Recognition Database", CoRR, abs/1604.02182, 2016.

[5] J. Lu, X. Zhou, Y. Tan, Y. Shang and J. Zhou, "Neighborhood Repulsed Metric Learning for Kinship Verification", IEEE Transactions on Pattern Analysis and Machine Intelligence, vol. 36(2), pp. 331–345, 2014.

[6] L. M. DeBruine, F.G. Smith, B. C. Jones, S. C. Roberts, M. Petrie and T. D. Spector, "Kin recognition signals in adult faces", Vision research - Elsevier, vol. 49(1), pp. 38–43, 2009.

[7] G. Kaminski, S. Dridi, C. Graff, and E. Gentaz, "Human ability to detect kinship in strangers' faces: effects of the degree of relatedness," Proceedings of the Royal Society B: Biological Sciences, vol. 276(1670), pp. 3193-3200, 2009.

[8] J. P. Robinson, M. Shao, Y. Wu, H. Liu, T. Gillis and Y. Fu, "Visual Kinship Recognition of Families in the Wild", IEEE Transactions on Pattern Analysis and Machine Intelligence, vol. 40(11), pp. 2624–2637, 2018.

[9] R. F. Rachmadi, I. K. E. Purnama, S. M. S. Nugroho and Y. K. Suprapto, "Family-aware convolutional neural network for image-based kinship verification", International Jour- nal of Intelligent Engineering and Systems, vol 13(6), pp. 20–30, 2020.

[10] F. Schroff, D. Kalenichenko and J. Philbin, "Facenet: A unified embedding for face recognition and clustering", IEEE Conference on Computer Vision and Pattern Recognition (CVPR), 2015.

[11] L. Dulčić, "Face Recognition with FaceNet and MTCNN - Ars Futura", https://arsfutura.com/magazine/face-recognition-with-facenet-and-mtcnn/, (Accessed on 23/06/2022).

[12] R. Fang, K. Tang, N. Snavely, and T Chen, " Towards computational models of kinship verification", IEEE International Conference on Image Processing, pp. 1577-1580, 2010.

[13] G. Guo and X. Wang, "Kinship measurement on salient facial features", IEEE Transactions on Instrumentation and Measurement, vol. 61(8), 2012.

[14] J. Liang, Q. Hu, C. Dang, and W. Zuo, "Weighted graph embedding-based metric learning for kinship verification", IEEE Transactions on Image Processing, vol. 28(3) pp. 1149–1162, 2019.

[15] R. Fang, A. C. Gallagher, T. Chen, and A. Loui, "Kinship classification by modeling facial feature heredity", IEEE International Conference on Image Processing, pp. 2983-2987, 2013.

[16] T. H. Nguyen, H. H. Nguyen and H. Dao, "Recognizing families through images with pretrained encoder", arXiv, 2020.

[17] Seldon, "Transfer learning for machine learning", https://www.seldon.io/transfer-learning/, June 2021, (Accessed on 23/06/2022).

Common Data Model for the Microservices of a Radiopropagation Tool

Adrián Valledor
Computer Science Dept.
Universidad de Alcalá
Madrid, Spain
e-mail: adrian.valledor@uah.es

Marcos Barranquero
Computer Science Dept.
Universidad de Alcalá
Madrid, Spain
e-mail: marcos.barranquero@uah.es

Juan Casado
Software Engineer at Starleaf
Starleaf, Building 7
United Kingdowm
e-mail: juan.ballesteros@starleaf.com

Josefa Gómez
Computer Science Dept.
Universidad de Alcalá
Madrid, Spain
e-mail: josefa.gomezp@uah.es

Abdelhamid Tayebi
Computer Science Dept.
Universidad de Alcalá
Madrid, Spain
e-mail: hamid.tayebi@uah.es

***Abstract*—This paper presents the development and improvement of a part of a Web simulation tool for radio propagation of 2D and 3D geospatial data. In particular, a fraction of its architecture, based on microservices, is shown. With our study, we encountered the need to use a common data model that allows the managment of the data throughout the tool. To solve this, some of the possible solutions to this problem are presented, such as the GraphQL Application Programming Interface (API) or the use of REpresentational State Transfer (REST) APIs and the use of Docker together with microservices. Finally, the implementation of a model supported by geometry specifications is provided as a solution and we conclude with the results obtained together with future work plans.**

Keywords—Microservices, radiopropagation tool, REST APIs, data model, GraphQL.

I. INTRODUCTION

In recent years, there has been a need, either because of time or because of the inability of maintenance during the software lifecycle, to migrate from the old monolithic systems to current microservices models. This is based on models in which the application was a single atomic unit, but complex and difficult to maintain and grow over time [1]. Therefore, nowadays the Service Oriented Architecture (SOA) model stands out, known for its great modularity and communication with other models. With this also comes the need to establish correct protocols for their communication with other models. At the moment, a microservice can be defined as "a small application that can be deployed independently, scaled independently and tested independently and that has a single responsibility" [1]. Despite all the benefits shown in the use of microservices, they also brings some problems to the table. One of them can be the inconsistency of the data model, since the microservices can be independent and, therefore, they may not share the same specifications. In this case, the improvement of a radio propagation simulation tool is being developed [2]. This Web simulation tool will allow the display of geospatial data through an interactive map in 2D and in 3D urban environments [3]. The tool uses several empirical and semi-empirical models for the computation of radiopropagation. In addition, it displays terrain-related information, e.g., height values, population density, terrain type or any other raster input that the algorithms may require. It also allows to represent and visualize the simulation results on the map in 2D for empirical methods or 3D for deterministic methods. Additionally, it allows the optimization of antenna positioning, by means of genetic algorithms, to provide the best coverage in a given area. In particular, the solution adopted for the development of this tool will be shown through the definition of a specification structure adapted to this need.

The remainder of this paper is organized as follows: Section II gives a short overview of work related to the idea to be put forward. Section III shows the devised solution of the specification structure as a data model. Section IV presents another solution related to microservices and Docker. Section V summarises the advantages and disadvantages of implementing this model. Finally, Section VI concludes the article and gives an outlook on future work.

II. STATE OF ART

Among the solutions that can be envisaged to solve the problem of the shared data model are the following.

A. GraphQL

GraphQL is a query-based language, in a JavaScript Object Notation (JSON) like format, for APIs and runtime that checks existing data. It provides a complete description of the data in its API, allowing users to request what they need [4]. Among its highlights is that in addition to getting the properties of a particular resource, it provides its references. This allows for quick queries, even if it relies on more limited network connections. Another point in favour is that it allows continuous adaptation to the types of data we need, i.e., if we need to add or remove specific fields, it would not be necessary to modify the existing queries.

On the contrary, this is not a suitable solution for the data model that is required for the simulation tool, as it may present one of the following problems:

- Performance problems, allowing the user to execute impermissible queries.
- It presents excessive complexity to solve this problem, making subsequent maintenance difficult.
- It has only one endpoint, making it difficult to use caching.
- Difficult error handling regarding other structures such as REST.

B. REST APIs

REST APIs represent a set of architectural principles that fits the specific needs of each application as defined by Dr. Roy Fielding et al. [5]. This provides a high level of flexibility and freedom for development of a microservices architecture. In addition, it must meet a number of requirements:

- Uniform interface: all requests must be the same, regardless of their origin.
- Decoupling of client-server, client and server applications must be independent of each other.
- Without status: each application must contain all the information necessary to process the query.
- Cacheability: resources must be able to be cached on the client or server side.
- Layered architecture: calls and responses will pass through different layers.
- Code on demand: in some cases responses may contain executable code.

REST APIs operation is based on communication through HTTP requests [6] that execute database functions, generally CRUD (Create, Read, Update and Delete).

In conclusion, the use of both GraphQL and the REST architecture is excessive or can become complex with respect to the development that is desired in the long term. For example, the need to provide a data model prior to GraphQL to be able to start working with it or the need to develop a larger architecture to be able to apply REST. For all these reasons, a better solution is proposed, in this case, the development of an own data model in the form of specifications.

III. Microservices with Docker

Another solution related to microservices is the use of Docker [7]. In this case, a small Dockerfile is designed that uses a couple of environment variables to define the port and the action to be performed. In this case, the action will be to launch one microservice or another depending on whether it is involved in the operation or not.

One of the benefits of using this framework is the possibility of implementing load balancing by launching or stopping microservices depending on their need.

Another great benefit of using Docker is that it will allow microservices to be scalable, easily upgradable and independently deployable.

As it can be seen from the code in Figure 1 referring to the Dockerfile, through this small development in Docker, it is possible to load the microservices components and code dynamically. That allows to have the same interfaces and code for all of the microservices, and loading only the part of the code relevant to that microservice encapsulated in one container. For the case shown in Figure 1, it is used with servers of different types depending on whether they are necessary or not.

```

FROM node:latest

ARG PORT
ARG ACTION
ARG ROOT=/app

ENV ACTION=${ACTION}
ENV PORT=${PORT}

RUN mkdir ${ROOT}
WORKDIR ${ROOT}

COPY package.json ${ROOT}
COPY index.js ${ROOT}
COPY load.js ${ROOT}
COPY ${ACTION}.js ${ROOT}
RUN npm install

EXPOSE ${PORT}
CMD npm start
```

Fig. 1. Dockerfile to launch a microservice.

To denote which elements will be loaded into the container, operating system environment variables with different values common to servers, such as the port or server name, are used. By reading these attributes in code, the code to be copied into the container is determined, thus loading only what is necessary for that microservice.

IV. Solution Specifications

At this point, we propose an application with an architecture divided into a front-end and a back-end. In the back-end is the set of servers that provide the microservices. The microservices, in turn, are responsible for providing the necessary data both to show the users of the application and to carry out internal operations, for example, obtaining building heights, optimising antennas locations or calculating the radiopropagation, among others. On the other hand, there is a front-end in charge of representing graphically in the browser the data collected from the servers in the form of geometries. As can be guessed, a common data model is needed that is recognised by both sides of this structure. In this way, through a single model, the different parties involved can communicate without the need to add extraneous elements or dependencies.

As a solution to the data model, it was decided to create a common data type that will be used transversally across the different microservices of the application and that has been defined as "Specification". This Specification is based on the common properties that all geometry is considered to have, geometry being a fundamental structure in the application. The Specification will have a similar structure to JSON type files and is defined by the type of geometry it represents, as well as the coordinates of the points that compose it. See, for example, if one wishes to represent the geometry of a rectangle, a specification will be generated in JSON format indicating the type of geometry, in this case rectangle, together with the coordinates of the four points that compose it. In this way, this specification can be shared and recognised in the same way in the different microservices that make up the application.

V. Advantages and Disadvantages

Having seen some of the different alternatives available, such as GraphQL or REST designs, together with the proposed solution, a set of advantages and disadvantages about them can be obtained.

The advantages include the following:

- Use of a common data model.
- No external dependencies.
- Easy to maintain structure.
- It provides a simple overview of the tool.

On the contrary, it has the following disadvantages:

- It does not have the possibility of being reusable in other developments.
- It has too concrete a design focused on the current tool.

VI. Conclusion

This work proposed the implementation of a common data model for radiopropagation tool. To do so, other models such as GrapQL or REST architectures have been discussed, reaching the conclusion of defining the Specification model, achieving a model recognised by the whole structure of its system. Moreover, it can be seen how beneficial it is for a framework like this tool the importance of maintaining an architecture through microservices.

The use of microservices has allowed the elimination of external dependencies, as well as the possibility of reusing them in the future and ensuring better maintenance over time. Plus, it adds modularization to the project, providing scalability and load balance between the front-end and the back-end. Parallel to the implementation of the microservices, it was necessary to use or develop a correct data model common to all of them in order to allow efficient communication. Along with this, current alternatives to this data model have been considered, but they do not fit with the situation of the tool being developed, either because of their size or because of future dependencies.

Once this problem has been solved, we propose as future work, the improvement of the user interface, as well as the relationship of this with the different libraries that allow the representation of maps in the browser. In addition, we intend to make use of the specifications designed in the data model, so that everything is communicated and perfectly integrated in the tool. The mentioned improvement will be based on the use of the OpenLayers [8] library, which allows maps to be represented in a browser and different operations to be carried out. Together with it, the React [9] framework will be used to transmit through forms, the coordinates that are intended to be represented on the map, which in turn will be represented by the data model of the specifications presented in this article. In this way, the data will be kept accessible throughout the entire structure of the tool.

Acknowledgement

This work was supported by the program "Programa de Estímulo a la Investigación de Jóvenes Investigadores" of Vice rectorate for Research and Knowledge Transfer of the University of Alcala and by the Comunidad de Madrid (Spain) through project CM/JIN/2021-033.

References

[1] J. Thönes, "Microservices," in IEEE Software, vol. 32, no. 1, pp. 116-116, Jan.-Feb. 2015, doi: 10.1109/MS.2015.11.

[2] A. Tayebi, J. Gomez, F. Saez de Adana, O. Gutierrez, and M. Fernandez de Sevilla, "Development of a Web-Based Simulation Tool to Estimate the Path Loss in Outdoor Environments using OpenStreetMaps [Wireless Corner]," IEEE Antennas and Propagation Magazine, vol. 61, no. 1, pp. 123-129, Feb. 2019, doi: 10.1109/MAP.2018.2883088.

[3] F. Saez De Adana, J. Gómez, A. Tayebi, and J. Casado, "Applications of Geographic Information Systems for Wireless Network Planning", Artech, 2020.

[4] GraphQL — A query language for your API. [Online]. Available from: http://www.Graphql.org. June, 2022.

[5] R. Fielding and R. Taylor, "Principled design of the modern Web architecture". ACM transactions on Internet technology, 2(2), pp.115–150, 2002, doi: 10.1145/514183.514185.

[6] J. Gómez, A. Tayebi, and J. Casado, "On the use of Websockets to maintain temporal states in stateless applications", in The 15th International Conference on Internet and Web Applications and Services ICIW 2020, pp. 21-24.

[7] X. Wan, X. Guan, T. Wang, G. Bai, and B. Choi, "Application deployment using Microservice and Docker containers: Framework and optimization". Journal of Network and Computer Applications, 119, pp.97-109, 2018, doi: 10.1016/j.jnca.2018.07.003.

[8] O. Zabala-Romero, E. Chassignet, J. Zabala-Hidalgo, P. Velissariou, H. Pandav, and A. Meyer-Baese, "OWGIS 2.0: Open source Java application that builds web GIS interfaces for desktop and mobile devices", SIGSPATIAL'14: Proceedings of the 22sn ACM SIGSPATIAL International Conference on Advances in Geographic Information Systems, 2014, pp. 311-320, doi:10.1145/2666310.2666381.

[9] C. M. Novac, O. C. Novac, R. M. Sferle, M. I. Gordan, G. Bujdoso, and C. M. Dindelegan, "Comparative study of some applications made in the Vue.js and React.js frameworks". 16th International Conference on Engineering of Modern Electric Systems (EMES), 2021, pp. 1-4, doi: 10.1109/EMES52337.2021.9484149.

Detecting Venous Disorders via Near-Infrared Imaging

Observation of Varicose Vein Development

Huseyin A. Erdem
Department of Computer Engineering, The Graduate School of Natural and Applied Sciences
Dokuz Eylul University
İzmir, Turkey
e-mail: huseyinaerdem@gmail.com

Semih Utku
Department of Computer Engineering, Faculty of Engineering
Dokuz Eylul University
İzmir, Turkey
e-mail: semih@cs.deu.edu.tr

***Abstract*—In this study, a method by which progression stages of venous disorders can be detected using the near-infrared vein images is proposed. For this purpose, the superficial vein surveillance system, which was developed within the scope of the ongoing doctoral thesis, was re-trained to find the telangiectasia and varicose vein patterns in the images. The trainings were carried out using the You Only Look Once version 3 (YOLOv3) object detection algorithm. Confidence values of 0.90 and above were achieved in object detection experiments performed with artificial telangiectasia and varicose vein patterns. According to the test results, the developed system can detect Chronic Venous Disorder patterns with Accuracy Rate (1), Misclassification Rate (0), Precision (1), Prevalence (0.5) and F-Score (1) values. With this system, the patient and physician will be informed about the development of venous disorders at an early stage and a pre-diagnosis data will be created for the physician.**

Keywords - vein imaging; near-infrared light; telangiectasia; varicose; YOLOv3.

I. Introduction

Medical imaging devices are one of the primary auxiliary methods used in hospitals to diagnose different diseases. The devices used in this context work on the basis of visualizing the area to be viewed with light or sound waves. Imaging with light is carried out by utilizing different wavelengths in the electromagnetic spectrum. Medical imaging devices currently in use are classified according to the body tissue they can monitor and the effects of the light used to illuminate the area of interest on the body. While the X-Ray device, which emits harmful rays (ionizing radiation) to the body, is dominantly used in the imaging of bone tissue and abdominal diseases, Computed Tomography is used for imaging both bone tissue and internal organs [1]-[3]. In addition, Magnetic Resonance Imaging provides imaging of tissues with magnetic waves, whereas Ultrasound uses high-frequency sound waves for imaging [1][2].

Although technology advances at a dizzying pace, many lives are still lost due to late detection of diseases that can be easily cured if detected earlier. Despite the efforts to increase the awareness of early diagnosis for all kinds of diseases, modern people do not abandon the habit of going to the doctor after the disease occurs and often neglect routine controls. In these omissions, the concern of triggering other diseases by imaging devices working with harmful rays to the body during controls has a large share. However, currently developing technology techniques give a chance to produce harmless alternatives to detect some diseases early. Among them, varicose disease, which is one of the vascular diseases and caused by the enlargement of the veins close to the skin surface (i.e., superficial veins), can be counted.

Computed Tomography or Magnetic Resonance Imaging techniques can be used for vein imaging [2]. However, both the negative effects of these devices on human health and their high costs limit their use to hospital environments only. In addition, although the ultrasound device, which provides visualization of blood flow [1][2], is harmless to the body, it has a high cost and can generally be used and interpreted by radiologists in hospitals. Near-infrared light, which is a type of light that is harmless to the body, is used in hospitals within the scope of superficial vein imaging, especially during vascular access procedures.

The main advantage of near-infrared light in the scope of vein imaging is that photons of this type of light can be absorbed by hemoglobin molecules in the vein [4]-[6]. In this way, the veins in the tissue area illuminated with near-infrared light of a certain wavelength (in the studies carried out in [5]-[7], a wavelength of 850 nm was used, which usually gives optimum results) can be viewed with a camera having the same wavelength filter. In this way, the visualization of the superficial veins can be easily performed with only the light source and the camera (even an ordinary camera can be turned into a simple near-infrared camera by changing the filter on it). By applying digital image processing filters on the obtained near-infrared image, some improvements can be made on the image. In this way, the edges of the veins can be sharpened, only the relevant vein patterns can be revealed by eliminating the surrounding tissues or the noise in the image can be removed. Processed near-infrared vascular images can be used for many different purposes from disease pre-diagnosis to biometric recognition [8]-[11]. For these purposes, deep learning techniques (such as classification or object detection/recognition) are applied on images.

The system, which was prepared within the scope of the ongoing doctoral study (near-infrared images of the right and left forearms were used) and which enables the superficial veins (in the near-infrared images) to be visualized as an e-health application in the home environment, was retrained in this study to monitor the vein enlargement. In this study, the vein enlargement patterns in the images are detected by the object detection algorithm. In addition, two artificial datasets (representing vein enlargements) to be used in training and testing of the YOLOv3 object detection algorithm [12] were created.

In Section 2, venous disorder stages are introduced and the re-trained YOLOv3 algorithm is explained so that the system can detect vein enlargement. How the datasets were created and the results obtained as a result of the trials are also stated in this section. In the last section, the study is discussed in general terms.

II. Vein Enlargement Detection: YOLOv3 Algorithm

Near-infrared imaging system is basically examined in two parts as hardware and software. While the hardware part is about the wavelength of the light source, Light Emitting Diode (LED) placements and camera features, the software part covers the extraction of vein patterns by making the veins in the obtained near-infrared images more prominent via digital image processing techniques. In this way, superficial veins can be visualized. The hardware part and digital image processing steps of this ongoing doctoral study were introduced in [10]. Also, the presentation of narrowing detections in processed images (using the YOLOv3 algorithm with a single class as stenosis_vein) to patients and physicians as a video-based indirect augmented reality environment was explained in [11]. In this study, the visualization of enlargements in superficial vein images is discussed.

When the valves of the superficial veins do not work properly, blood accumulations occur, and as a result, the veins expand and elongate, and form twisted folds, resulting in varicose veins [13][14]. Although varicose veins are most commonly observed in leg veins (which are under more pressure than other veins [13]), varicose veins can be encountered in every part of the body [15]. In general, however, the development of vascular disease in hand veins does not give results as dramatic as in leg veins. Chronic Venous Disorders (CVDs) affecting millions of people worldwide are caused by morphological and functional abnormalities of the venous system [16][17]. Risk factors, such as heredity (family history, height), lifestyle (long term standing/sitting, occupation, smoking), gain (age, pregnancy, obesity, deep vein thrombosis) or hormones (female gender, progesterone) can lead to venous disorders, such as vein enlargement [18][19]. CVD clinical stages are defined by the CEAP (Clinical, Etiological, Anatomical and Pathophysiological [16]) classification system: C0 (no visible signs of venous disease), C1 (visible veins, telangiectasia/spider veins), C2 (varicose veins), C3 (swelling/edema), C4 (changes to skin quality), C5 (healed ulceration), C6 (active ulceration) [17][20]. CVD is often overlooked in its early stages [16]. In case of early diagnosis, advanced symptoms, such as edema, skin changes or leg ulcers can be alleviated with the support of lifestyle changes [17][19]. The incidence of vascular disorders in adults in urban and rural Bonn area is 59% for telangiectasia vein and 14% for varicose vein, respectively [17].

As most superficial veins, varicose veins are also not easily visible to the naked eye, so near-infrared light is used to visualize these veins [21]. In this study, the hand vein dataset obtained with the superficial vein surveillance system developed within the scope of the ongoing doctoral study was used for the trials of the YOLOv3 algorithm, which was re-trained to detect CVD in the C1 (telangiectasia/spider veins) and C2 (varicose veins) stages. An example image from the dataset and its processed version are given in Fig. 1.

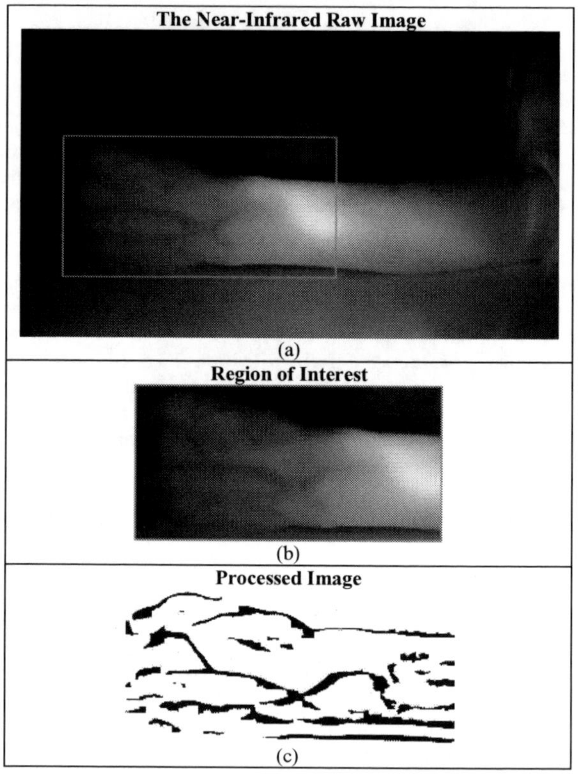

Figure 1. The near-infrared vein image. (a) The near-infrared raw image of hand dorsum. (b) Region of interest, containing only the veins to be examined. (c) Vein patterns obtained by digital image processing.

The YOLOv3 is a deep learning algorithm that performs object detection. With object detection algorithms, training can be performed for multiple objects (up to 80 classes [12] placed at certain locations on the image) that can represent different classes. In this study, the YOLOv3 algorithm was used for CVD detection in vein patterns obtained by image processing steps. The developed near-infrared imaging system was retrained in this study to detect CVD progression using two separate classes (spider_vein and varicose_vein).

There is currently no venous disorder dataset consisting of near-infrared images, available to the public. For this, a two-class training dataset was prepared (The dataset was created by the method of obtaining images from the video recordings described in the study [11]) by adding artificial spider_vein and varicose_vein patterns on the near-infrared images. In this context, 5 spider_vein and 5 varicose_vein patterns were added onto 150 near-infrared images. Furthermore, 50 additional images were created from the existing images by data augmentation methods (10 degrees rotation, 30 degrees rotation, mirroring, noise addition and downscaling). In this way, an artificial training dataset containing 1000 spider_vein and 1000 varicose_vein patterns was obtained. The patterns in the images were labelled with the free (under General Public License version 3) makesense [22] web-based application.

A second dataset consisting of 300 images containing artificial vein enlargement patterns was prepared for the test process to be carried out after the trainings. The dataset was created by adding only a single spider_vein or varicose_vein pattern to each image in random rotations and locations (maintaining a certain figural format). In this way, 150 test images containing the spider_vein class and 150 test images containing the varicose_vein class were obtained. The confusion matrix of the object detection results of the YOLOv3 algorithm, obtained using the test dataset, is given in Table 1. As can be seen from the matrix, all of the searched objects (spider_vein and varicose_vein patterns) in the test images were detected correctly. The developed system can detect CVD patterns in C1 and C2 stages with Accuracy Rate (1), Misclassification Rate (0), Precision (1), Prevalence (0.5) and F-Score (1) values.

The YOLOv3 algorithm marks the locations of the objects detected onto the image with bounding boxes. In addition, the name of the class with the highest probability and the detection rate (confidence value is shown between 0.00 and 1.00 in the study) are printed on the box.

Two sample result images of the YOLOv3 algorithm test process (venous disorder detection with confidence value of 0.99 for spider_vein and 0.90 for varicose_vein classes) are shown in Fig. 2.

Although all classes in the test images were predicted correctly, the YOLOv3 algorithm had a lower confidence value for some patterns. Among 150 images containing spider_vein patterns, 130 had a confidence value in the range of 0.95-1.00, 13 in the range of 0.90-0.94, 6 in the range of 0.80-0.89, and 1 of them was determined as 0.32. When the pattern with the confidence value of 0.32 is examined, it is determined that it is not much different from the patterns in the training dataset (mostly large-sized patterns were used) or other test patterns, but it is smaller in size, as can be seen in Fig. 3. It was evaluated that this situation may result in a low confidence value.

TABLE I. THE CONFUSION MATRIX OF YOLOV3 ALGORITHM RESULTS OBTAINED WITH SPIDER_VEIN AND VARICOSE_VEIN CLASSES

n=300		Predicted Class	
		Positive (spider_vein)	*Negative (varicose_vein)*
Actual Class	*Positive (spider_vein)*	True Positive=150	False Negative=0
	Negative (varicose_vein)	False Positive=0	True Negative=150

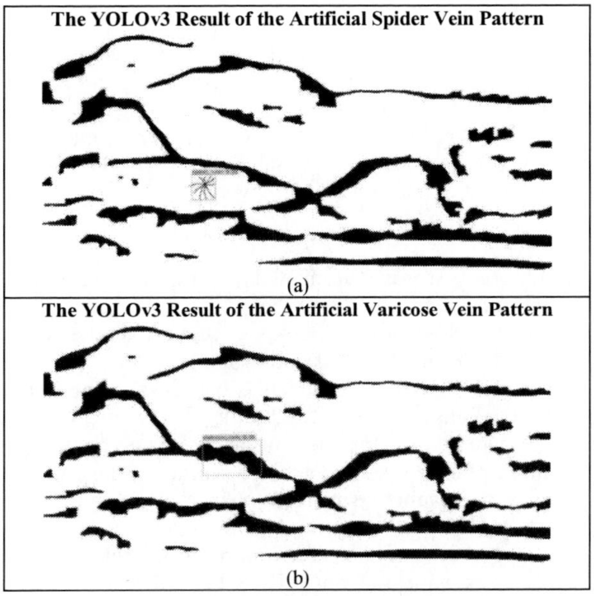

Figure 2. The YOLOv3 algorithm test process result images. (a) 0.99 confidence valued result for spider_vein class. (b) 0.90 confidence valued result for varicose_vein class.

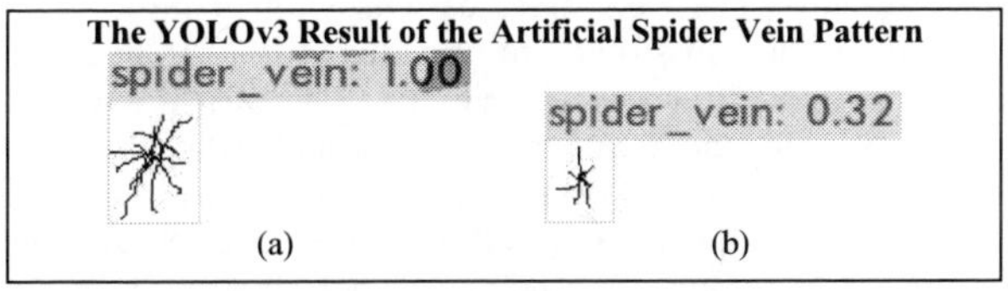

Figure 3. Artificial spider_vein patterns shown in accordance with their actual dimensions. (a) Pattern with the confidence value of 1.00. (b) Pattern with the confidence value of 0.32.

Among the 150 images containing varicose_vein pattern, 126 had a confidence value in the range of 0.95-1.00, 6 had a range of 0.90-0.94, 11 had a range of 0.80-0.89, and 7 had a range of 0.79-0.30. When the 7 patterns with the lowest confidence values are examined, it is determined that these patterns are slightly different (U-shaped, twisted) from the patterns in the training dataset or other test patterns (mostly linear line patterns were used) which can be seen in Fig. 4. It was evaluated that this condition may lead to a low confidence value.

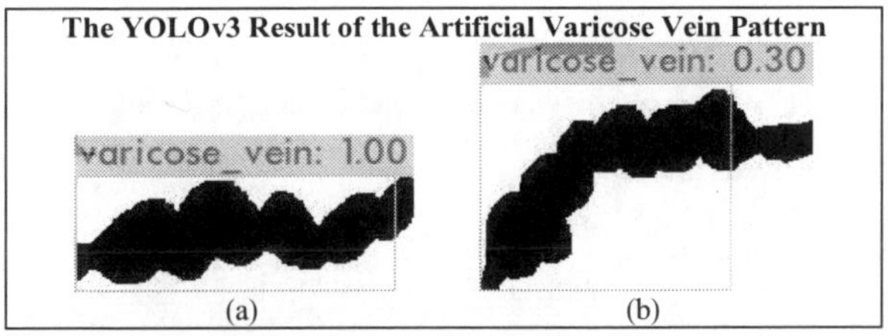

Figure 4. Artificial varicose_vein patterns are shown in accordance with their actual dimensions. (a) Pattern with the confidence value of 1.00. (b) Pattern with the confidence value of 0.30.

Since small-sized spider_vein patterns represent the early stages of CVD and varicose_vein patterns can also twist and fold (may not follow a linear line) over time, such patterns are important in the detection system. Therefore, in order to overcome the low confidence values of spider_vein and varicose_vein classes, smaller-sized patterns and new patterns in different rotations (U-shaped) will be added to the training dataset as part of the future work.

III. CONCLUSION

In this study, it was investigated how the superficial vein surveillance system, which was prepared within the scope of the ongoing doctoral study, could be expanded to detect vein enlargement. The study is based on superficial vein imaging by using near-infrared light which is harmless to the body. The YOLOv3 algorithm was used to detect Chronic Venous Disorder patterns in the near-infrared images obtained. According to the test results obtained with artificial patterns including spider_vein and varicose_vein classes, confidence values of 0.90 and above were achieved in object detection. The developed system could perform object detection of the related classes with Accuracy Rate (1), Misclassification Rate (0), Precision (1), Prevalence (0.5) and F-Score (1) values. In this way, a system in which the development of Chronic Venous Disorder can be followed within the scope of pre-diagnosis has been created. It is vital to inform the doctor about the possibility of the detected telangiectasia vein turning into a varicose vein. In this way, it will be possible to start the treatment without delay. Within the scope of future studies, the system will be tested with real patient data. Also, the vein enlargement detection feature will also be integrated into the superficial vein surveillance system that offers video-based indirect augmented reality, therefore informing the patient and physician.

ACKNOWLEDGMENT

The authors would like to thank Işıl Erdem (Civil Engineer, MSc) for making the final edits of this paper.

REFERENCES

[1] M. Y. M. Chen, T. L. Pope, and D. J. Ott, Basic Radiology, 2nd ed., McGraw Hill: Lange Clinical Medicine, 2011.

[2] Inside View: A Blog For Our Patients, From UVA Radiology and Medical Imaging. *Different Imaging Tests, Explained.* 17.Sep.2017. [Online]. Available from: https://blog.radiology.virginia.edu/different-imaging-tests-explained/ [retrieved: July, 2022]

[3] Bravo Imaging. *Medical Imaging Modality Options and Their Uses.* 20.Jul.2008. [Online]. Available from: https://www.bravoimaging.com/medical-imaging-equipment-miami/medical-imaging-modality-options-and-their-uses/ [retrieved: July, 2022]

[4] V. P. Zharov, S. Ferguson, J. F. Eidt, P. C. Howard, L. M. Fink, and M. Waner, "Infrared Imaging of Subcutaneous Veins", Lasers in Surgery and Medicine: The Official Journal of the American Society for Laser Medicine and Surgery, 34(1), pp. 56-61, 2004, doi.org: 10.1002/lsm.10248.

[5] R. Fuksis, M. Greitans, O. Nikisins, and M. Pudzs, "Infrared Imaging System for Analysis of Blood Vessel Structure", Electronics and Electrical Engineering, System Engineering, Computer Technology, 97(1), pp. 45-48, 2010.

[6] N. Bouzida, A. H. Bendada, and X. P. Maldague, "Near-Infrared Image Formation and Processing for the Extraction of Hand Veins", Journal of Modern Optics, 57(18), pp. 1731-1737, 2010, doi.org: 10.1080/09500341003725763.

[7] Y. Ayoub et al., "Diagnostic Superficial Vein Scanner", International Conference on Computer and Applications (ICCA 2018), IEEE, Aug. 2018, pp. 321-325, doi.org: 10.1109/COMAPP.2018.8460229.

[8] C. L. Lin and K. C. Fan, "Biometric Verification Using Thermal Images of Palm-Dorsa Vein Patterns", IEEE Transactions on Circuits and Systems for Video Technology, 14(2), pp. 199-213, 2004, doi.org: 10.1109/TCSVT.2003.821975.

[9] R. Garcia-Martin and R. Sanchez-Reillo, "Vein Biometric Recognition on a Smartphone", IEEE Access, 8, pp. 104801-104813, 2020, doi.org: 10.1109/ACCESS.2020.3000044.

[10] H. A. Erdem, I. Erdem, and S. Utku, "Near-Infrared Mobile Imaging Systems for e-Health: Lighting the Veins", The Twelfth International Conference on eHealth, Telemedicine, and Social Medicine (eTELEMED 2020), IARIA, Valencia, Spain, November 21-25, 2020, pp. 80-84.

[11] H. A. Erdem and S. Utku, "Augmented Reality Aided Pre-Diagnosis Environment for Telemedicine: Superficial Vein Surveillance System", European Journal of Science and Technology, 2022.

[12] J. Redmon and A. Farhadi. "Yolov3: An Incremental Improvement", arXiv preprint arXiv:1804.02767, 2018.

[13] N. Özbayrak, "Varis Çoraplarının Performans Özelliklerinin İncelenmesi (An Investigation About Performance Properties of Compression Stockings)", Master's Thesis, Uludag University, Bursa, Turkey, 2009. Thesis in Turkish with an abstract in English.

[14] A. E. Gabbey and J. Marcin (reviewed by), Healthline. *Varicose Veins.* 8.Mar.2019. [Online]. Available from: https://www.healthline.com/health/varicose-veins [retrieved: July, 2022]

[15] Health. Johns Hopkins Medicine. *Varicose Veins.* [Online]. Available from: https://www.hopkinsmedicine.org/health/conditions-and-diseases/varicose-veins [retrieved: July, 2022]

[16] T. Feodor, S. Baila, I. A. Mitea, D. E. Branisteanu, and O. Vittos, "Epidemiology and Clinical Characteristics of Chronic Venous Disease in Romania", Experimental and Therapeutic Medicine, 17, pp. 1097-1105, 2019, doi.org: 10.3892/etm.2018.7059.

[17] H. Partsch, "Varicose Veins and Chronic Venous Insufficiency", Vasa: European Journal of Vascular Medicine, 38(4), pp. 293-301, 2009, doi.org: 10.1024/0301–1526.38.4.293.

[18] G. Piazza, "Varicose Veins", Circulation, 130(7), pp. 582-587, 2014, doi.org: 10.1161/CIRCULATIONAHA.113.008331

[19] N. Labropoulos, "How Does Chronic Venous Disease Progress from the First Symptoms to the Advanced Stages? A Review". Advances in Therapy, 36(1), pp. 13-19, 2019, doi.org:10.1007/s12325-019-0885-3.

[20] S. Behring and A. Gonzalez (reviewed by), Healthline. *What Are the Stages of Chronic Venous Insufficiency?.* 10.Jun.2021. [Online]. Available from: https://www.healthline.com/health/chronic-venous-insufficiency-stages [retrieved: July, 2022]

[21] N. Kahraman et al., "Detection of Residual Varicose Veins with Near Infrared Light in the Early Period After Varicose Surgery and Near Infrared Light Assisted Sclerotherapy", Vascular, 2021, doi.org: 10.1177/17085381211051489.

[22] P. Skalski, Makesense, Alpha. *Free To Use Online Tool For Labelling Photos.* [Online] Available from: https://www.makesense.ai/ [retrieved: July, 2022]

Flexibility of Modular and Accountable MLOps Pipelines for Cyber Physical Systems

Philipp Ruf, Christoph Reich
Institute for Data Science, Cloud Computing and Security *(IDACUS)*
Hochschule Furtwangen University (HFU)
Furtwangen, Germany
email: {Philipp.Ruf, Christoph.Reich}@hs-furtwangen.de

Djaffar Ould-Abdeslam
IRIMAS
Université de Haute-Alsace (UHA)
Mulhouse, France
email: djaffar.ould-abdeslam@uha.fr

***Abstract*—Operations within a Cyber Physical System (CPS) environment are naturally diverse and the resulting data sets include complex relations between sensors of the shopfloor devices setup, their configuration respectively. As Machine Learning (ML) can increase the success of industrial plants in a variety of cases, like smart controlling, intrusion detection or predictive maintenance, clarifying responsibilities and operations for the whole lifecycle supports evaluating the potentially feasible scenarios. In this work, the need for highly configurable and flexible modules is demonstrated by depicting the complex possibilities of extending simple Machine Learning Operations (MLOps) pipelines with additional data sources, e.g., sensors. In addition to the particular modules core functionality, arbitrary evaluation logic or data structure specific anomaly detection can be integrated into the pipeline. With the creation of audit-trails for all operational modules, automated reports can be generated for increasing the accountability of the different physical devices and the data related processing. The concept is evaluated in the context of the project Collaborative Smart Contracting Platform for digital value-added Networks (KOSMoS), where a sensor is part of an ML pipeline and audit trails are realized using Blockchain (BC) technology.**

***Keywords*—CPS; ML; MLOps; Deployment; Modularization.**

I. INTRODUCTION

In a fast evolving and interconnected world of user-specific needs, spontaneous demands on individually or rarely manufactured goods and the time span of completing such an order are new challenges to industrial operations. The fourth industrial revolution, known as *Industry 4.0* may be interpreted as the integration of interconnected systems and Internet of Things (IoT) in manufacturing [1]. Also known as CPS, this trend focuses on the deep integration of physical artifacts and informational entities [2], producing a huge amount of operational data. As research in this field is ongoing and concepts are refined continuously, topics like *cobots* (e.g., co-operating robots), further personalization, bio-economy, green computing and other sophisticated technology is summarized as *Industry 5.0* [3].

The usage of ML technology is always dependent on the theoretical feasibility of a respective scenario, the operational infrastructure, applied field devices and overall quality requirements. As production data originated within an organization's CPS plants, the dedicated combination of physical infrastructure and software is geared to the specific setup. While the field of ML emerges in the CPS domain, many Artificial Intelligence (AI)-driven use cases, as for example automated traffic signaling systems or Wireless Sensor Network (WSN) security and privacy enhancement, as outlined in [4], have been implemented in real-world scenarios. Such smart environments are also sometimes termed Artificial Intelligence of Things (AIoT) [5].

As the solutions to the respective problems are often depicted in detail, most literature lacks of comparable integration and management steps of devices in ML environments. It is more common to apply well-known data sets for demonstration and evaluation purposes. Another aspect of related work is executing ML operations on commercial infrastructure or services, as in [6]. In this context, an organization's data privacy policies are often threatened or cannot be met. Engineering an ML task results often in a static implementation and work is carried out within a dedicated environment, comprising specific hardware properties and libraries. Solving an ML problem is not an atomic task, but consists of a pipeline which can be interpreted as a domain-specific and integrated ML platform [7], containing various sub-processes.

When performing maintenance in a CPS plant, both the digital and physical shopfloor configuration must be tested extensively before production can continue. By serving a modular digital environment for CPS operations, an order-specific configuration of shopfloor devices can be dynamically deployed. The accountability and reliability of modules may impact the decision of pipeline compositions, too. In the case of on-demand manufacturing, many common tasks of the devices in a production-line can be automated.The whole pipeline must be held accountable, e.g., audit trails for each involved module operation must be persisted. When considering the obstacles around creating even simple ML pipelines [8], modularization of operations can improve stability and reliability when environmental circumstances change.

In the work on hand, the combination of CPS, ML and required quality aspects, is depicted by related work in Section II. By clarifying MLOps principles with respect to CPS in Section III, the foundation for discussing flexible ML pipelines in Section IV is given. The work is concluded in Section V.

II. Related Work and State-of-the-Art

As AI-based systems become more and more part of modern society, there are also public competitions backed and promoted by governments, e.g., as illustrated in [9]. In order to assure the participation and success of such events, up-to-date and user-friendly topics, as for example MLOps or AutoML, enable non-technical interested parties. A comprehensive overview of ML algorithms and their applications in real-world scenarios was given by Sarker in [10]. In outlining the most common algorithms functionality and intended usage, the importance of characteristics in data to be processed was accentuated. The different phases of MLOps and responsibilities of involved actors were clarified in [11]. With presenting a comparable list of supportive tools, an overview of ML-related environments, appropriate for different tasks was given. Although the work on hand describes an accountable and modular approach of defining MLOps pipelines, capable of implementing a variety of real-world setups, only a theoretical evaluation is performed and no involvement in public competitions took place.

A. Machine Learning for IoT and CPS

The utilization of ML techniques on data originating from industrial devices, e.g., mills, laser cutters, etc., has been implemented within many organisations so far. Sharma et ala [4] surveyed different efforts of ML with respect to IoT, e.g., different embedded devices and cloud-IoT platforms. Fei et al. [12] gave a comparative overview of ML-enabled data stream analytics. In the current literature for the most typical ML applications in CPS (smart grid, intelligent transport systems and smart manufacturing), various tasks and the respective ML techniques are depicted including the algorithms time complexity. In addition to basic ML techniques, incremental- and online learning is overviewed by the authors. In [3], use cases and further aspects of the *Industry 5.0* paradigm are clarified and an overview of technologies applied in the field of CPS is presented. In general, this is a refinement, and utilization of its predecessor, Industry 4.0, where interconnection of devices, humans and AI is extensively applied to industrial processes and scenarios. A containerized AIoT framework for enabling Continuous Integration, Continuous Delivery (CI/CD) of ML models and their deployment on highly configurable edge environments was shown by Raj et al. in [5]. When presenting an air-quality control system scenario in a distributed environment, e.g., conditions of different rooms, the model drift at the respective edges and a retraining with location-specific information was discussed. As outlined in [13], when developing a CPS operation, Digital Twin (DT)s are commonly applied in order to combine an abstraction of physical assets with the industrial application. Using a set of digital representations of a physical device, e.g., a module pipeline, production lines can be abstracted and actuated. Although there is an overlap with CPS operations, no holistic view on possible scenarios or specific deployment setups is considered in the work on hand. Rather, a bottom-up approach for modularization and deployment of modules using the KOSMoS framework is shown. As a management system and synchronization among DTs are some of the biggest challenges for the overall quality in a scenario [13], their composition of well defined and evaluated pipeline modules is one possible flexibility enhancement.

B. ML Quality and Deployment

The integration of trained ML models in preexisting logic is always application-dependent and, therefore, different quality requirements exist. For example, it may be required to deploy modules with consideration of certain restrictions or properties like scalability and serverless execution. The deployment of ML models as a nano-service was proposed by Paraskevoulakou et al. [14], where hardware resources were abstracted in order to provide a massive-scaleable *ML-*Function as a Service (FaaS), using the Apache OpenWhisk framework. Therefore, the same preprocessing pipeline of an offline-trained model is applied to unseen input data and forwarded via Representational State Transfer (REST) calls until the pre-trained model is invoked. Dependent on the technology stack of an operation or organization, such FaaS strategies may be integrated within the underlying infrastructure system itself. An overview and comparison of four open-source serveless platforms was given by Li et al. [15]. Mechanisms like the kubernets Horizontal Pod Autoscaler (HPA) automate resource-based scaling of pods by interpreting gathered metrics. On the other hand, stateful modules must be implemented with respect to such environmental conditions. A multi-target compiler for ML-model deployment was introduced in [16], where Predictive Model Markup Language (PMML)-compatible models are represented as a set of templates. These building blocks are applied in code generation for efficient production execution on single- and multi Central Processing Unit (CPU) and Graphics Processing Unit (GPU) systems. With respect to quality management systems, various real-world examples were outlined by Lee et al. [17], targeting the predictive maintenance in Industry 4.0. Amongst others, external data and multiple sensors represent the benefit of sensor fusion techniques. A comprehensive overview of quality dimensions, e.g., intrinsic, contextual, accessible and representational, with respect to *Big Data* was given in [18]. In addition to discussing data quality metrics for measuring the dimensions, quality scores are proposed for evaluation. A variety of quality attributes for microservice architectures is described in [19]. Architectural design decisions must be taken into consideration for classic requirements like the scalability or availability of an application, too. Aspects of a CPS demonstration cell were discussed in [20], where different devices simulated a production line and the generated data was used to predict the quality of a workpiece. While utilizing different ML techniques for the various CPS parts, there were challenges regarding the synchronizations and inconvenient labeling procedures. As the work on hand focuses on the deployment and interaction schemes of modularized ML pipeline parts, no attention is given to framework details or cross compilation. Due to the possible and likely fusion of datasets originated from different sensors, difficulties can occur when synchronizing events. As the data and modules implementation quality is vital to the success of AIoT and CPS operations, domain-specific quality dimensions and requirements must be engineered beforehand.

III. Environments of ML Pipelines for CPS

A. ML in Hierarchical CPS Environments

The physical and digital setup and configuration of a shop floor is always specific to the CPS operations and architectures are often presented in a high-level manner. In literature, the commonality is often a top-down *1-to-n* connection of clouds, edges or fogs, CPS nodes, shopfloor devices and their integrated sensors and actuators respectively. Using such a basic depiction of an CPS constellation allows for clear and simplistic (re-)design of an operations digital infrastructure. Constant monitoring of the whole system on different levels enables a holistic view of current and historical operations [11]. As shown in Figure 1, the constellation of an organization's CPS and the placement of ML-related modules is driven by and dependent on domain- and scenario-specific expert knowledge. As illustrated, the depicted phases of a pipeline, which are clarified in the following, are impacted by their respective locations within a CPS. As the MLOps configuration is based on this CPS inventory, scenario-specific decisions which impact the stability of the whole workflow must be identified during project requirement engineering. With respect to the overall architecture, antipatterns, e.g., as in [19], and technical ML depts, e.g., as in [8], must be taken into consideration, too. In order to ensure usable datasets for model training, the data management phase aims for the fulfillment of different requirements, including domain specific evaluation on raw data. A a basic data quality analysis indicates the usability of a dataset version, where different techniques, processes and metrics exist for structured, e.g., text, or unstructured data like images [11]. Triggering and (re)configuring modules in an shopfloor environment, alarming for required maintenance or contribution to production pipeline management decisions are possible effects. When device-specific quality dimensions are identified, appropriate metrics, as outlined in [18], can be configured with scenario-specific attributes and indicate usable data and data to be reevaluated, respectively. There are many technical solutions to store versionable data, e.g., Data Version Control (DVC), problem-specific databases, distributed file systems or Copy-On-Write (COW) block devices, but dependent on the type of data, amount, frequency and usage of versions from different times, only a few of them will scale. Another aspect is the tenant-specific access of data, privacy concerns and the integration into existing digital environments. As the access to problem-specific data versions is not trivial, a high-level access or data stewardship support is appropriate for data-intense and dynamic pipelines. Operations in the preprocessing phase, e.g., labeling or generating appropriate features, can be automated to a certain extent, dependent on the underlying problem and involved sensors. The configuration of ML architectures optimal hyperparameters cannot be derived from operational data [21] and is problem-specific. The training processes are deployed to more or less potent hardware, possibly executed in parallel with respect to multiple versions or hyperparameter configurations. The metrics and model training runs may vary in requirements, as for example time constraints for the training, the models execution time or accuracy demands. With the definition of an applications access to the model, e.g., the model's inference, the problem-specific input data can be evaluated by modules from the training pipeline. A complete flow from sensing data to the usage of a resulting model is depicted and formalized by expert knowledge. As the environmental quality of each sensor, device, node, edge or cloud system is of relevance to the compliance with defined Key Performance Indicator (KPI)s, constant monitoring and quality assessment of the systems must be assured. With enough computation power, CPS nodes, edge devices or cloud environments are capable of data preprocessing tasks. As the training of ML models often requires Graphics Processing Unit (GPU) resources, more powerful edge devices and cloud environments are attractive locations. The model integration, inference respectively, can be enabled within CPS devices, nodes, edges or the cloud. Training a model on CPS devices data and applying the resulting ML implementation requires domain-specific knowledge of various shopfloor configurations in the first place. The dynamic deployment of ML tasks in CPS is based on the concatenation of containers, respective KPIs and an association with data structures of the actual shopfloor devices.

B. Generic composition of Modules

The declaration of an ML pipeline, e.g., a module composition, is comparable to creating a Directed Acyclic Graph (DAG) of predefined functions. In general, a module receives some kind of information, executes its dedicated processing and finally produces an output to be interpreted by its successor. Therefore, the actual module logic simply has to utilize such interfaces in order to serve as a composable and exchangeable part of the system. As a pipeline module tackles a specific problem, results can be treated as independent parts of the overall solution. When splitting the functionality of an application into an appropriate number of modules, their composition may enable more flexible, diverse and reliable operations. As every ML-related task fits best to a specific algorithm, as overviewed in [10] and [4], the granularity of a module is impacted by the respective scenario. Although a specific module implementation structure and its overall purpose depends on the problem on hand, common interfaces and communication patterns for interaction within the pipelines enhance the overall structure and configuration. As the design of the phases modules may require automated scaling, deployment strategies and applied technologies differ. Although autoscaling features are present in Kubernetes-based serverless platforms, as shown in [15], e.g., comparing *Nuclio, OpenFAAS, KNative* and *Kubeless*, the overall communication and management patterns must still be defined. When *interact-*

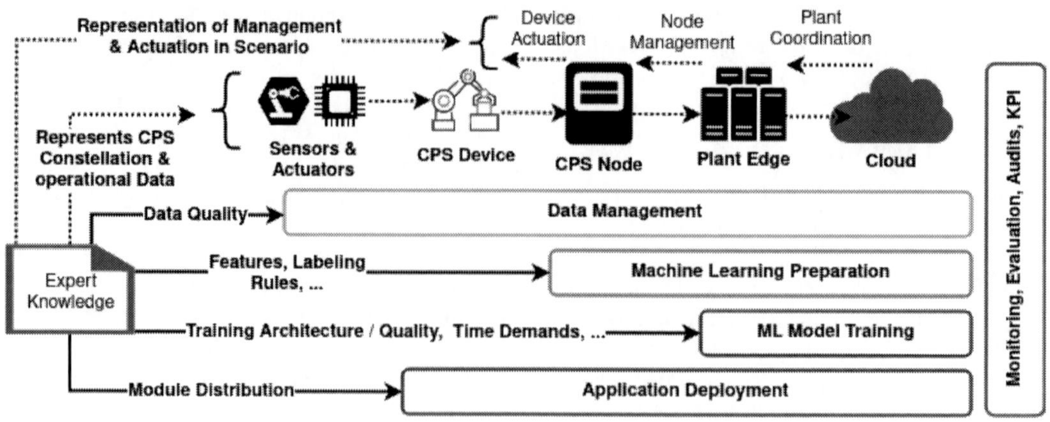

Figure 1. ML Tasks in CPS driven by formalized Expert Knowledge

ing with foreign systems, e.g., interfacing shopfloor devices or digital enterprise services, the respective module environment must be able to securely communicate with its counterparts in the first place. Especially, when a module is the origin of a pipeline, the data source is either produced by code, read from existing data structures or received via a foreign system by applying specific libraries. In addition to passive operations like reading a file from disk or pulling data from an endpoint, a module may be asynchronously triggered by a foreign system or an alien pipelines module respectively, or impact the environment by actuation. In contrast, a *module input* represents a connection to a specific storage, which enables the usage of previously persisted and task-related data. As the operations within a pipeline are often based on data science operations, common functionality like treating data to be persisted or read as *DataFrame* is viable. Such utilization will enhance convenience when applying the information within a subsequent module. When task-specific operations are designed in a generic way, whole modules may also be more flexible due to their parameterization. The *module output*, e.g., the persistence of module results in a task specific storage, can range from primitive datatypes to high-level objects, byte-code or trained models. By ensuring *module accountability*, each module instance can be audited separately. The logs can be of any kind and may also relate to custom operations for preceding modules in a specific pipeline setup. When consequently applying such logging patterns, the significance of task-specific audit-trails can be increased. Also, different parts of the *module evaluation* can be automatically executed when specified circumstances are met. They may strike when receiving data or as early as during their configuration with respect to fellow pipeline modules. Therefore, it is vital to the success of a module that metrics, parameters and custom tests are present for each implemented operation. Treating the various containers as independent *standalone* applications allows for implementing the whole learning pipeline as a dynamic and exchangeable configuration. The scheduling and deployment of tasks can also be carried out with respect to priorities and quality demands, as well as hardware requirements or modules in a pipeline. With executing the trained model version, an ecosystem of various monitoring hooks and mechanisms for assuring the specified KPIs is implied. Depending on the overall application goals, assertions of the declared ML tasks quality metrics influence the systems decision of automatically retaining the utilized model or performing actuation actions on the shop floor, respectively.

IV. Flexible Pipelines for ML in CPS

A. Exemplary Deployment and Accountability with KOSMoS

Depending on the complexity of data and the algorithms applied during processing, the optimal deployment technologies and techniques, the DAG of modules and the persistence of data varies. In the context of the KOSMoS project, a framework for the server-side management of client-side ecosystems was designed with respect to the CPS and shopfloor environments. By creating containers for each dedicated module, a communication protocol for interaction among them and defining a storage procedure, pipelines are depicted as JavaScript Object Notation (JSON) objects. As shown in Figure 2, a global platform (upper part) allows for the configuration of modules for pipelines which are applied in the digital environment of a system (bottom right part) and relates to a physical shopfloor (bottom left part). In such a KOSMoS setup, accountability of executed module operations, as well as significant device behaviour can be realized by providing pipeline- and tenant-specific access to the cloud-based BC technology. On the other hand, regular events can be transmitted to the BC as a hash, e.g., representing a interval of sensor data. Later on, the hashes can be compared to the respective data versions intervals at the pipelines local environments storage. There is a *n-to-n* relation between sensors and ML pipeline modules, as well as for modules among themselves. Basically, one or more sensors from one or more devices are configured with one or more pipeline modules. Therefore, sensor- and data-fusion is possible and likely to occur in CPS scenarios. When an applications infers a shopfloor-related AI-based model, automated actuation may occur at physical machines. As one promising area of CPS

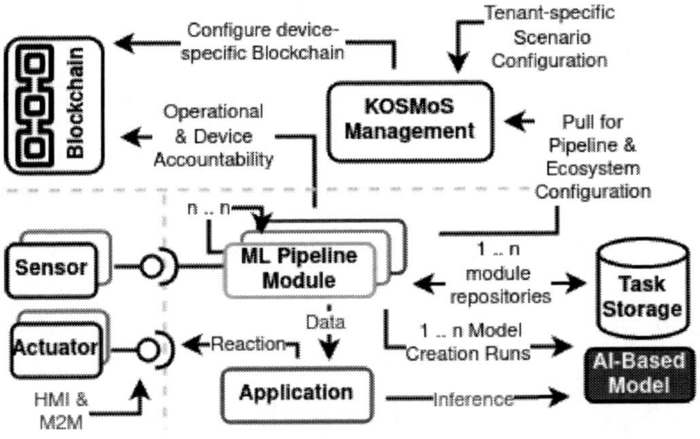

Figure 2. Accountable module Deployment with KOSMoS

is the human-robot coworking [3], the utilization of Human Machine Interface (HMI) can enhance productivity. When Machine to Machine (M2M) communication takes place on the shopfloor, authorized devices may reconfigure a production line's parameters, or interfere in dangerous situations. This is similar to another aspect of KOSMoS, where the possibility of cross-tenant cooperation is realized.

B. Simple Pipelines

In the following, a simple ML scenario is described, where the structure of each separate module comprises overall configuration parameters, as well as the interfaces described in Section III-B. In Figure 3, a temperature sensor is the origin of environmental data and the depicted ML pipeline implements the prediction of labels for the environment's next interval. Therein, every communication must be taken into consideration during evaluation of a module (e.g., Foreign System interaction, Configuration, input, Logging and Results). In the following, the assumption is that data quality requirements for this problem are known and an algorithm takes care of automated labeling of the sensors intervals. Therefore, the various preprocessing operations can be completely automated and a well-formalized *timeseries* data structure arises. Another aspect of this pipeline construction technique is the independence and dynamicity of module instances, enabling a high degree of interoperability and exchangeability of modules. The implementation of preprocessing device data and the model training will presumably differ for each type of ML task and requires the respective domain knowledge as well as software engineering and data-science capabilities. As implied in Figure 2, the digital shopfloor environment is capable of actuating the same devices from which data is already sensed. In controlling and reconfiguring physical surroundings, specific circumstances will require an adjustment of preexisting pipeline modules, too. The generic implementation of modules and asynchronous communication patterns allow for specific databases which are used for persisting a module's result and receiving the preceding outcomes, respectively. In the following, each module involved in the mentioned scenario is described.

a) Receive Sensor Temperature: In order to utilize CPS data, a reference to the respective devices has to be a declared for initially loading the correct data into the pipeline. When assuming a shopfloor device comprises primitive communication mechanisms, direct access to data via Universal Asynchronous Receiver / Transmitter (UART), Inter-Integrated Circuit (I2C), Serial BUS or other technologies is probable. As in the context of a CPS, industry standards for communication with such devices like *Simens S7* or Open Platform Communications Unified Architecture (OPC-UA) are more likely to occur and many libraries and communication models, e.g., pull vs. subscribe, exist. When deciding for a specific communication protocol, as OPC-UA was chosen for this example, various technology-specific parameters, e.g., how to connect to the specific machine in order to retrieve the required data, must be set. On the other hand, the received data and the data versions respectively, must be persisted within the task-specific storage and annotated with metadata related to this specific data version, e.g., module runtime, possible anomalies, and others. In addition to persisting task-specific operations, the logging of the operational context, e.g., the OPC-UA servers statistics for the respective interval, enhances the accountability and debugging of this specific module configuration.

b) Temperature Data Quality: When handling domain-specific hardware such as a temperature sensor, the respective datasheet most certainly clarifies circumstances in which the product works best. By performing checks for anticipated behavior of the dataset, basic data quality assessment can be carried out. In separating the domain-specific checks from well-formatted dataset versions, spontaneous exchanges or additional assertions related to scenario-specific quality assurance are made possible. Naturally, the access to previously sensed and persisted task-specific data, e.g., referencing the former modules output, must be configured in order to fulfill the processing of this module. In addition, by defining value ranges as well as other sensor-, scenario-, or domain-specific completeness indicators, a basic data quality assessment can be implemented. Additionally, techniques for *repairing* obvious outliers or anomalies in a dataset version may help in creating more reliable operations. In addition to creating an evaluated version of previously sensed data ready for preprocessing, various module-specific pieces of information, e.g., the justification of the data quality assessment, occurred anomalies, etc., allow for a more fine-grained monitoring, reporting and accountability.

c) Temperature Data Preprocessing: As the preprocessing of a dataset determines the ability of being used during ML model creation, the data structure originating from preceding modules must be interpretable, appropriate for the specific scenario, and allow for (semi)automated feature generation or engineering. When data cannot automatically be labeled and unsupervised learning is not an option, a *lambda*-like architectures can be applied. Therein, the base-knowledge, e.g., training-, test- and validation-dataset is extended with *new*

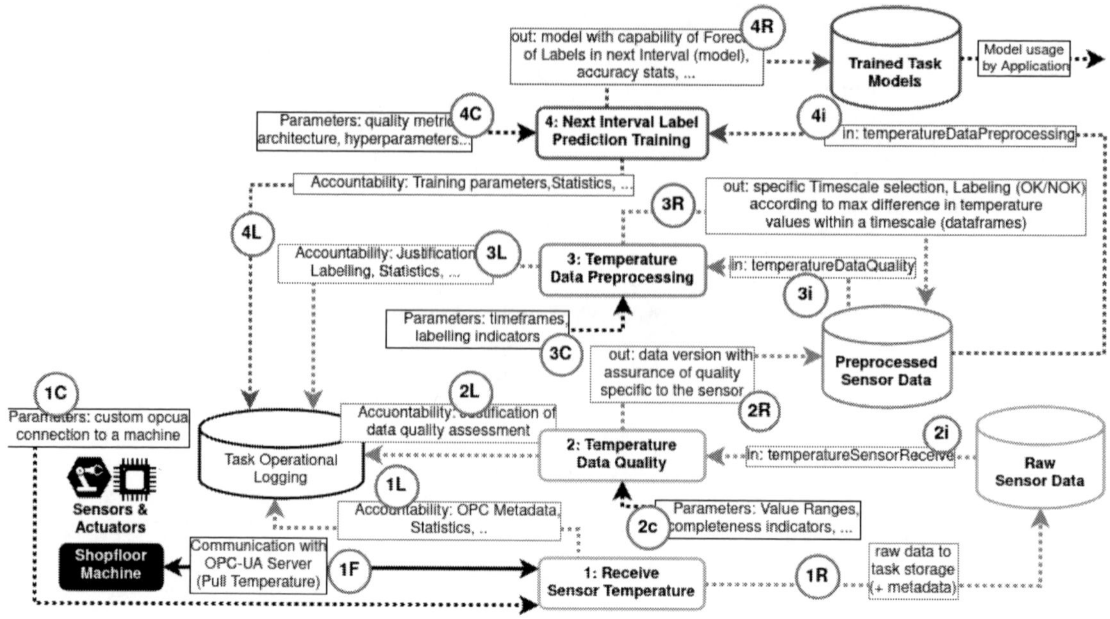

Figure 3. Module Pipeline Example for Temperature Label Prediction

sample-sets, whenever manual processing, e.g., boxing specific areas in images, is done. Either this event may trigger the re-training of a previously trained model or activate a transfer-learning process. A manual start of the learning process or periodically executed training runs are also viable options. The sensed temperature data is up to this point ensured to correspond to a certain pattern. Therefore, a simple labeling script which determines if a period is to be treated as *OK* or not, can be easily formalized and applied to the current base-knowledge. In addition to the persistence of the labeled timescale selections, module-internal statistics and justification of the labeling outcome can help in *up-to-date* decisions regarding a pipeline. For example, it can be asserted if a module's version, algorithm and the selected parameter are feasible for the utilization with a specific kind of data version.

d) Next Interval Label Prediction Training: Within this crucial step, the cleansed and ready-to-use dataframes are separated into test-, training- and validation-datasets and processed by the modules ML framework, e.g., generate the actual ML model. The feasibility within a scenario dependents on the module's implementation, its configuration of the learning architecture and feasible hyperparameters, as well as quality metrics for determining the model's performance with respect to the problem at hand. As the applied ML technologies and libraries impact the implementation complexity and required resources, this kind of module is most likely to be adjusted over time in order to reach the best performing outcome. This is also one of the modules where it is feasible to utilize *AutoML* functionality in parallel with hand-selected ML architectures and their hyperparameters, respectively. In addition to generating a model with the capability of forecasting labels for the next interval, the accuracy of a model and other technology-, custom-, domain- or quality-specific evaluation outcomes are versioned alongside.

e) Model Usage by Application: Once there is a suitable model available within the task-specific repository, its integration into the overall application takes place. According to whether the application itself is required to be recompiled for utilization of the new model or an additional independent lightweight execution environment module is created for its inference on demand, dynamic deployment of the up-to-date versions is possible. When referring to on-the-fly exchangeability, either the DevOps pipeline states how to dynamically use a model version or the application itself provides 'online'-configuration possibilities, e.g., changing a REST endpoint and other parameters. In addition to the model's specific ML-framework libraries, the logic for preprocessing or referencing the input parameters, e.g., data used for predictions, must be available to the module. When providing the module via REST, many additional parameters like listening ports, key material for transport encryption, allowed routes, e.g., calling modules and applications and other custom application-specific configurations must be defined. In addition to the model's usage and basic statistics, domain-specific information and inference results may be persisted in the dedicated task-specific repositories. Based on these events, it is possible to generate additional insights, or process information within a novel pipeline's modules.

C. Dynamic and Extensible Pipelines

As outlined previously, any generated data version can be applied to any module. By reusing pipelines up to a specific point, new scenarios, versions of scenarios or experiments are configurable with minimum effort, e.g., implementing a new module while considering accountability guarantees. As imaginable, the possibilities and complexity for configuring an MLOps pipeline rise when there are multiple origins of data, e.g., available sensors. When an additional sensor becomes available on the shopfloor, the respective data management- and preprocessing-modules must be implemented while respecting the overall scenario's quality requirements [17] and demands on data quality [18]. In order to train a new model based on the combined sensor sources, existing workflows can be extended. This is similar to when a sensor is replaced by a different type, but proved parts of the workflow can be reused. On the other hand, a dedicated pipeline results in a sensor-specific model which can be combined with other existing models in the application phases. Also, attention should be payed to the many pitfalls of the sensor-data fusions data management and preprocessing phases, like scenario-specific requirements or timestamp synchronization, as in [20]. Dependent on the overall technology stack, existing management systems, as in [15], can be used as automated deployment manager, too. While the preexisting modules of a pipeline can transparently continue to process dedicated data versions and serving resulting information, additional pipelines, pipeline variants or module configurations can be defined for other scenarios. With ensuring the regular productive workflow and being able to experiment with potential improvements, the utilization of modules comprising Automated Machine Learning (AutoML) functionality becomes a promising aspect.

V. Conclusion

In this work, an approach of a flexible, module-based and accountability-enhanced pipeline definition for MLOps-conform implementation was described. In addition to clarify requirements to CPS-related module interactions, details on operations and persistence strategies were exemplary depicted and benefits of formalizing ML scenarios were highlighted. The different devices on a shopfloor can be rearranged, replaced or used in a novel way, which is why the possibility of dynamic updates to existing pipelines was briefly discussed. As the resulting dynamic pipelines may involve complex relations and dedicated meaning within a CPS, it is a challenge to provide accurate monitoring of each component. Although management frameworks for such distributed digital environments exist, hardware restrictions and threats to operations, e.g., bottlenecks or deadlocks, must be considered and modules should be adjusted accordingly. In future work, the integration of AutoML capabilities and an assertion of most feasible frameworks for different types of tasks are promising topics. Another aspect of using such a flexible structure is the possibility of evaluating quality attributes of pipeline compositions with respect to specific scenarios beforehand, due to using simulators for environments and device data.

Acknowledgement

This work is funded by the Federal Ministry of Education and Research (BMBF) under reference number 02P17D022 and supervised by Projektträger Karlsruhe (PTKA), Germany. The content was developed within the research project KOSMoS - (https://www.hs-furtwangen.de/en/research/forschungsprojekte/kosmos/).

References

[1] J. Lee, "Smart Factory Systems," *Informatik-Spektrum*, vol. 38, no. 3, pp. 230–235, jun 2015.

[2] S. Wang, J. Wan, D. Li, and C. Zhang, "Implementing smart factory of industrie 4.0: An outlook," *Int. J. Distrib. Sen. Netw.*, vol. 2016, pp. 7:7–7:7, Jan. 2016, accessed: 24.06.2022. [Online]. Available: https://doi.org/10.1155/2016/3159805

[3] B. Chander, S. Pal, D. De, and R. Buyya, "Artificial intelligence-based internet of things for industry 5.0," in *Artificial Intelligence-based Internet of Things Systems*. Springer, 2022, pp. 3–45.

[4] K. Sharma and R. Nandal, "A literature study on machine learning fusion with iot," in *2019 3rd International Conference on Trends in Electronics and Informatics (ICOEI)*, 2019, pp. 1440–1445.

[5] E. Raj, D. Buffoni, M. Westerlund, and K. Ahola, "Edge mlops: An automation framework for aiot applications," in *2021 IEEE International Conference on Cloud Engineering (IC2E)*, 2021, pp. 191–200.

[6] P. Singh, *Machine Learning Deployment Using Kubernetes*. Berkeley, CA: Apress, 2021, pp. 127–146, accessed: 24.06.2022. [Online]. Available: https://doi.org/10.1007/978-1-4842-6546-8_5

[7] H. E, K. Zhou, and M. Song, "Spark-based machine learning pipeline construction method," in *2019 International Conference on Machine Learning and Data Engineering (iCMLDE)*, 2019, pp. 1–6.

[8] e. a. Sculley, D, "Hidden technical debt in machine learning systems," *NIPS*, pp. 2494–2502, 01 2015.

[9] E. J. Maier, "Advancing artificial intelligence and machine learning in the us government through improved public competitions," *arXiv preprint arXiv:2112.01275*, 2021.

[10] I. H. Sarker, "Machine learning: Algorithms, real-world applications and research directions," *SN Computer Science*, vol. 2, no. 3, pp. 1–21, 2021.

[11] P. Ruf, M. Madan, C. Reich, and D. Ould-Abdeslam, "Demystifying mlops and presenting a recipe for the selection of open-source tools," *Applied Sciences*, vol. 11, no. 19, 2021, accessed: 24.06.2022. [Online]. Available: https://www.mdpi.com/2076-3417/11/19/8861

[12] X. F. et al., "Cps data streams analytics based on machine learning for cloud and fog computing: A survey," *Future Generation Computer Systems*, vol. 90, pp. 435–450, 2019, accessed: 24.06.2022. [Online]. Available: https://www.sciencedirect.com/science/article/pii/S0167739X17330613

[13] M. W. Hoffmann, S. Malakuti, S. Grüner, S. Finster, J. Gebhardt, R. Tan, T. Schindler, and T. Gamer, "Developing industrial cps: A multi-disciplinary challenge," *Sensors*, vol. 21, no. 6, p. 1991, 2021.

[14] E. Paraskevoulakou and D. Kyriazis, "Leveraging the serverless paradigm for realizing machine learning pipelines across the edge-cloud continuum," in *2021 24th Conference on Innovation in Clouds, Internet and Networks and Workshops (ICIN)*. IEEE, 2021, pp. 110–117.

[15] J. Li, S. G. Kulkarni, K. K. Ramakrishnan, and D. Li, "Analyzing open-source serverless platforms: Characteristics and performance," *CoRR*, vol. abs/2106.03601, 2021, accessed: 24.06.2022. [Online]. Available: https://arxiv.org/abs/2106.03601

[16] O. Castro-Lopez and I. F. Vega-Lopez, "Multi-target compiler for the deployment of machine learning models," in *2019 IEEE/ACM International Symposium on Code Generation and Optimization (CGO)*, 2019, pp. 280–281.

[17] S. M. Lee, D. Lee, and Y. S. Kim, "The quality management ecosystem for predictive maintenance in the industry 4.0 era," *International Journal of Quality Innovation*, vol. 5, no. 1, pp. 1–11, 2019.

[18] I. Taleb, M. A. Serhani, and R. Dssouli, "Big data quality: A survey," in *2018 IEEE International Congress on Big Data (BigData Congress)*. IEEE, 2018, pp. 166–173.

[19] T. Schirgi and E. Brenner, "Quality assurance for microservice architectures," in *2021 IEEE 12th International Conference on Software Engineering and Service Science (ICSESS)*. IEEE, 2021, pp. 76–80.

[20] P. e. a. Burggräf, "Predictive analytics in quality assurance for assembly processes: lessons learned from a case study at an industry 4.0 demonstration cell," *Procedia CIRP*, vol. 104, pp. 641–646, 2021.

[21] P. Janardhanan, "Project repositories for machine learning with tensorflow," *Procedia Computer Science*, vol. 171, pp. 188–196, 2020.

Early Risk Detection of Bachelor's Student Withdrawal or Long-Term Retention

Isaac Caicedo-Castro[123], Oswaldo Vélez-Langs[23], Mario Macea-Anaya[235],
Samir Castaño-Rivera[23], Rubby Castro-Púche[14]
[1]*Research Group: Development, Education, and Healthcare*
[2]*Socrates Research Group*
[3]*Faculty of Engineering*
[4]*Faculty of Humanity and Social Science*
[5]*CINTIA, Center of INnovation in Technology of Information to support the Academia*
University of Córdoba
Carrera 6 No. 76-103, 230002, Montería, Colombia
emails: {isacaic, oswaldovelez, mariomacea, sacastano, rubycastro}@correo.unicordoba.edu.co

***Abstract*—In this research, we study the problem of forecasting recently admitted students at risk of withdrawing from the university or being long-term retained in a bachelor's program. We conduct research to study the case of students enrolled in courses up to the ninth semester, in the Department of Systems Engineering at the University of Córdoba in Colombia. At most universities throughout Colombia, including the University of Córdoba, the standardized and official admission test Saber 11 has been adopted for bachelor's program admissions. Therefore, we address the following research question: Might the admission test Saber 11 be used to forecast if the recently admitted student will be at either withdrawal or long-term retention risk, in the foreseeable future, before starting the first semester? We are motivated to solve the previously mentioned question because once the admitted students at risk have been identified, the University might make choices to help such students. To this end, we collected a dataset from 86 surveyed students. Although the original dataset has 86 records, after cleaning the dataset, and removing records with missing or inconsistent values, the final version of the dataset contains records of 47 students. According to the results of this research, given the student's test admission outcomes, machine learning algorithms learn regular patterns for forecasting if a recently admitted student is at withdrawal or long-term retention risk with a mean accuracy of about 72.5% (i.e., mean error of approximately 27.5%).**

***Keywords*—machine learning; educational data mining; classification algorithm; University admission test; student withdrawal; student long-term retention.**

I. INTRODUCTION

Universities offer bachelor programs that provide people, who have finished school, with higher education or vocational training for contributing to society in several sectors such as, e.g., healthcare, education, agronomy, industry, building, business management, government, and so forth. The education quality at schools (besides other factors) influences the student's performance at university. Moreover, university resources are limited, hence, each cannot admit an unlimited number of students. As a consequence, universities perform a selection process, where applications are usually studied according to the candidate's performance during the admission test, interviews, and other criteria. With the admission test, the goal is to evaluate if the candidate has reached the appropriate level to pursue a bachelor's program. Nevertheless, some students lack the required competencies, skills, or knowledge to succeed in the bachelor's program, albeit they have passed the admission test.

Those students who are not properly prepared, either might fail courses or might abandon them. In the former case, such students face the risk of losing their student status, when their performance is lower than required according to the university rules. This problem is known as *student withdrawal*. On the other hand, those students who leave courses without completion will eventually take more time than required to finish the bachelor's program. This problem is known as *long-term retention*. In this research, we study the problem of forecasting recently admitted students at risk of withdrawing from the university or being long-term-retained in a bachelor's program.

In Section I-A, we state the problem and research context. Section I-B discusses the arguments that motivate us to conduct this research. The key assumptions and motivations considered in this research are mentioned in Section I-C. In Section I-D, we present the contributions of this research and outline the rest of this article.

A. Research Context and Problem Statement

The problem addressed in this research is to predict if an admitted student might be at risk of withdrawing from the university or being long-term-retained in the bachelor's program, before starting the first semester. Herein, predicting means to classify the admitted student according to two classes as follows: (i) student at risk or (ii) student at no risk. Therefore, the problem is to classify the admitted students according to the previous two classes given the student's admission test outcomes.

The target variable is the class of students, whereas the student's admission test outcomes are input variables. Thus, in order to classify a student, the problem is to find the functional dependency between the target variable and input variables from the history of previously admitted students, who have finished at least the first semester. In machine learning, this is a classification problem, because the target variable is discrete.

We conducted this research, by studying the case of students enrolled in the bachelor of science in engineering, who chose the major in systems engineering, in the context of the University of Córdoba in Colombia, which is a public university.

In Colombia, Saber 11 is the standardized and official test adopted for bachelor program admission, as well as Scholastic Assessment Test (SAT), is used for the same purpose in the United States. Therefore, candidates at the University of Córdoba are admitted or rejected, taking into account their outcomes obtained in the Saber 11 test.

The test Saber 11 evaluates four areas as follows: (i) mathematics, (ii) critical reading, (iii) social sciences, and (iv) English language. The Colombian education ministry assumes these areas are the foundation that every school student must learn properly to pursue a bachelor's program.

The problem is formally defined as follows: let $\{(\mathbf{x}^t, r^t)\}_{t=1}^{N}$ be the training dataset, where $\mathbf{x}^t \in \mathbb{R}^d$ and $r^t \in \{0,1\}$. Henceforth, t is a super index rather than an exponent, for $t = 1, \ldots, N$. The d-dimensional vector $\mathbf{x}^t$ represents the t-th student's admission test outcomes. For instance, the j-th component, i.e., x_j^t, represents the resulting score in the mathematics area achieved by the t-th student in the admission test. $r^t = 1$ means the t-th student is at academic risk, whereas $r^t = 0$ means otherwise.

Given the previously described dataset, the learning problem is to find the functional dependency between the (independent) variables in $\mathbf{x}^t$ (or the student's features) and the target variable r^t (a.k.a., dependent variable). In other words, the problem is to find the function g such that $g : \mathbb{R}^d \to \{0,1\}$. Thus, once the function g is found, given the input variables in the d-dimensional vector $\mathbf{x}$, corresponding to a new student, we can classify the student as follows: $g(\mathbf{x}) = y$, where y is the output variable, and $y = 1$ if the function g classifies the new student as one at risk, otherwise $y = 0$.

The above-described problem leads us to ponder the following research question: Might the student's outcome, achieved from the admission test, be used to forecast if the recently admitted student will be at either withdrawal risk, or long-term retention risk, in the foreseeable future, before starting the first semester?

B. Motivation

We are motivated to conduct this research to help universities (in particular the University of Córdoba in Colombia) at identifying those students at risk, who might leave their academic programs without completion, in the foreseeable future, as well as those students who might be retained in their bachelor's programs, beyond the expected time. Both cases are caused because such students were admitted lacking key competencies, or knowledge, to attain the required performance, which allows them to keep their student status, and finish their programs in the expected time. As a consequence, this causes students psychological issues, frustration, and financial loss.

If stakeholders at the university know in advance, who are those students at academic risk, they can carry out plans of action and strategies to handle the above-mentioned issues (e.g., the student's frustration, and financial loss), in order to help students, before starting their bachelor career, to keep their student status, and complete their programs within the expected time.

Strategies for coping with the risk might be such as, e.g., psychological support or extra courses to cover those topics that such students did not learn properly before being admitted to the university. Thus, eventually, students' withdrawal and long-term retention rates might decrease, considering that both problems are a serious concern in the higher education systems and for policy-making stakeholders at universities (cf., [1]).

C. Key Assumptions and Limitations

In this research, we have considered the following assumptions:

(i) We assume the test called Saber 11 actually measures the knowledge and competencies, which students ought to attain for pursuing a bachelor's degree. Indeed, article 17-*th* of the student code at the University of Córdoba states that candidates are admitted according to their score achieved in the test Saber 11.

(ii) We assume that a student at academic risk leaves at least one course without completing the first semester because such courses might be prerequisites for attending further ones, or the student might face a high workload later, in another semester, enrolling unfinished courses (or equivalent courses to fulfill the graduation requirements). Therefore, eventually, the overwhelmed student will need more time than required to conclude the program.

(iii) We assume that a student at academic risk fails at least one course the first semester because this causes the same issues faced by another student who leaves at least one course without completion starting the bachelor's career. Moreover, there is a chance the student's global average grade decreases below the minimum required, compromising its student status after finishing the first semester, or later.

(iv) We assume the student at academic risk obtains a global average grade lower or equal to the required for keeping the student status. Bachelor students at Colombian universities are graded in the range from 0 up to 5. In the specific case of the University of Córdoba, according to the student's code (cf., article 16-*th* in [2]), each student ought to achieve a global average grade equal to or greater than 3.3, otherwise, this one might be dropped out from the university. According to article 28-*th* of the same code, if a student's global average grade is between 3 and 3.3, this one must increase the global average grade at least up to 3.3 the next semester, otherwise, the student is dropped out. Finally, if any student achieves a grade lower than 3, this one is withdrawn from the university.

(v) We assume the student might be at academic risk if this one might lose the student status, or the student takes more time in the academic program than the expected time.
(vi) We assume accuracy is more relevant for improving the user's experience than the interpretation of the forecasting algorithm.
(vii) We assume that classifying students at risk, who are not at risk whatsoever (i.e., false positive) is as inconvenient as classifying them without risk, though they are at an actual risk (i.e., false negative). In the first case, both students and the University will spend unnecessary resources. In the second case, students at risk will face the consequences of poor preparation for pursuing the bachelor's degree, and the University will not be able to plan how to deal with such students.

The scope limitations of this research are as follows:

(i) We shall not predict the student's grades in bachelor courses given their admission test performance.
(ii) We shall not aim at interpreting the functional dependency between the academic risk, i.e., the target variable, and student's performance in the admission test, i.e., the input variables.

D. Contributions and Outline

The contributions of this research are as follows:

(i) A dataset with 47 records. This includes the student's profile and academic history. These students have attended courses from the second up to the ninth semester. Besides, the dataset includes their respective outcomes from the standard admission evaluation Saber 11, which is taken into account in Colombia, to study applications for bachelor's degrees.
(ii) The proof-of-concept of an intelligence system, written in Python, that learns regular patterns from the outcome achieved by the students, during the University admission test, and their performance during the first semester. Such regular patterns are learned in order to forecast if a recently admitted student might be at academic risk of leaving the bachelor's career, due to low performance, or taking more time to finish the bachelor's career, than the expected one.
(iii) An empirical study that reveals the multilayer perceptrons algorithm outperforms support vector machines, logistic regression, and decision trees. The multilayer perceptrons net reaches a mean accuracy of about 72.5% (i.e., mean error about 27.5%)

The remainder of this article is outlined as follows: in Section II, we discuss the prior research. In Section III, we explain the research method we adopted for conducting this study. In Section IV, we present the experimental setting, including dataset features, adopted evaluation procedure, and which hyper-parameters are tuned for each model. Moreover, in the same section, we present and discuss the results of the experiments. Finally, Section V concludes the article with the findings drawn from the results and we discuss perspectives for further research.

II. Prior Research

This research belongs to the domain of educational data mining, which is a discipline whose goal is to adopt machine learning algorithms to large-scale datasets collected from educational settings in order to better understand students and the way they learn. Educational data mining includes (although not limited to) the following research direction: analyzing educational datasets, studying pedagogical theories through data mining, contributing to understanding the students' domain representations, evaluating the students' engagement in the learning tasks, and so forth.

Herein, we are focused on analyzing an educational dataset by training machine learning algorithms to find regular patterns, in order to classify a recently admitted student according to two classes, i.e., i) student at withdrawal or long-term retention risk, and ii) student at no risk.

In this research direction, the performance of American students at school, and their cognitive abilities, have been used for predicting the student's persistence in a bachelor's career, unfortunately, the prediction accuracy was unfeasible [3].

Another related research has been taken into the student's performance, during the Dutch pre-university secondary education, for prediction purposes. The prediction is done before the student starts the first semester. The goal is to forecast if the student might be at risk of leaving a bachelor's program without completion later. [4]. The drawback of this research approach is, that it is fitted to the particular Dutch pre-university educational system, hence, it is not feasible to be reproduced in other contexts, such as, e.g., the Colombian one.

The outcomes of the standard American admission test, known as SAT, have been used in prior research to predict if students will withdraw from the bachelor's program [5], [6]. tests, SAT and Saber 11, evaluate mathematics knowledge and communication skills. However, the test Saber 11 evaluates social science knowledge as well as communication competencies in two tongues, i.e., the English and Spanish languages. SAT is designed to evaluate just the communication skills in the English language.

So, the test SAT and the performance during the freshman year at university, have been used to predict if a student will withdraw from the bachelor's program [5]. However, predicting student withdrawal after the freshman year does not aid in anticipating the student's long-term retention issues. A similar approach also includes the student's demographic information, besides the pre-university student's performance information, for forecasting purposes. [6]. This research endeavor is similar to our study, although our goal is to carry out the prediction before the student starts the freshman year.

Moreover, using demographic information for prediction is beyond our research scope because it is not related to our research question. Another relevant difference is that we use the actual admission test outcomes for training and prediction, whereas Lovenoor et al. carried out data imputation for completing 40% of the missing admission outcomes in their dataset [6].

Another research direction is taking into account emotional intelligence measurements for predicting bachelor students withdrawal [7]. However, our research is rather focused on the relationship between the test Saber 11 outcomes and the risk of long-term retention and bachelor's career withdrawal.

On the other hand, academic and personal data have been used for predicting the bachelor's student withdrawal rate in the context of a Colombian university [8]. Unfortunately, the final dataset used in this research is not publicly available, for experimental reproduction purposes. Besides, we do not aim at estimating the withdrawal rate, instead, we are focused on the risk prediction of each recently admitted student in a bachelor's program.

As far as we know, no prior research has studied if only the admission test is sufficient for forecasting whether a recently admitted student might face the risk of withdrawing from the bachelor's program or being long-term retained beyond the expected time.

III. RESEARCH METHOD

We adopted a quantitative research approach, using machine learning algorithms for predicting if a bachelor's degree student will be at academic risk, given their outcomes in the admission test called Saber 11. To this end, we collected a dataset for training these algorithms. The procedure to collect this dataset is described in Section III-A.

The machine learning algorithms used for prediction in this research are supervised learning algorithms for classification. We discuss them in Section III-B.

A. Collecting the Dataset

We collected the required information for this study through Google Form. We surveyed 86 students enrolled in the bachelor's program of Systems Engineering at the University of Córdoba in Colombia. These students are attending courses from the second up to the eighth semester. The information collected from each student includes the outcome achieved from the admission test. Thus, a t-th student's features are represented through a four-dimensional vector, i.e., $\mathbf{x}^t \in \mathbb{R}^n$ (here $n = 4$ and t is a super index instead of an exponent), where its components correspond to the following areas of the test: (i) mathematics, whose student's score is denoted as x_1^t, (ii) critical reading, whose student's score is denoted as x_2^t, (iii) social sciences, whose student's score is denoted as x_3^t, and (iv) English language, whose student's score is denoted as x_4^t. These variables do not depend on other ones (i.e., independent variables), where each one is in the range from 0 up to 100.

We also collected the following information for each student: (i) the number of students' failed courses in the first semester, (ii) the number of the students' canceled courses in the first semester, and (iii) the student's global average grade achieved the first semester. These variables are used to determine the target variable r^t (once again, t is a super index) considering the following conditions:

- If the t-th student does not approve all the courses the first semester, then this one might be at risk of being retained or losing the student status due to poor performance, i.e., $r^t = 1$ as long as the t-th student fulfills this condition, otherwise $r^t = 0$.
- The t-th student is at risk of being retained in the program if this one cancels at least one course since the first semester, i.e., $r^t = 1$ as long as the student t-th fulfills this condition, otherwise $r^t = 0$.
- The student might be at risk of being withdrawn from the university as well, if this one achieves a global average grade lower than the minimum required to keep the student status according to the rules of the University of Córdoba in Colombia, in this case, the t-th student is at risk of being dropped out if this one achieves an average grade lower than 3.3, where grades are in the range from 0 up to 5, i.e., $r^t = 1$ as long as the t-th student fulfills this condition, otherwise $r^t = 0$.

Once we collected the dataset, we removed those records with inconsistent data such as, e.g., those records whose sum of the score per area is different from the total score. After this procedure, the dataset contains 47 records, furthermore, each student was de-identified to keep their identity anonymous. Currently, the dataset is available on the web, to allow the reproduction of our study, and for further research [9].

Figure 1 depicts the proportion of students at academic risk from the remaining records. The final dataset is rather balanced due to almost half of the records corresponding to students at risk, while the remainder dataset does not.

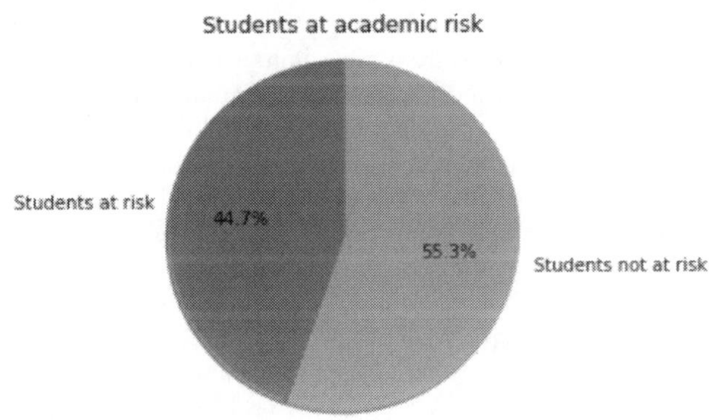

Figure 1. In the final dataset, 21 out of 47 surveyed students are at academic risk.

B. Classification Algorithms

We have adopted four supervised machine learning algorithms for predicting if an admitted student will be at risk, i.e., support vector machines, logistic regression (a.k.a., logistic discrimination), multilayer perceptrons, and decision trees. These algorithms carry out the prediction by classifying the student according to two classes, namely i) student at risk or ii) student at no risk.

So far, the support vector machines algorithm is the best theoretical motivation and the most successful one in the practice of modern machine learning [10, pg. 79]. This algorithm is based on convex optimization, as a consequence, there is a global maximum solution to be found, i.e., there is only one optimal solution, which is its main advantage. Nonetheless, this algorithm does not suit for interpretation in data mining, hence, this is not appropriate for discovering knowledge but for training accurate intelligence systems. A broader description of this algorithm is provided by Cortes and Vapnik [11].

With both classification algorithms, support vector machines, and logistic regression, it is assumed the input vector space can be separated through a linear decision boundary (or a hyperplane in the case of a multidimensional space), thereby, these algorithms are known as linear discrimination algorithms. Nevertheless, when this assumption is not satisfied the support vector machines algorithm is used with kernel methods (see Cortes and Vapnik [11] for further details).

In the case of logistic regression, the input space can be mapped to another vector space, where this assumption is set. Another option is adopting artificial neural networks, where each neuron is actually a logistic discriminator. The neuron outputs in the middle of the network become inputs of the neurons that actually classify. Thus, the original input variables are mapped into a new vector space, through the neurons in the middle, where the previously mentioned assumption is fulfilled. Anderson and McLachlan delve into the details of logistic regression [12], [13], besides, we trained the logistic regression classifier through Limited-memory Broyden-Fletcher-Goldfarb-Shanno (L-BFGS) algorithm [14], [15].

Although support vector machines is considered the most successful algorithm in the practice of modern machine learning, the multilayer perceptrons algorithm, which is an artificial neural network, is the most successful algorithm in the practice of deep learning and big data [16, pg. 3]. In this research, we have adopted the multilayer perceptrons algorithm trained through back-propagated cross-entropy error [17], and the optimization algorithm known as Adam [18]. We used one hidden layer due to the high time complexity of the back-propagation algorithm.

The multilayer perceptrons algorithm is a universal approximator (i.e., this is able to approximate any function for either classification or regression), which is its main advantage, whereas its main disadvantage is the objective function (a.k.a., loss function) based on the cross-entropy error is not convex, therefore, the synaptic weights obtained through the training process might not converge in the most optimum solution because there are several local minimums in the objective function. Thus, finding a solution depends on the random initialization of the synaptic weights. Furthermore, the multilayer perceptrons have more hyper-parameter to be tuned than other learning algorithms (e.g., support vector machines or naive Bayes), which is an additional shortcoming.

Finally, the decision tree algorithm is the most common learning algorithm adopted for mining data or knowledge discovery because this one is simple to interpret. It is possible to visualize trees, which is a desirable feature for making decisions, and its best advantage. Decision trees are trained through heuristic algorithms, such as greedy algorithms, where there are several local optimal solutions at each node. Therefore, there is no guarantee the learning algorithm converges in the most optimal solution, as well as the multilayer perceptrons algorithm. So, this is the main drawback of the decision trees, and it also causes completely different tree shapes due to small variations in the training dataset (as we shall see in Section IV-C). The decision tree algorithm was proposed in 1984, Breiman *et al.* delve into its details (cf., [19]).

IV. Evaluation

A. Experimental Setting

To evaluate the machine learning algorithms used for predicting if a student is at withdrawal or long-term retention risk, we need several pairs of training and test datasets. To this end, we carried out experiments based on K-Fold Cross-Validation (KFCV), thus, from the original dataset, we get K pairs of training and test datasets. We chose $K = 10$, where it is usually 10 or 30. We did not choose $K = 30$ because the dataset is small. Thus, we test each algorithm K times through KFCV. With the test outcomes, we calculate the mean error to compare the learning algorithms, and choosing the algorithm hyper-parameters (e.g., the regularization parameter in the multilayer perceptrons and logistic regression). Besides the mean error, we also measure the mean of precision and recall.

With support vector machines, we tested two kernels, namely, polynomial and Gaussian kernel (a.k.a., radial basis function kernel).

We tested two decision trees with two impurity functions, namely, entropy and Gini function.

Moreover, we tested multilayer perceptrons with several neurons within one hidden layer. We evaluated three activation functions in the hidden layer, i.e., ReLU (Rectified Linear Unit), hyperbolic tangent, and sigmoid function. Besides, we tested various regularization parameter values for logistic regression and multilayer perceptrons net. Both algorithms have been trained for minimizing the sum of cross-entropy errors. The sigmoid function is the activation function in the output layer of the multilayer perceptions net. By definition, the same function is the generalization function in logistic regression.

Finally, we have programmed all the experiments with Python, using the Scikit-Learn library [20], in Google Colaboratory [21].

B. Results

According to the results shown in Table I, the multilayer perceptrons algorithm outperforms the other tested learning algorithms, despite the t-test revealing there is no statistical evidence that the mean error of the multilayer perceptrons algorithm is far lower than the one obtained through the other algorithms, i.e., the resulting p-value is greater than 0.05 (see Table II).

TABLE I
PERFORMANCE OF THE MACHINE LEARNING ALGORITHMS ADOPTED IN THIS RESEARCH

Machine Learning Algorithm	Mean error (%)	Mean precision (%)	Mean recall (%)
MP[a]	**27.5**	55	43.33
SVMPK[b]	30	**63.33**	**65.83**
SVMGK[c]	34.5	**63.33**	62.5
LR[d]	32.5	**63.33**	**65.83**
DTE[e]	34	46.33	58.33
DTGI[f]	40.5	48.33	46.67

[a]MP stands for Multilayer Perceptrons.
[b]SVMPK stands for Support Vector Machine and polynomial kernel.
[c]SVMGK stands for Support Vector Machine and Gaussian kernel.
[d]LR stands for Logistic Regression.
[e]DTE stands for Decision Tree with Entropy impurity function.
[f]DTGI stands for Decision Tree with Gini impurity function.

Thus, according to the experiments, the multilayer perceptrons algorithm achieved the lowest mean error with the following setting:

- The regularization parameter selection for decaying the synaptic weights in the multilayer perceptrons algorithm is sketched in Figure 2, where the best setting is obtained when the regularization parameter is equal to 10^{-2}.
- Another weight decay method used is early stopping.
- The lowest mean error was achieved using ReLU activation function with 600 neurons within the hidden layer, whereas we use sigmoid function with the neuron in the output layer.
- We used the Adam algorithm for training, where the initial learning rate is equal to 10^{-2}. The exponential decay rate for estimating the first and second moment vectors are equal to 0.9 and 0.999, respectively. The numerical stability in Adam is equal to 10^{-8}.
- We used a batch size of 8 examples.

TABLE II
STUDENT'S PAIRED T-TEST ON MEAN ERROR TO COMPARE THE MULTILAYER PERCEPTRONS ACCURACY WITH OTHER MACHINE LEARNING ALGORITHMS ADOPTED IN THIS RESEARCH

Machine Learning Algorithm	Mean error (%)	p-value
Multilayer Perceptrons	27.5	–
Support Vector Machine with Polynomial Kernel	30	0.82
Support Vector Machine with Gaussian Kernel	34.5	0.55
Linear Regression	32.5	0.68
Decision Tree with Entropy impurity function	34	0.53
Decision Tree with Gini impurity function	40.5	0.24

Support vector machines with a polynomial kernel is the next best choice according to the experiments. The best results for this learning algorithm is achieved with the following setting:

- The best degree value for the polynomial kernel is equal to 2.

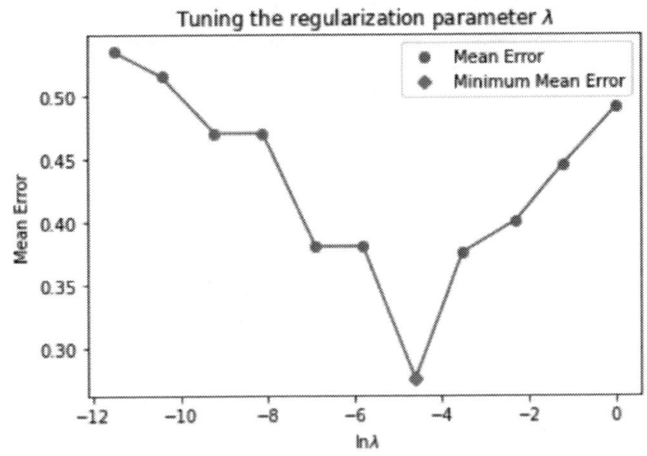

Figure 2. Tuning the multilayer perceptrons through 10-Fold Cross-Validation for choosing the regularization parameter λ according to the elbow rule. The minimum mean error is achieved when $\lambda = 10^{-2}$

- The best regularization parameter of the support vector machines algorithm with polynomial kernel is equal to 0.5. (i.e., $C = 0.5$)

On the other hand, the best setting for the support vector machines algorithm with a Gaussian kernel is as follows:

- The best gamma parameter for the Gaussian kernel is equal to 10^{-4}.
- The best regularization parameter of the support vector machines algorithm with Gaussian kernel is equal to 32×10^4 (i.e., $C = 32 \times 10^4$).

Finally, with logistic regression, the best regularization parameter is equal to 10^{-2}, whereas the entropy impurity function in decision trees performs better than Gini impurity function.

C. Discussion

The results reveal that, given the student's test admission outcomes, machine learning algorithms learn regular patterns for forecasting if a recently admitted student is at withdrawal or long-term-retention risk with a mean accuracy of about 72.5% (i.e., mean error of approximately 27.5%), which is much more accurate than tossing an unbiased coin, despite the dataset containing few instance numbers. Therefore, it is expected that the bigger dataset is, the better the mean accuracy will be.

On the other hand, the t-test that reveals there is no statistical evidence to prove that the multilayer perceptrons algorithm is significantly far more accurate than the other machine learning algorithms tested in this research because the p-value greater is than 0.05 (see Table II). This might lead us to think that in this case, adopting the decision trees algorithm is the right choice due to this is simple to interpret. Nevertheless, the variations in the training dataset caused by the 10-fold cross-validation, the tree shape changes drastically, as shown in Figure 3. This does not allow generalizing the rules for estimating the student's

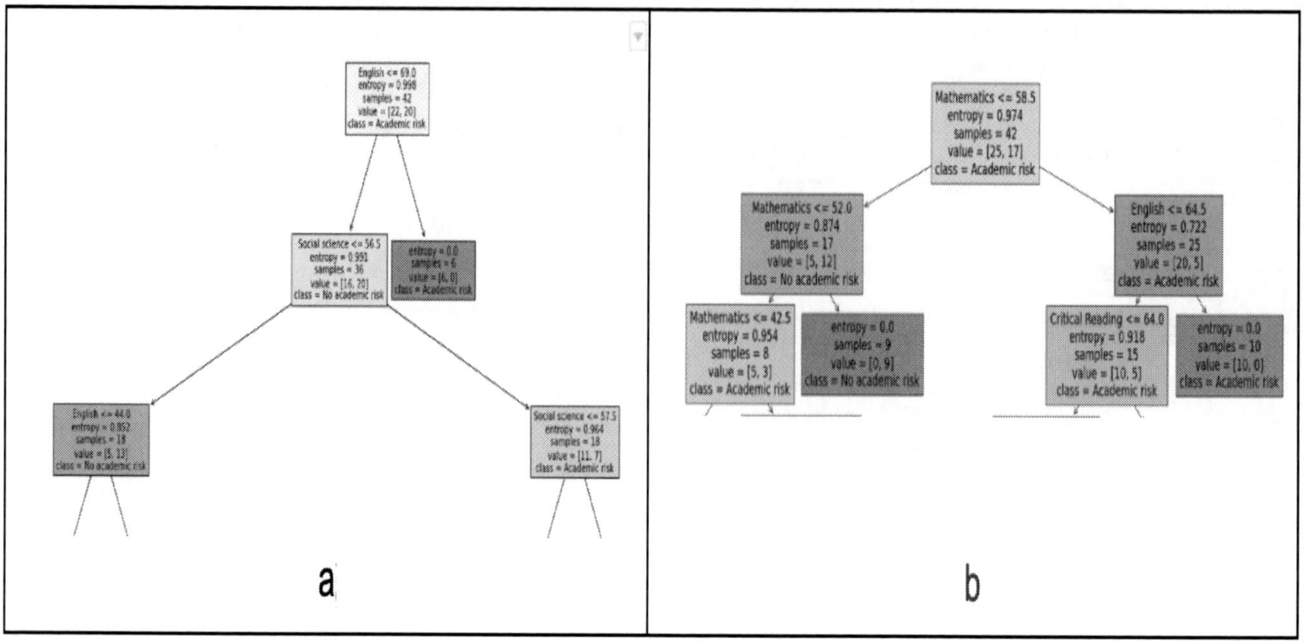

Figure 3. a) Part of the resulting decision tree shape during the first iteration of the 10-Fold Cross-Validation. b) Part of the resulting decision tree shape during the second iteration of the 10-FCV.

risk. Therefore, the reason for recommending the multilayer perceptrons algorithm to tackle the problem addressed in our research is twofold:

(i) Experiments in other domains have evidenced that the bigger the dataset is, the more accurate the multilayer perceptrons algorithm is, even more than other machine learning algorithms [16, pg. 3]. As a consequence, we expect significant improvement of the multilayer perceptrons accuracy, compared with the other tested learning algorithms, as we collect more examples for training it.
(ii) Taking into account the sixth assumption mentioned in Section I-C, the multilayer perceptrons algorithm is the better choice than decision trees, according to the results,because the prediction accuracy is more desirable than an interpretative prediction, that is less accurate.

Finally, regarding the test Saber 11 is similar to SAT, the outcomes of this research might be extended to the context of American Colleges or Universities. Indeed, by adopting the multilayer perceptrons algorithm, the knowledge it attains might be transferred to similar contexts, using the pre-trained synaptic weights, so it is not required to train a new multilayer perceptrons net from scratch likewise this is done in other domains, such as, e.g., computer vision.

V. CONCLUSIONS AND PERSPECTIVES

In this research, we addressed the following question: Might the student's outcome, achieved from the admission test called Saber 11, be used to forecast if the recently admitted student will be at either withdrawal or long-term retention risk, in the foreseeable future, before starting the first semester?

Anticipating the student's risk might allow the Universities to take precautions necessary to prevent the issues related to these risks, such as, e.g., the student's frustration, financial loss, and so forth.

Some precautions might be such as, e.g., psychological advice, and courses that let the student overcome the associated risk.

Herein, the addressed problem is to find the functional dependency between the admission test outcomes achieved by the student, and its withdrawal or long-term-retention risk. We have tackled this problem, by using supervised machine learning algorithms for classification, i.e., multilayer perceptrons, support vector machines, logistic regression, and decision trees.

To train and evaluate machine learning algorithms, we collected a dataset by surveying 86 students. After cleaning the dataset, we removed 39 records, resulting in a dataset containing 47 records.

We draw the following conclusions from the experimental evaluation (through K-fold cross-validation):

(i) The polynomial kernel is a better choice than the Gaussian kernel for adopting the support vector machines algorithm.
(ii) Support vector machines and logistic regression have the same mean precision, while the former algorithm with the polynomial kernel has the same mean recall that the latter.
(iii) The decision tree with the entropy impurity function

performs better than the one with the Gini impurity function.

(iv) The multilayer perceptrons algorithm outperforms the other studied learning algorithms, despite the t-test revealing there is no statistical evidence that the mean error of the support vector machines algorithm is far lower than the one obtained through the other algorithms, i.e., the resulting p-value is greater than 0.05.

(v) Concerning the research question, with machine learning, it is possible to predict if a recently admitted student in a bachelor's program will be at withdrawal or long-term-retention risk with a mean accuracy of about 72.5% (i.e., a mean error of approximately 27.5%).

(vi) The results reveal that the multilayer perceptrons algorithm is the best choice for facing the problem addressed in this research, regarding also the experience in other domains, where the bigger the dataset is, the more accurate deep neural networks based on the multilayer perceptrons algorithm are, even far more accurate than other learning algorithms [16, pg. 3]

(vii) The multilayer perceptrons algorithm is a better choice than decision trees, according to the results, because it is more desirable accurate forecasting than a less accurate prediction based on an interpretative model.

For further research, we shall collect more data, including more variables, such as, e.g., demographic, economic, emotional, psychological, environmental variables, and so forth. Thus, we can study their influence on the student's performance. On the other hand, a dataset with more records will reduce the classification error and improve the forecasting accuracy.

Finally, we propose other research directions based on the following open questions:

(i) Might the admission test Saber 11 be used for suggesting bachelor's degrees, according to the risk faced by the student in pursuing such bachelor's careers? Arguably, a candidate who has poor performance in the mathematics area of the admission test might be at risk if, for instance, this person pursues a bachelor of engineering. Nevertheless, if the same candidate has a good outcome in the critical reading area, might not be at risk, as long as this person chooses a bachelor's degree that does not require advanced quantitative competencies such as, e.g., a bachelor's degree in literature.

(ii) Will the accuracy increase as more areas are included in the test Saber 11? For instance, if general science is evaluated, this might help to predict the student performance in bachelor of science with majors in either science (e.g., physics, chemistry, biology, and so forth) or engineering (e.g., computer science, electrical and electronic engineering, etc.).

(iii) Might the accuracy of the learning algorithms increase above 90% by training them with more examples, without including more variables (e.g., demographic data or emotional measurements)? If so, might variables such as, e.g., demographic, psychological, emotional, economic, and so forth, be latent factors that can be inferred from the test Saber 11 outcomes? For example, recommender systems might infer latent factors such as, e.g., movie genre from the rating given by the user to movies.

(iv) In Colombia, there is a standardized test called Saber Pro, which is taken by bachelor's students before fulfilling the requirements to receive a bachelor's degree. The test Saber Pro is similar to Saber 11, and it is designed to evaluate the critical reading, quantitative reasoning, citizenship competencies, Spanish written communication, and English communication skills. Might the test Saber Pro be used to forecast if a recently admitted graduate student (e.g., enrolled in either a master's or a Ph.D. program) will be at risk of withdrawing from the University, or being long-term-retained in the graduate program?

ACKNOWLEDGMENT

Caicedo-Castro thanks the Lord Jesus Christ for blessing this project. We thank Universidad de Córdoba in Colombia for the financial support to this research (grant FE-06-17). In special, our deepest appreciation goes to Dr. Jairo Torres-Oviedo, University of Córdoba president, who has always helped us and supported us throughout this research. We thank all students who collaborated with us, answering the survey conducted for collecting the dataset, used to train the learning algorithms adopted in this research. Finally, we thank the anonymous reviewers for their comments that contributed to improve the quality of this article.

REFERENCES

[1] C. Demetriou and A. Schmitz-Sciborski, "Integration , Motivation , Strengths and Optimism : Retention Theories Past , Present and Future," in *Proceedings of the 7th National Symposium on Student Retention*, 2011, pp. 300–312.

[2] I. Pacheco-Arrieta *et al.* (2004) Agreement No. 004: Student's code at the University of Córdoba in Colombia. Retrieved on June 14. [Online]. Available: http://www.unicordoba.edu.co/wp-content/uploads/2018/12/reglamento-academico.pdf

[3] J. B. Berger and J. F. Milem, "The Role of Student Involvement and Perceptions of Integration in a Causal Model of Student Persistence," *Research in Higher Education*, vol. 40, no. 6, pp. 641–664, 1999.

[4] G. Dekker, M. Pechenizkiy, and J. Vleeshouwers, "Predicting Students Drop Out: A Case Study." *Computers, Environment and Urban Systems*, pp. 41–50, 01 2009.

[5] J. Lin, P. Imbrie, and K. Reid, "Student Retention Modelling: An Evaluation of Different Methods and their Impact on Prediction Results," in *Research in Engineering Education Symposium*. Curran Associates, Inc., 2009.

[6] L. Aulck, N. Velagapudi, J. Blumenstock, and J. West. (2016) Predicting Student Dropout in Higher Education. Retrieved on December 10. [Online]. Available: https://arxiv.org/abs/1606.06364

[7] J. Parker, M. Hogan, J. Eastabroo, A. Oke, and L. Wood, "Emotional intelligence and student retention: Predicting the successful transition from high school to university," *Personality and Individual Differences*, vol. 41, pp. 1329–1336, 2006.

[8] B. Pérez, C. Castellanos, and D. Correal, *Predicting Student Drop-Out Rates Using Data Mining Techniques: A Case Study: First IEEE Colombian Conference, ColCACI 2018, Medellín, Colombia, May 16-18, 2018, Revised Selected Papers*. IEEE, 05 2018, pp. 111–125.

[9] I. Caicedo-Castro. (2022) Dataset for Early Risk Detection of Bachelor Student Withdrawal or Long-Term-Retention. Retrieved on March 15. [Online]. Available: https://sites.google.com/correo.unicordoba.edu.co/isacaic/research

[10] M. Mohri, A. Rostamizadeh, and A. Talwalkar, *Foundations of Machine Learning*, 2nd ed. The MIT Press, 2018.

[11] C. Cortes and V. Vapnik, "Support Vector Networks," *Machine Learning*, vol. 20, pp. 273–297, 1995.

[12] J. A. Anderson, *Logistic Discrimination*. North Holland, 1982, pp. 169–192.

[13] G. J. McLachlan, *Discriminant Analysis and Statistical Pattern Recognition*. Wiley, 1992.

[14] D. C. Liu and J. Nocedal, "On the limited memory BFGS method for large scale optimization," *Mathematical Programming*, vol. 45, no. 3, (Ser. B), pp. 503–528, 1989.

[15] R. Byrd, P. Lu, J. Nocedal, and C. Zhu, "A Limited Memory Algorithm for Bound Constrained Optimization," *SIAM Journal on Scientific Computing*, vol. 16, no. 5, pp. 1190–1208, 1995.

[16] C. C. Aggarwal, *Neural Networks and Deep Learning*. Springer, 2018.

[17] D. E. Rumelhart, G. E. Hinton, and R. J. Williams, "Learning Representations by Back-propagating Errors," *Nature*, vol. 323, no. 6088, pp. 533–536, 1986.

[18] D. P. Kingma and J. Ba. (2014) Adam: A method for stochastic optimization. Retrieved on December 10. [Online]. Available: http://arxiv.org/abs/1412.6980

[19] L. Breiman, J. H. Friedman, R. A. Olshen, and C. J. Stone, *Classification and Regression Trees*. Monterey, CA: Wadsworth and Brooks, 1984.

[20] F. Pedregosa *et al.*, "Scikit-learn: Machine Learning in Python," *Journal of Machine Learning Research*, vol. 12, pp. 2825–2830, 2011.

[21] (2017) Google Colaboratory. Retrieved on June 14. [Online]. Available: https://colab.research.google.com/

A Data-Reuse Approach for the RLS-DCD Algorithm

Ionuţ-Dorinel Fîciu, Cristian-Lucian Stanciu, Camelia Elisei-Iliescu, Cristian Anghel, and Constantin Paleologu
Department of Telecommunications, University Politehnica of Bucharest, Romania
Emails: ionut.ficiu22@gmail.com, cristian@comm.pub.ro, camelia.elisei@romatsa.ro, canghel@comm.pub.ro, pale@comm.pub.ro

***Abstract*—The mitigation of input signal correlation is one of the main advantages associated with the Recursive Least-Squares (RLS) algorithms. This paper proposes a low-complexity RLS adaptive algorithm based on the Dichotomous Coordinate Descent (DCD) iterations, with a Data-Reuse (DR) approach. In this way, the corresponding convergence speeds in tracking and low signal-to-noise scenarios are improved, with overall attractive costs in terms of chip areas for hardware implementations.**

***Index Terms*—adaptive algorithms; Data-Reuse (DR); low Signal-to-Noise Ratio; Recursive Least-Squares (RLS); Dichotomous Coordinate Descent (DCD); tracking.**

I. INTRODUCTION

In recent times, considerable research efforts were concentrated on improving convergence rates and tracking capabilities for practical implementations of adaptive systems. The Recursive Least-Squares (RLS) family of adaptive algorithms is a good way to accomplish this goal, unfortunately, with the cost of an increased arithmetic workload and numerical stability issues. The current industry workhorse is the Least-Mean-Square (LMS) algorithm [1], which has poor results when working with correlated input signals. To overcome these impediments, two versions of the RLS method have been previously introduced: the RLS adaptive algorithm combined with the dichotomous coordinate descent iterations (RLS-DCD) [2], [3], respectively the RLS adaptive algorithm based on the data-reuse approach (DR-RLS) [4].

The RLS-DCD has been designed to match the performance of classical RLS versions, and also to avoid the necessity of handling prohibitive amounts of arithmetic operations (usually, proportional to the square of the filter's length or even more complex) associated with the computation of the inverse correlation matrix. The usage of the DCD iterations exchanges the correlation matrix inversion with a solution based only on additions and bit-shifts, corresponding to an auxiliary system of equations, which exploits the statistical properties of the input signal [2]. Thus, hardware costs become appealing for practical applications.

The DR-RLS adaptive algorithm improves performance of the RLS method in tracking scenarios [4]. Along with the forgetting factor, the DR parameter can be used to compromise between convergence speeds and filter accuracy at steady-state, with just a minimal increase in terms of complexity (proportional to the filter's length).

In this paper, we analyze a new version of the RLS adaptive algorithm, based on the combination between the DCD iterations and the DR principles, and we study the corresponding performances in scenarios with tracking, respectively low Signal-to-Noise Ratio (SNR) conditions. Section II introduces the system model, which is employed in Section III to describe the proposed algorithm. Simulation results are discussed in Section IV, and conclusions are drawn in Section V.

II. SYSTEM MODEL

Starting with the estimated impulse response $\widehat{\mathbf{g}}(n)$ (of length L), we define the $a\ priori$ error signal as:

$$e(n) = d(n) - \widehat{y}(n) = d(n) - \widehat{\mathbf{g}}^T(n-1)\mathbf{x}(n), \quad (1)$$

where $\widehat{y}(n)$ is the output signal estimate obtained using the adaptive filter coefficients, $\mathbf{x}(n)$ is the $L \times 1$ input signal vector, and $d(n)$ represents the desired (or *reference*) signal [1].

The minimization of the cost function [1], [5], with respect to $\widehat{\mathbf{g}}(n)$, leads to the set of normal equations

$$\mathbf{R}(n)\widehat{\mathbf{g}}(n) = \mathbf{p}(n) = \lambda\mathbf{p}(n-1) + \mathbf{x}(n)d(n), \quad (2)$$

where λ is the forgetting factor, $\mathbf{R}(n)$ expresses the $L \times L$ correlation matrix, and $\mathbf{p}(n)$ represents the cross-correlation vector between $\mathbf{x}(n)$ and the reference signal $d(n)$.

When working with the RLS-DCD algorithm, we write the *residual vector* using the solution provided at previous time index of the filter:

$$\mathbf{r}(n-1) = \mathbf{p}(n-1) - \mathbf{R}(n-1)\widehat{\mathbf{g}}(n-1). \quad (3)$$

By using the DCD method, we aim to reduce the complexity of updating the filter coefficients through the estimation of the *solution* vector $\Delta\mathbf{g}(n)$, and adding it to the previous filter set of coefficients, such that $\widehat{\mathbf{g}}(n) = \widehat{\mathbf{g}}(n-1) + \Delta\widehat{\mathbf{g}}(n)$ [2], [3].

Consequently, the RLS-DCD solves the auxiliary set of normal equations:

$$\mathbf{R}(n)\Delta\mathbf{g}(n) = \mathbf{p}(n) - \mathbf{R}(n)\widehat{\mathbf{g}}(n-1) \overset{not}{=} \mathbf{p}_0(n), \quad (4)$$

and the computation of a direct solution is avoided [3].

After some calculations, the residual vector can be expressed as:

$$\mathbf{r}(n) = \mathbf{p}_0(n) - \mathbf{R}(n)\Delta\widehat{\mathbf{g}}(n). \quad (5)$$

Finally, we obtain:

$$\mathbf{p}_0(n) = \lambda\mathbf{r}(n-1) + e(n)\mathbf{x}(n) \overset{not}{=} \lambda\mathbf{r}(n-1) + \mathbf{r}_{e,x}(n). \quad (6)$$

The DCD method has two empiric roles for (4): it estimates the solution vector $\Delta\widehat{\mathbf{g}}(n)$ and it updates the residual values associated with the vectors $\mathbf{p}_0(n)$, respectively $\mathbf{r}(n)$.

III. DR-RLS-DCD ALGORITHM

We propose to apply the DR method [4] over the RLS-DCD adaptive algorithm. The goal is to employ N_{it} updates for $\widehat{\mathbf{g}}(n-1)$ in order to obtain $\widehat{\mathbf{g}}(n)$. Firstly, the error signal can be written in a recursive way [4]:

$$e_k(n) = \begin{cases} d(n) - \widehat{\mathbf{g}}^T(n-1)\mathbf{x}(n) = e_0(n), & k = 0 \\ e_{k-1}(n) - \Delta\widehat{\mathbf{g}}_{k-1}^T(n)\mathbf{x}(n) & k \geq 1 \end{cases} \quad (7)$$

where $k = 0 \ldots N_{it} - 1$ represents the current step. It is obvious that for $N_{it} = 1$ the algorithm is equivalent to the RLS-DCD approach.

Since we have used the DR method to update the error signal, we need to adapt the update of the residual vector in a similar manner [4]:

$$\mathbf{r}_k(n) = \begin{cases} \lambda\mathbf{r}_{N_{it}-1}(n-1) + \mathbf{r}_{e,x,0}(n), & k = 0 \\ \mathbf{r}_{k-1}(n) + \mathbf{r}_{e,x,k}(n), & k \geq 1, \end{cases} \quad (8)$$

where $\mathbf{r}_{e,x,k}(n) = e_k(n)\mathbf{x}(n)$.

Considering the worst case scenario, the newly introduced DR-RLS-DCD method supposes more $(N_{it} - 1)N_u L$ additions, with respect to the RLS-DCD approach. However, in real applications, since $N_u \ll L$ and $N_{it} \ll L$, the global complexity of this new adaptive algorithm is still proportional to the filter's length multiplied by a small factor. The performances of the algorithm, in terms of tracking capabilities/convergence rate, are improving with the increase of the DR control parameter N_{it}. The sequential behavior of the DR-RLS-DCD adaptive algorithm is presented in Table I.

IV. SIMULATION RESULTS

We used as an input signal a Gaussian noise with the length of 280000 samples and SNR = 20 dB filtered through an autoregressive AR(1) model with the pole 0.9. The unknown system was chosen to be the forth impulse response from the G.168 ITU-T Recommendation [6], with the length $L = 128$.

We performed a simulation by combining two types of scenarios: tracking and temporary low SNR conditions. In the first part of the scenario, abrupt changes in the unknown system were triggered by changing the sign of the corresponding impulse response coefficients at the time index 60000. In the low SNR part of the scenario, the additive noise was experimentally changed from SNR = 20dB to SNR = -20dB, for a duration of 5000 samples, starting with time index 180000. The performance has been measured with the normalized misalignment [3]. The forgetting factor is the same in all circumstances, $\lambda = 1 - 1/(KL)$, with $K = 128$. The DCD parameters were set to $N_u = 4$, $M_b = 16$, and $H = 1$. The simulations results are illustrated in Figure 1.

TABLE I: DR-RLS-DCD ADAPTIVE ALGORITHM

Step no.	Step action
Init.	Set $\widehat{\mathbf{g}}(0) = \mathbf{0}_{L\times 1}; \mathbf{r}(0) = \mathbf{0}_{L\times 1}$ $\mathbf{R}(0) = \delta\mathbf{I}_L$, with $\delta > 0$
	For $n = 1, 2, \ldots,$ number of iterations :
A	Update vector $\mathbf{x}(n)$ and matrix $\mathbf{R}(n)$
B	For $k = 1, 2, \ldots, N_{it} - 1$:
1	Compute $e_k(n)$ using (7)
2	Compute $\mathbf{p}_k(n)$ using (8)
3	$\mathbf{R}(n)\Delta\mathbf{g}_k(n) = \mathbf{p}_k(n) \xrightarrow{\text{DCD}} \Delta\widehat{\mathbf{g}}_k(n), \mathbf{r}_k(n)$
C	$\widehat{\mathbf{g}}_k(n) = \widehat{\mathbf{g}}_k(n-1) + \Delta\widehat{\mathbf{g}}_k(n)$

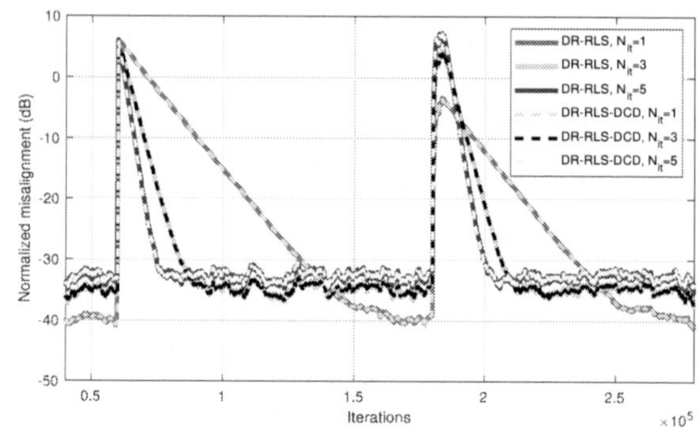

Figure 1. Performance of the DR-RLS and DR-RLS-DCD algorithms for different values of N_{it}. The unknown system changes at time index 60001, and the SNR is decreased for 5000 iterations, starting with index 180001.

V. CONCLUSIONS

The algorithm introduced in this paper is an efficient combination between the exponentially weighted RLS algorithm based on the DCD method [2], [3], enhanced by a data-reuse approach. The DR-RLS-DCD adaptive algorithm has proven to offer a useful compromise between tracking capabilities and estimation accuracy. The trade-off is controlled from the DR part of the algorithm through the number of iterations N_{it}.

ACKNOWLEDGEMENT

This work was supported by two grants of the Romanian Ministry of Education and Research, CNCS–UEFISCDI, project number PN-III-P1-1.1-TE-2019-0529, and PN-III-P4-PCE-2021-0438, within PNCDI III.

REFERENCES

[1] S. Haykin, *Adaptive Filter Theory*. Fourth Edition, Upper Saddle River, NJ, USA: Prentice-Hall, 2002.

[2] Y. V. Zakharov, G. P. White, and J. Liu, "Low-complexity RLS algorithms using dichotomous coordinate descent iterations," *IEEE Trans. Signal Processing*, vol. 56, pp. 3150–3161, July 2008.

[3] C. Stanciu, J. Benesty, C. Paleologu, T. Gänsler, and S. Ciochină, "A widely linear model for stereophonic acoustic echo cancellation," *Signal Processing*, vol. 93, issue 2, pp. 511-516, 2013.

[4] C. Paleologu, J. Benesty, and S. Ciochină, "Data-Reuse Recursive Least-Squares Algorithms," *IEEE Signal Processing Letters*, vol. 29, pp. 752-756, 2022.

[5] P. S. R. Diniz, *Adaptive Filtering: Algorithms and Practical Implementation*. Fourth Edition, New York, NY, USA: Springer-Verlag, 2013.

[6] Digital Network Echo Cancellers. ITU-T Recommendations G.168. Available online: https://www.itu.int/rec/T-REC-G.168/en (accessed on June 22 2022)

Enhanced Robust Convex Relaxation Framework for Optimal Controllability of Certain Large Complex Networked Systems

An Accelerant Amalgam and Bespoke Numerical Stability Paradigm for a Decoupled and Sequenced Control Strategy on Dense and Homogeneous Temporal Networks

Steve Chan
Decision Engineering Analysis Laboratory, VTIRL, VT
Orlando, USA
e-mail: schan@dengineering.org

Abstract— **Efficient Controllability Problems (ECP) for Large Complex Networked System (LCNS) often involve solving a succession of convex optimization problems, with varied approaches to optimally resolve each problem. In various cases, even when the input set is specifically designed/architected to segue to a convex paradigm, the resultant output set may still turn out to be nonconvex. Further processing is necessary to reach the desired convex paradigm, such as via certain relaxation techniques. However, the involved transformation, during the processing, may result in further nonconvex optimization problems, thereby highlighting the need/opportunity to utilize an Enhanced Robust Convex Relaxation (ERCR) framework. In this paper, we illuminate how leveraging such an ERCR framework, to discern how the involved LCNS's topological structure, facilitates or prevents the diffusion of control signals and/or augmented control signals, which in turn informs the computations related to an accelerant amalgam and numerical stability paradigm for effectively leveraging a set of control/driver nodes to influence yet another set of control/driver nodes so as to steer the LCNS to a target state, if a decoupled and sequenced control strategy is utilized. The numerical stability paradigm employed by the ERCR framework is, potentially, of scientific gain and shows promise in contending with certain round-off errors, thereby better facilitating the transformation of certain uncontrollable cases into controllable cases, if temporal networks are considered. For those paradigms, wherein the Bak–Tang–Wiesenfeld (BTW) sandpile cascading effect is a potentiality, this facilitation may be quite significant.**

Keywords-Cyber-physical systems; cyber-physical power system; large complex networked systems; temporal networks; supply chain vulnerability; efficient controllability; strong controllability; control signal energy cost; robust convex relaxation; accelerant amalgam; numerical stability; neural network; controllability Gramian; Gramian submatrices.

I. Introduction

Interest in the controllability problem of complex networks is burgeoning. Some studies have posited that while control of a substantive portion of the nodes may be ideal in the cases of some smaller networks, controlling a smaller subset of nodes may be more practical for larger, more complex networks. Accordingly, various studies have examined the problem set of influencing or controlling Large Complex Networked Systems (LCNS) with limited external Control Signals (CS) [1], which is often referred to as the Network Controllability Problem (NCP) [2]. Along this vein, other works have tackled the problem of selecting the smallest number of CS to ensure controllability of such LCNS [3]. Yet, the solving of such Minimum Controllability Problems (MCP) is just one step [4]. A further step involves solving related Efficient Controllability Problems (ECP), which focus on minimizing both the number of control nodes needed, as well as minimizing the control signal energy needed. However, these ECP have been shown to exhibit Non-deterministic Polynomial-time Hardness (NP-Hardness). Various approximation algorithms and heuristical approaches have been utilized to achieve sub-optimal solutions to these NP-Hard ECPs [1]. To aggravate matters, these sub-optimal approaches tend to falter further when elevated notions of specific (e.g., output) controllability [5][6] are contended with, and, practically speaking, actual controllability is difficult to achieve (as contrasted to merely mathematical controllability [7]).

More robust approaches have been proposed for tackling the NP-Hard ECPs as well as the issue of actual controllability. Various works have focused on augmenting the set of input CS on "properly chosen" control or "driver nodes" [6], which connotes the paradigm of certain nodes within the network having the potential of control authority to drive [8]. Yet, even if the control/driver nodes are "properly chosen" — and even if the LCNS is controllable (putting aside the issue of mathematical versus actual controllability) — via the chosen control/driver nodes, the Control Signal Energy Cost (CSEC) that those nodes require may be "unrealistically large" [8]; in other words, "if the number of control signals is small, the energy cost demanded … could be prohibitively high" [9]. There is yet another issue; a substantive portion of the studies are focused upon linear systems because, at least over short time scales, continuous nonlinear systems are approximated as linear [10]; for this reason, the involved networks are approximated and assumed to have n-dimensional Linear Time-Invariant (LTI) dynamics [2]. To further the discussion regarding practicality, just as a prohibitively high CSEC would not be practical, controllability over only short time scales would be comparably impractical (e.g., the inability to exert control at a desired time, as the window of control may have already passed). This further extends the problem, as temporal considerations are at play, into the realm of Temporal Problems (TPs); moreover, as the temporal duration is uncertain, the problem is that of TP with uncertainty (TPU) [11]. Not only does the controllability need to persist over a sufficiently long time scale or reasonable extended period of time, the actual ability to control, when desired, needs to occur in a finite period of time (i.e., immediately or As Soon As Possible — ASAP). Hence, it seems that the revised optimality problem becomes one of ascertaining the sufficient number of input CS to steer a minimal number of control/driver nodes at a reasonable energy cost ($CSEC_{OPT}$), over an extended period of time (TPU_{OPT}) (as contrasted to TPU_{max}), but which can be activated and effectuated within a finite period of time (e.g., ASAP). Accordingly, the main contribution of the paper is to introduce a strategy for transforming optimization problems to convex form so as to reduce the complexity class from NP-Hard to polynomial time, such as for the ECP-related computations, using an Enhanced Robust Convex Relaxation (ERCR) framework equipped with a bespoke numerical stability paradigm.

The paper is structured as follows. Section I introduces the controllability problem of complex networks. Section II presents relevant background information and discusses the operating environment and the state of the controllability challenge. Section III provides some theoretical foundations and the utilized approach. Section IV delineates a strategy for a sequence of transformations and presents some preliminary experimental findings from using an ERCR framework on dense and homogeneous temporal networks. Section V provides some reflections on potential further heuristical processing, such as by way of LCNS partitioning and the practicality of TN_{Bno} expansion for some real-world applications, such as assessing Supply Chain Vulnerability (SCV). Section VI concludes with some reflections, puts forth some envisioned future work, and the acknowledgements close the paper.

II. BACKGROUND INFORMATION

In accordance with control theory, a system is deemed to be controllable, if it can be driven from an initial state to a desired state with suitable input(s) [4]. It then follows that if the nodes of a LCNS can be steered from an arbitrary initial state vector towards a predefined goal state vector within a finite period of time, then the network is deemed to be controllable [9]. The positing of the actual controllability is another matter; the positing of the accuracy of the controllability is still yet another matter. Among other frameworks, structural controllability had been put forth as a potentially viable analytical framework for ascertaining the controllability of LCNS. However, Cowan et al. have noted the limitations of structural controllability [12] as well as certain of its associated paradoxes; for example, in some cases, the CSEC of a structurally controllable system can be higher than that of a "structurally" uncontrollable system [8]. Alternative frameworks have been proposed, such as by Yuan et al., to include exact controllability (i.e., arbitrary link structures [e.g., directed, undirected] and link weights [e.g., weighted, unweighted] [13]), which better reflects the directed and weighted network configurations found in most real-world systems [35].

With regards to CSEC, Chen et al. asserted that "if the number of control signals is small, the energy cost demanded ... could be prohibitively high;" conversely, the energy cost is reduced exponentially as the number of input CS increases [9]. It should, therefore, be axiomatic that the ascertaining of the sufficient number of input CS and their optimal "distribution throughout the complex network" (CS_{opt}) is "vitally important to the feasibility and the efficiency of a Control Action" (CA) [1], which is defined to be the achieving of a predefined goal state vector; along this vein, a "Control Maneuver" (CM) might be comprised of several CAs [1], which at some point might arrive at CA_{OPT} (ascertained over time). Effective CAs and/or their CMs can lead to faster network control/collapse [14. The Target Nodes (TN) involved in the achieving of the predefined goal state vector are deemed to have been subjected to "Targeted Control" (TC) [9]. The computational aims, then, seem to be that of ascertaining a minimum number of optimal control/driver nodes, such as proposed by Gao et al. [9], and their placements, such as proposed by Lindmark et al. [8], that, with sufficiently distributed and available CS, such as proposed by Klickstein et al., would only require a minimum CSEC ($CSEC_{min}$) [8], but the optimal [and practical] CSEC ($CSEC_{OPT}$) would include augmentation CS. In accordance with self-organization theory, a series of small events can cause a chain reaction that can affect any number of components in the system, as delineated by the well-known Bak–Tang–Wiesenfeld (BTW) sandpile effect [15] of non-equilibrium systems in which sand is dropped, one grain at a time, onto the same spot until the addition of one more grain of sand causes an avalanche to slide down the slopes of the growing sandpile; this avalanche also tends to burgeon into a cascading series of avalanches that can grow in size and intensity (i.e., similar to the notion of a cascading effect) [36]. Cascading effects (e.g., cascading failures) have manifested themselves, such as via Northeast Blackout of 2003 and 2012 India Blackouts, wherein the "failure of one or a few components" ... triggered the ... "successive failures of other components" [16].

The identification of control/driver nodes has been a longstanding goal of many Complex Network Analysis (CNA) efforts [17], such as for Supply Chain Vulnerability (SCV) analysis efforts within the rubric of Supply Chain Risk Management (SCRM). These SCRM efforts have become more complicated, as physical systems and information systems are increasingly being fused into Cyber-Physical Systems (CPS), wherein it is possible to control physical systems, via cyber systems [18]. The implication should be clear; prospective input CS can emanate from either the cyber or physical domains. Both these domains are considered in Guo et al.'s Cyber-Physical Power System (CPPS) model, which touches upon the notion that while current CPPS can provide a modicum of resiliency for high-indexed nodes, they are much less resilient (i.e., vulnerable) to malicious attacks (i.e., targeted attacks) [14]. The implications of the varied attack surfaces of Multi-Domain Operations (MDO) should be axiomatic.

In either case, the previously cited MCP, as applied to the approximated LTI paradigm, can be construed to be a minimum Constrained Input Selection (minCIS) problem [19][20]. With CSEC constraints, the minCIS then becomes a minimum Cost Constrained Input Selection (minCCIS) problem [21][22]. Among other methods, the Projected Gradient Method (PGM) has been used to solve the constrained optimization problem of minCCIS [2][23], which can also be recast as a constrained convex minimization/optimization problem [23]. In essence, PGM endeavors to find locally optimal solutions to a continuous relaxation of the convex optimization problem [1]. While PGM can be useful for convex optimization problems with simple constraints, such as minCCIS with LTI dynamics, other methods may be needed given more complex constraints. For example, various works are examining minCCIS amidst uncertainties (minCCIS-u), such as time delays [24] (e.g., does the ability to effectuate a CM persist beyond the immediate time period, and is it available when desired). The aforementioned paradigm is delineated in Fig. 1 below.

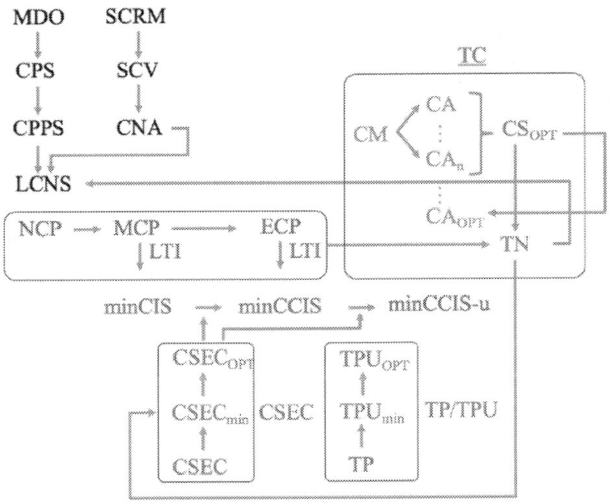

Figure 1. Targeted Control (TC), via Targeted Nodes (TN), in the Described Environs of minCCIS-u and TPU_{OPT}

Given the myriad of uncertainties for the minCCIS-u problem, the continuous relaxations involve successive convex optimization problems, wherein varied approaches might be utilized to optimally resolve each problem. After all, as previously observed in [25], even when the input set is specifically formulated to segue to a convex optimization problem, the resultant may still turn out to be nonconvex, thereby necessitating a transformation to the desired form of a convex optimization problem, via certain relaxation techniques; however, the transformation itself may spawn other nonconvex optimization problems. In fact, when the objective and constraint functions are nonconvex, these problems turn out to be NP-Hard Mixed Integer Non-Linear Programming (MINLP) nonconvex optimization problems that need to be optimally solved.

The referenced ERCR, which was equipped with a bespoke numerical stability paradigm, was utilized to handle these nonconvex optimization problems and reduce the complexity class from NP-Hard to polynomial time; to further unpack this handling, by way of background information, pertinent approach vectors are typically classified into two methods: (1) exact (i.e., complete), and (2) relaxed (i.e., incomplete). Prototypical exact verifiers are predicated upon Mixed Integer Programming (MIP) (specifically, MINLP, for the experimentation discussed herein), Branch-and-Bound (BnB), or Satisfiability Modulo Theories (SMT) (which, by definition, are not beset by false positives or false negatives). The challenge of utilizing exact verifiers is that they must contend with resolving NP-hard optimization problems, which in turn, obviates their scalability. Prototypical relaxed verifiers are predicated upon Mixed Integer Convex Programming (MICP) or Mixed Integer Linear Programming (MILP). MILP/MICP can be more quickly resolved and are more scalable, but the effectiveness (i.e., increased false negative rates) degrades quickly [42], thereby potentially obviating the ability to verify robustness. Hence, addressing robustness, such as via robust convex relaxations (i.e., effectuating the tightest possible relaxation [42]) becomes central for the experimentation/simulation. The utilized pathways to a convex paradigm are set within a Discrete, Continuous/Discontinuous (y-axis) and Non-Linear, Linear (x-axis) quad chart shown in Fig. 2 below.

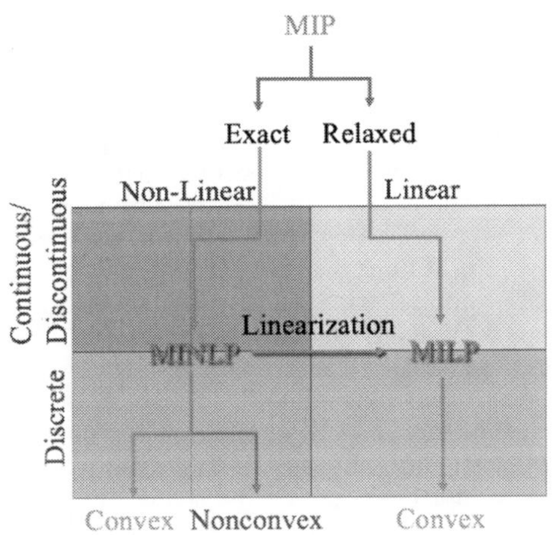

Figure 2. Computational Pathways for Attaining a Convex Paradigm

Let us then take the case of a prototypical Command and Control (C2) architecture (even an advanced one [26]), such as within the energy ecosystem, which typically involves Control Center (CC)-related node data and remote, distributed hyper-locale (specific to the area conditions) node data that need to be effectively fused so as to create actionable quality data [27]. Under exigency circumstances, control may devolve to Back-up CCs. If the exigency is limited, the devolution may only involve one Back-up CC. However, if the exigency is large-scale and widespread, the needs may be varied, and, consequently, multiple Back-up CCs may be involved.

Throughout it all, the interests of the original CC likely remain overarching (if not paramount), thereby necessitating non-zero-sum game theory success (i.e., ideally, all winners and no losers among the involved original CC, regional/area CCs, and Back-up CCs) [27]. However, this is often not the case due to the practicality of limited capacities and capabilities during large-scale and widespread exigencies. For example, some involved areas may have not blackstart (i.e., the ability to restart and recover from a blackout without external reliance) or quickstart (i.e., the ability to come back on-line quickly) capabilities. As has been observed from various Just-In-Time (JIT) case studies, issues with even a single component within the supply chain can have a cascading effect and impact a myriad of organizations [40]; this paradigm can, potentially, lead to a decrease in a country's overall total industrial output. Thus, if the criticality of a particular component is known, and the involved manufacturing resides in an area with no blackstart or quickstart capabilities, then the original CC may prioritize that area; alternatively, the CC may prioritize other areas, as the circumstances and/or involved decision engineering posits dictate. In any case, the follow-on research of [28] in 2020 and 2021 have shown that the involved objective and constraint functions, which include TPU and minCCIS-u-related considerations, are likely to be nonconvex.

As the involved circumstances change with time, the involved MINLP problems will vary. For example, the CSEC associated with minCCIS-u might be considerably higher when the normal CCs are at play than when the Backup-up CCs are at play. Regardless, prototypical approaches to solving these nonconvex MINLP problems involve transforming them into convex surrogates (e.g., via reformulations, convex approximations, or a series of convex relaxations) [25]. It turns out that the particular instantiation of the ERCR utilized, with the bespoke numerical stability paradigm, is well suited for this requisite series of convex relaxations. The utilized ERCR, which was based on [25], could not only resolve the minCCIS-u problem, but it could also leverage the same ERCR mechanisms for tuning its own hyperparameters; the utilized ERCR architectural stack achieved this with three key design/architectural elements: (1) effectuating an ERCR paradigm, via a bespoke Modified Squeezed "You Only Look Once" (YOLO) v3 (a PyTorch implementation, as contrasted to, for example, v4, which is a Darknet implementation) [Deep Convolutional Generative Adversarial Network (DCGAN)] Implementation (MSY3I), (2) utilizing Particle Swarm Optimization (PSO) to tune the MSY3I so as to reduce the associated computational costs, and (3) operationalizing the PSO via an Adaptive Inertial Weighting Mechanism (AIWM) (to mitigate against potential stagnation at local optima) facilitated by a modified GNU Octave platform (m-GNU-O). The particulars of this ERCR architecture are delineated in [25]; the utilized architectural stack and components are presented, the experimental setup of a stable RCR, composed of two MSY3I implementations that are augmented with a third DCGAN is delineated, and a sampling of the numerical issues found in various ML libraries/toolkits is discussed.

III. THEORETICAL APPROACH

The theoretical approach centers upon the issue of the accuracy of the controllability (as the actual controllability is also probabilistic). As discussed, an ERCR framework, as shown in Fig. 3, is utilized, and enhancing the tightness of the ERCR bounds is an ongoing challenge. The PSO and AIWM tuning of the involved MSY3Is is central, as is minimizing the convex relaxation barrier, the inherent gap between the actual and lower bound of robustness provided by verifiers (i.e., verification algorithms for verifying the involved DCGANs, or MSY3Is in this case).

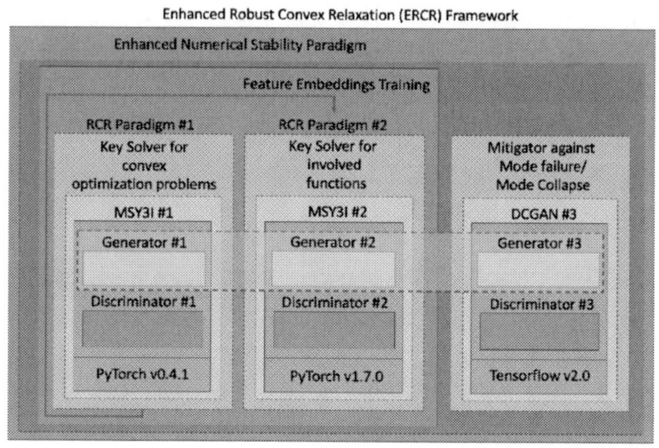

Figure 3. Enhanced Robust Convex Relaxation (ERCR) Architectural Stack Utilized

As contextualizing background information, Machine Learning (ML) is a subfield of Artificial Intelligence (AI). In turn, Deep Learning (DL) is a subfield of ML, and DL Neural Networks (NN) are a mainstay of DL algorithms ("deep" refers to the number of layers of the involved NN). A NN with just a few layers may produce a model that is not quite acceptable for the task at hand. Conversely, a NN that is fully connected, with many layers, dramatically increases the computational complexity and cost. Consequently, the goal is to arrive at a DNN architecture with sufficiently reduced connectivity, and therefore, reduced computational complexity and cost, that is still fit for purpose and, ideally, sufficiently robust. A commonly used DNN, with such reduced connectivity, is a Convolutional Neural Network (CNN). By way of example, Zhu et al. have asserted that CNNs are promising for condition monitoring [49]. Huang et al. have noted that specific implementations of CNN, such as the Multi-Scale Cascade CNN (MC-CNN), can robustly classify faults [50]. Others have noted that CNNs are the architectural elements of choice for Generative Adversarial Networks (GANs). Radford et al. have noted that a Deep Convolutional GAN (DCGAN) can produce robust results that were not present in the training set [51].

The utilized ERCR framework, which is underpinned by DCGANs (or MYS3Is, in this case) was utilized to tackle the Complex Network Analysis (CNA) challenge of optimal controllability of certain Large Complex Networked System (LCNS), particularly a Cyber-Physical Power System (CPPS) within the overarching rubric of Cyber-Physical Systems (CPS). An underlying challenge was to identify control/driver Target Nodes (TN) that are amenable to "Targeted Control" (TC). Other underlying challenges included discerning the topological structure of the LCNS-CPPS, as the structure diffusiveness (a.k.a., permeability) can facilitate or prevent the diffusion of control signals (CS) and/or augmented control signals (ACS), which in turn informs the computations, which leverage a set of control/driver TN_{n-1} to influence yet another set of control/driver TN_n so as to steer the LCNS-CPPS to a target state. Further granularity regarding the topological structure (e.g., directed/ undirected links; weighted/unweighted links) is necessary to address the issues of exact controllability, actual controllability, and accuracy of controllability. The involved sub-challenges include, among others, the Network Controllability Problem (NCP), Minimum Controllability Problem (MCP), Efficient Controllability Problems (ECP), Control Signal Energy Cost (CSEC) problem, minimum Constrained Input Selection (minCIS) problem, minimum Cost Constrained Input Selection (minCCIS) problem, minCCIS amidst uncertainties (minCCIS-u) (e.g., time delays), and adequately addressing the associated Temporal Problems (TPs) with uncertainty (TPUs). Essentially, the aforementioned problems can be recast as constrained convex minimization/optimization problems.

In addition to analyzing its performance as pertains to the convex optimization problems, the involved MSY3Is of the ERCR framework must be examined for robustness. As noted in [25], this often relates to the performance of the layer-wise optimal convex relaxations implemented within the involved DCGAN (also MSY3Is in this case); in essence, a certain convex relaxation is posited for the purpose of ascertaining an upper bound for a worst-case instability scenario. This is of critical import, as prototypical DCGANs exhibit non-graceful degradation in performance even at imperceptible perturbation levels, which results in numerical instability; this is also why the bespoke numerical stability paradigm discussed in [25] is invaluable. For this paper, the numerical stability paradigm employed by the ERCR framework is, potentially, of scientific gain and shows promise in contending with certain round-off errors, thereby better facilitating the transformation of certain uncontrollable cases into controllable cases; moreover, Ohtsuka et al. has noted there is equivalence between the convex relaxation and sparsity constrained controllability problems, wherein the controllability Gramian is used as a metric for the ease of control [52]. In essence, the discernment of the controllability Gramian is directly related to the involved convex relaxation. In particular, the minimum/optimal TN selection (i.e., sparsity constraint) is, in essence, a selection problem, wherein TNs are selected for their efficacy of control while minimizing CSEC. This sparse optimization problem, as applied to a LCNS-CCP controllability maximization problem, has equivalency to its convex relaxation. As a consequence, the ERCR — conjoined with its bespoke numerical stability paradigm — by its very design (i.e., more robust convex relaxations) might, potentially, warrant further examination for its efficacy in treating sparse optimization controllability maximization problems.

IV. EXPERIMENTATION

A. Heuristical Pre-Processing

For the 2020 follow-on work from [28], three regions were examined: A, B, and C. It was found that B had no blackstart and quickstart capabilities. Yet, B contained manufacturing sites producing components that would impact the supply chain affecting A, B, and C. In many ways, B's criticality surpassed that of A and C, and from a SCV Criticality (SCVC) perspective — for the specific manufacturing analysis at hand — B was, potentially, the most vulnerable. For this case, the aggregate network of A, B, and C, hereinafter $LCNS_{ABC}$, did not have to be treated in its entirety. The heuristical determination was that an examination of the sub-network of B ($LCNS_B$), would suffice. Hence, it was not necessary to compute the CSEC for $LCNS_{ABC}$ ($CSEC_{ABC}$); computing the CSEC for $LCNS_B$ ($CSEC_B$), would suffice. Also, by simply treating $LCNS_B$, the considered time frame could be further constrained (as contrasted by treating the entirety of $LCNS_{ABC}$); hence, the involved TPU component could be reduced and simplified (TPU_B), and accordingly, the involved CSEC could also be reduced and simplified ($CSEC_B$). Moreover, Chen et al. had found that CSEC could be reduced significantly when the addition of input CS could be accomplished while minimizing the path lengths from control/driver nodes to non-control/driver nodes, via optimal placements of the involved nodes [29]; the longest path of the set of involved paths is known as the Longest Control Chain (LCC). As $LCNS_B$ was considered in isolation, as contrasted to considering $LCNS_{ABC}$, it was found that the LCC_B for $LCNS_B << LCC_{ABC}$ for $LCNS_{ABC}$; correspondingly, $CSEC_B << CSEC_{ABC}$.

B. Algorithmic Pre-Processing

To further minimize $CSEC_B$ and attain $CSEC_{OPT}$, algorithmic processing was used to ascertain the potentially greatest impact $LCNS_{Bn}$ (a sub-region of $LCNS_B$). In this way, LCC_{Bn} for $LCNS_{Bn} << LCC_B$ for $LCNS_B$, $CSEC_{Bn} << CSEC_B$, and correspondingly, TN_{Bn} for $CSEC_{Bn} << TN_B$ for $CSEC_B$. With the same mechanism utilized for [30], selective updating of an optimal Adaptive Impact Vector (AIV_{OPT}) was undertaken for helping derive the potentially greatest impact $LCNS_{Bn}$. In essence, AIV_{Bn} can be derived, via minimizing a recast TN_{Bn} criterion subject to a similarity constraint; the AIV can also be validated, and more finely-tuned, via a decomposition-based evolutionary algorithm coupled with the AIV. The associated constrained paradigm can be transformed into a convex optimization problem, via various Semi-Definite Programming (SDP) algorithms, which were implemented on a m-GNU-O as delineated in [30]. Then, a Quadratically Constrained Quadratic Programming (QCQP) Step-Down Algorithm (QCQP-SDA) can compute the [QCQP special class] resultant convex optimization problem in polynomial time; historically, this had been tested in Ilog Cplex Optimizer (a commercial software package for optimization); subsequent testing migrated to AD Model Builder (ADMB) (an open source software package for non-linear statistical modeling) as well as Interior Point OPTimizer (IPOPT) (a software package for large-scale nonlinear optimization) [31], and experimentation has also been conducted with Advanpix (a multi-precision computing toolbox for Matlab). The significance of deriving $CSEC_{Bn}$, and subsequently, TN_{Bn}, is to have a sufficiently small TN, such that a particular approach proposed by Klickstein et al., the controllability Gramian of lattice graphs [33], could be practically used for further testing and winnowing to a TN_{Bno} of $LCNS_{Bno}$ (a sub-area of $LCNS_{Bn}$), as graph-related computations can be computationally less prohibitive as contrasted to algebraic computations and is well suited to the task at hand [45]. While certain methods, such as greedy approximation algorithms, which have been proposed by Summers et al. [32] and others, as well as low-rank approximation algorithms, which have been proposed by Benner et al. and others, are of mathematical interest, as noted by Klickstein et al., they do not necessarily provide the requisite discernment into the connections among the optimal distribution of input CS (i.e., CS_{OPT}) and the topological properties of the involved LCNS [33]; this discernment is necessary, as it is an important aspect of the assessment process [34]. Ultimately, it provides validation that, by way of example, $LCNS_{Bno}$ has been "properly selected" [6], that $CSEC_{Bno}$ is reasonable, and that TN_{Bno} makes practical sense.

C. *Hybridized Processing*

For the involved experimentation, the full node set of $LCNS_{ABC}$ had been heuristically reduced to $LCNS_{Bno}$, its corresponding $CSEC_{Bno}$, and its corresponding TN_{Bno}. Li et al. had previously proposed PGM to iteratively search for the energy optimal placement of CS [2] (i.e., for an optimized CSEC or $CSEC_{OPT}$). Ding et al. proposed a Revisited Projected Gradient Method Extension (R-PGME) for even better performance [4]. Numerous other works have also contributed to deriving $CSEC_{OPT}$. However, generally speaking, the notion of complete control is typically considered, wherein the CS steer the full node set towards the predefined goal state vector. Klickstein et al. have noted that a smaller TN set, such as TN_{Bno}, might be all that is needed [4][33] to effectuate the cascading effect of $LCNS_{Bno}$, $LCNS_{Bn}$, $LCNS_B$, and $LCNS_{ABC}$ converging to the desired "final state in the prespecified time within a predefined precision" [7], thereby providing a physically controllable case. A TN_{Bnp} accelerant might also serve to assist TN_{Bno} (i.e., TN_{Bno}-TN_{Bnp} Amalgam) in effectuating this paradigm, which is depicted in Fig. 4 below. Ideally, the TN_{Bno}-TN_{Bnp} Amalgam still remains optimally small (i.e., TN_{OPT}). In this case, the involved Gramian matrix is well-behaved (i.e., the condition number or sensitivity of the least squares polynomial approximation and the CSEC are not unrealistically large), which is the desired state [7]. This is contrasted to the case of when the Gramian matrix is ill-conditioned (i.e., the condition number and CSEC are unrealistically large), wherein, the LCNS is unable to reach the "final state in the prespecified time within a predefined precision" [7]. Hence, a suitable approach to addressing the Gramian matrix is critical; after all, some approaches, as noted by Lindmark et al., can only be "computed in closed form … when the time of the transfer tends to infinity" [8] (i.e., actual control will likely never devolve).

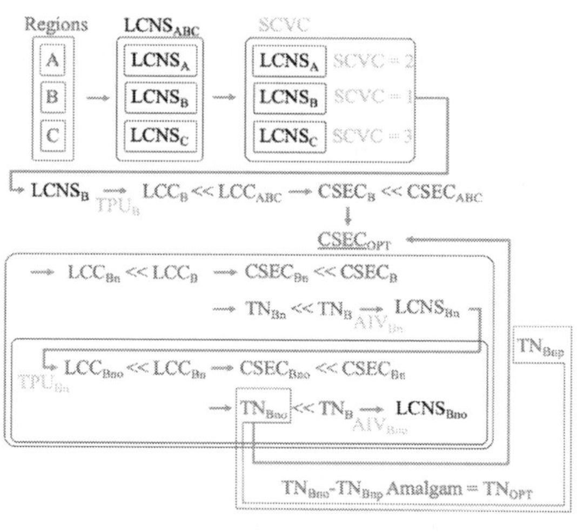

Figure 4. TN_{Bno}, $CSEC_{OPT}$, and the Cascading Effect for Convergence to the Desired Final State, while the Amalgam of TN_{Bno} and TN_{Bnp} (TN_{OPT}) Still Remains Small

Arriving at a well-behaved controllability Gramian matrix when using $CSEC_{OPT}$ illuminates the value of TN_{Bnp}, as an augmentation and accelerant to TN_{Bno}, to enhance the likelihood of actual controllability. This TN_{Bno}-TN_{Bnp} Amalgam may have an even higher likelihood of actual controllability (i.e., robust controllability) and accurate controllability, particularly in the case of dense and homogeneous networks [35] (as contrasted to sparse and heterogeneous networks) with clustered sub-networks [48]. Moreover, temporal networks seem to be more controllable than their static counterparts, such as when considering link temporality for network controllability; Zhang et al. have noted that link temporality, such as by weight variation, can be equated to "attaching a virtual driver node to that link"

[43]. Hence, the TN computational approach can also be used for specific optimal Target Links (TL_{OPT}). The TN_{Bno}-TN_{Bnp} Amalgam (a.k.a., TN_{OPT}) can be revised to include TL_{OPT} for a more accurate amalgam descriptor: TN_{Bno}-TN_{Bnp}-TL_{OPT} or TN_{OPT}- TL_{OPT} Amalgam. The TN_{Bno}-TN_{Bnp}-TL_{OPT} Amalgam need not necessarily effectuate an overarching controlling or cascading effect on $LCNS_B$ and/or $LCNS_{ABC}$; if TN_{Bno} can impact a peer TN (e.g., TN_{Bnn}, TN_{Bnm}, TN_{Bnl}, etc.) or other (e.g., TN_{Bn}, TN_{Bm}, TN_{Bl}, etc.) (i.e., one set of control/driver nodes influencing yet another set of control/driver nodes) so as to steer $LCNS_{Bn}$ and/or other pertinent peer LCNS and/or higher-order LCNS to a target state, then the desired state might be achieved.

As noted by Roy et al., central to this task seems to be the principal submatrices of the controllability Gramian [37]. In particular, these Gramian submatrices well inform various metrics and optimal inputs. The LCNS diffusiveness (a.k.a., permeability) for CS and/or augmented CS (collectively, CS_{opt}) can be calculated in a variety of ways [38]; in turn, the permeability can be emblematic of the readiness of the LCNS to be controllable. For the specific cases studied, when the LCNS is uncontrollable, the inverse Gramian does not exist and CSEC approaches infinity [39]; conversely, when the LCNS is controllable, the inverse Gramian does exist. On the basis that a corresponding vanishing moment recovery matrix is a suitable approximation to the inverse Gramian and "guarantees n vanishing moments of the irregular framelets" [40], the ERCR framework endeavors to capitalize upon its efficacy for handling wavelet tight frames with n vanishing moments; as the number of vanishing moments increases, the polynomial degree of the wavelet increases and the involved underlying graph becomes smoother. The potential advantage of this is that, theoretically, wavelet tight frames can be derived from any multiresolution analysis [47].

Architecturally, to facilitate the requisite discernment into the LCNS diffusiveness, autodiff libraries (e.g., a C++ library that facilitate automatic differentiation of mathematical functions) are utilized by the ERCR framework to enable large-scale tuning of the myriad of parameters utilized, and the specialized workflow is comprised of the following: (1) iterative convolutions with ever smaller filters (wherein the filter depth is smaller than the input layer depth, such that kernel size is less than the channel size), (2) pointwise nonlinearities (which are relationships that are already equivariant to permutations of the input/output indices), and (3) constrained subsampling operations, such that, collectively, the resultant paradigm nicely bears semblance/emulates the wavelets [41]. Overall, the enhanced numerical stability paradigm utilized by the ERCR framework, which is based upon [25], shows promise in contending with select round-off errors, thereby facilitating the transformation of certain uncontrollable cases into controllable cases. For those paradigms, wherein the BTW cascading effect is a potentiality, this facilitation may constitute a deciding factor.

For the experiments described herein, two different ERCR paradigms with different versions of components at the MSY3I level (i.e., ERCR Component #1: MSY3I-1 and ERCR Component #2: MSY3I-2) were augmented with a TensorFlow-based DCGAN implementation. MSY3I-1 was utilized for solving the controllability-related convex optimization problems. As such, it required a high degree of numerical stability; accordingly, PyTorch v0.4.1 was utilized. MSY3I-2 was utilized for solving ERCR-related optimization problems. PyTorch v1.7.0 was utilized, which allowed MSY3I #2 to focus on its intrinsic stability training, so as to mitigate against numerical instability issues from PyTorch v1.7.0 (as contrasted to v0.4.1). A "forward stable" TensorFlow-based DCGAN implementation (i.e., ERCR Component #3: DCGAN) was utilized via an additional generator (hence, a mixture of generators) to assist in mitigating mode failure (a.k.a., mode collapse), which can occur when two competing neural networks that are being trained concurrently fail to converge or have an unusual convergence [25]. In addition, to validate the results for reasonableness, Advanpix was utilized for its multi-precision computation of the eigen-decomposition of the controllability Gramian (W_p), the invertible matrix (U_p), and the matrix M_p, where $M_p = U_p^{-1} W_p U_p^{-1}$ is the p x p symmetric, real, semi-positive definite matrix and has the same set of eigenvectors as W_p (W_p also has the same set of eigenvectors as U_p) [44]. As the Gramian is approximately proportional to the covariance matrix, sample covariance matrix computations were performed for Quality Assurance/Quality Control (QA/QC).

V. FURTHER HEURISTICAL PROCESSING FOR LCNS PARTIONING AND POTENTIAL TN_{BNO} EXPANSION

The process involved in the derivation of TN_{Bno}, $CSEC_{OPT}$, etc. is invaluable for it gives insight into the notion of network partitioning (i.e., LCNS partitioning) and the potential significance of various involved clusters. Of note, Pasqualetti et al. had proposed a decoupled control strategy that was scalable and amenable to a distributed implementation; central to the strategy was LCNS partitioning into strongly connected components [46]. Restated, interconnection matrices needed to be computed for the various involved clusters. Also of note, works in the area of control theory typically focus on simultaneous control of the clusters. Yet, certain prescient works in the area of SCV have noted the potential potency related to sequential control of the clusters. For example, Zhu et al. have noted that "the sequential attack is demonstrated to be statistically stronger than the simultaneous attack" [45]; along this vein, sequential control is likely to have more efficacy than simultaneous control of the clusters. A final point to note, Liu et al. have noted that "dense and homogeneous networks can be controlled using a few driver nodes" [35], and this sets the stage for the clustered sub-network and TL virtual driver experimentation for a decoupled and sequenced control strategy on a dense and homogeneous temporal LCNS described herein.

Particular attention was paid to those clusters, whose associated CSEC were abnormally low. These might constitute areas of SCV, which might warrant further examination. When honing in on these areas, it might be prudent to review the relative criticality of vulnerability of the prospective control nodes via the Analytical Hierarchy Process (AHP). In particular, Sharma, et al. noted that the following factors might be non-trivial: (1) type of supply chain relationship (e.g., transactional, collaborative), (2) transparency with regards to supply chain-related information (e.g., ambiguity, uncertainty), (3) degree of control over alerting systems [6]. Amaeshi et al. had noted "boundaryless responsibility" and the potential liability associated with the actions of the suppliers' suppliers, and Liao et al. [41] had noted that "firms are building stronger relationships with their supply chain suppliers in order to gain flexibility, efficiency," etc.; the combination of these notions may have enticed larger organizations to migrate from transactional to more collaborative relationships. In some cases, collaborative relationships have led to more ambiguity, and Luthra, et al. have noted that "data vagueness and inaccuracy" … "may affect the results of AHP" [35]. Limited Vulnerability Design (LVD) efforts may also be affected by a skewed AHP.

Accordingly, in the treatment of abnormally low values related to CSEC, the principal submatrices of the Gramian and their inverses were treated. This informed the involved TC metrics and CS_{OPT}, which in turn informed the derivation of CA_{OPT} and the upstream CM. Hence, the overall notional sequence of involved transformations (not necessarily in this computational order), among others, is shown in Fig. 5 below.

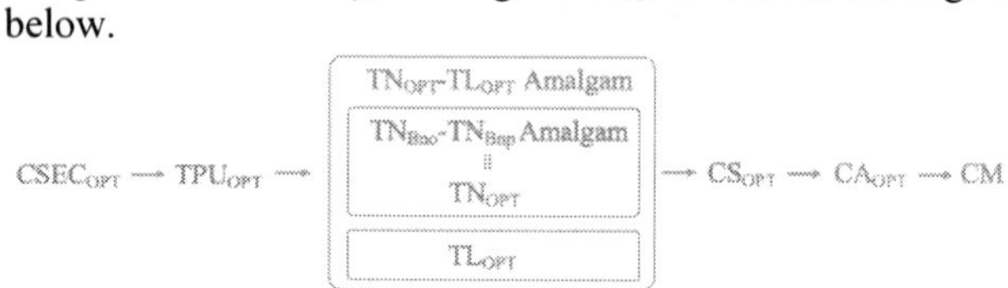

Figure. 5. Notional Sequence of Involved Transformations (Not Necessarily in this Computational Order)

Overall, this paradigm contributes towards informing both the actual as well as the accuracy of controllability.

VI. CONCLUSION

Optimal controllability of certain LCNS involves solving a succession of convex optimization problems. Since further nonconvex problems may be spawned amidst the solving of these convex optimization problems, an ERCR framework is leveraged. The utilized ERCR's bespoke numerical stability paradigm was useful in the facilitation of certain uncontrollable cases into controllable cases, and it was also able to facilitate discerning the involved LCNS's permeability so as to yield the apropos accelerant amalgam for use in the determination of $CSEC_{OPT}$, TPU_{OPT}, TN_{OPT}, TL_{OPT}, among others. Accordingly, in the treatment of abnormally low values related to CSEC, the principal submatrices of the Gramian and their inverses were treated. This helped to inform the involved TC metrics and CS_{OPT}, which in turn informed the derivation of CA_{OPT} and the upstream CM. The involved sequence of transformations contributed to enhancing the actual and accuracy of controllability (i.e., optimal controllability) of the LCNS involved in the preliminary experimentation described in this paper. Also of interest, it turns out that the involved interconnection matrices can well inform a potential TN_{Bno} expansion [46], as the clusters discerned from the LCNS portioning need to be assessed by their efficacy, as sequencing changes; conversely, the involved TN_{Bno} might also be winnowed as each cluster is assessed. Future work will involve more quantitative experimentation in this area.

ACKNOWLEDGMENT

This research is supported by the Decision Engineering Analysis Laboratory (DEAL), an Underwatch initiative of VTIRL, VT. This is part of an ongoing VTIRL technical series, on behalf of the Quality Assurance/Quality Control (QA/QC) unit, to advance the involved TRLs.

REFERENCES

[1] I. Klickstein and F. Sorrentino, "Selecting Energy Efficient Inputs using Graph Structure," International Journal of Control, vol. 8, pp. 36009-36028, 2022, doi: 10.1080/00207179.2021.2022218

[2] G. Li, et al., "Minimum-cost Control of Complex Networks," New Journal of Physics, vol. 18, 2016, pp. 1-12, doi: 10.1088/1367-2630/18/1/013012.

[3] Y. Liu and A. Barabasi, "Control Principles of Complex Systems," Reviews of Modern Physics, vol. 88, 2016, pp. 1-55, doi: 10.1103/RevModPhys.88.035006

[4] J. Ding, C. Wen, G. Li, and Z. Chen, "Key Nodes Selection in Controlling Complex Networks," IEEE Transactions on Cybernetics, vol. 51, pp. 52-63, 2021, doi: 10.1109/TCYB.2018.2888953.

[5] Z. Yuan, et al., "Exact Controllability of Complex Networks," Nature Communications, vol. 4, 2013, doi: https://doi.org/10.1038/ncomms3447

[6] Z. Commault, J. Woude, and T. Boukhobza, "Exact Controllability of Complex Networks," Systems & Control Letters, vol. 102, pp. 42-47, 2017, doi: https://doi.org/10.1016/j.sysconle.2017.01.002

[7] L. Wang, Y. Chen, W. Wang, and Y. Lai, "Physical Controllability of Complex Networks," Scientific Reports, vol. 7, 2017, pp. 1-14, doi: https://doi.org/10.1038/srep40198

[8] G. Lindmark and C. Altafini, "Minimum Energy Control for Complex Networks," Scientific Reports, pp. 1-4, 2018, doi: https://doi.org/10.1038/s41598-018-21398-7

[9] H. Chen and E. Yong, "Optimizing Target Nodes Selection for the Control Energy of Directed Complex Networks." Scientific Reports, vol. 10, 2020, doi: https://doi.org/10.1038/s41598-020-75101-w

[10] I. Klickstein, A. Shirin, and F. Sorrentino, "Locally Optimal Control of Complex Networks," Physical Review Letters, vol. 119, 2017, doi: https://doi.org/10.1103/PhysRevLett.119.268301

[11] A. Cimatti, A. Micheli, and M. Roveri. "Solving Strong Controllability of Temporal Problems with Uncertainty using SMT," Constraints, vol. 20, pp. 1-29, 2015, doi: https://doi.org/10.1007/s10601-014-9167-5

[12] N. Cowan, E. Chastain, D. Vilhena, J. Freudenberg, and C. Bergstrom, "Nodal Dynamics, Not Degree Distributions, Deter Structural Controllability of Complex Networks," PLOS One, 2012, doi: https://doi.org/10.1371/journal.pone.0038398

[13] Z. Yuan, C. Zhao, Z. Di, W. Wang, and Y. Lai, "Exact Controllability of Complex Networks," Nature Communications, 2013, doi: 10.1038/ncomms3447

[14] S. Li, Y. Chen, X. Wu, X. Cheng, and Z. Tian, "Power Grid-Oriented Cascading Failure Vulnerability Identifying Method Based on Wireless Sensors," Recent Advances in Security and Privacy for Wireless Sensor Networks vol. 2021, 2020, doi: https://doi.org/10.1155/2021/8820413

[15] P. Cui, P. Zhu, P. Xun, and C. Shao "Power Grid Cascading Failure Blackouts Analysis," AIP Conference Proceedings, 2019, doi: https://doi.org/10.1063/1.5089088

[16] Y. Zhu, J. Yan, Y. Tang, Y. Sun, and H. He, "The Sequential Attack against Power Grid Networks," 2014 IEEE International Conference on Communications (ICC), pp. 616-621, 2014, doi: 10.1109/ICC.2014.6883387.

[17] G. Pagani and M. Aiello, "The Power Grid as a Complex Network: A Survey," Physica A: Statistical Mechanics and its Applications, vol. 392, pp. 2688-2700, 2013, doi: https://doi.org/10.1016/j.physa.2013.01.023

[18] P. Cui, P. Zhu, P. Xun, and C. Shao, "Robustness of Cyber-Physical Systems against Simultaneous, Sequential, and Composite Attack," Electronics, vol. 7, pp. 196, 2018, https://doi.org/10.3390/electronics7090196

[19] A. Jadbabaie, A. Olshevsky and M. Siami, "Limitations and Tradeoffs in Minimum Input Selection Problems," 2018 Annual American Control Conference (ACC), pp. 185-190, 2018, doi: 10.23919/ACC.2018.8431306.

[20] S. Pequito, S. Kar, and A. Aguiar, "On the Complexity of the Constrained Input Selection Problem for Structural Linear Systems," Automatica (Journal of IFAC), vol. 62, 2015, pp. 193-199, doi: https://doi.org/10.1016/j.automatica.2015.06.022

[21] S. Moothedath, P. Chaporkar, and M. Belur, "Approximating Constrained Minimum Input Selection for State Space Structural Controllability," 2017, doi: https://doi.org/10.48550/arXiv.1712.01232

[22] S. Moothedath, P. Chaporkar and M. N. Belur, "A Flow-Network-Based Polynomial-Time Approximation Algorithm for the Minimum Constrained Input Structural Controllability Problem," IEEE Transactions on Automatic Control, vol. 63, pp. 3151-3158, 2018, doi: 10.1109/TAC.2018.2797210.

[23] J. Cruz and W. Oliveira, "On Weak and Strong Convergence of the Projected Gradient Method for Convex Optimization in real Hilbert Spaces," Numerical Functional Analysis and Optimization, vol 37, pp. 129-144, 2015, doi: https://doi.org/10.48550/arXiv.1402.5884

[24] Z. Liu, et al., "Minimal Input Selection for Robust Control," IEEE 56th Annual Conference on Decision and Control (CDC), pp. 2659-2966, 2017, doi: https://doi.org/10.1109/CDC.2017.8264090

[25] S. Chan, M. Krunz, and B. Griffin, "AI-based Robust Convex Relaxations for Supporting Diverse QoS in Next-Generation Wireless Systems," Proc. of the IEEE ICDCS Workshop - Next-Generation Mobile Networking and Computing (NGMobile 2021), pp. 1-8, 2021, doi: doi: 10.1109/ICDCSW53096.2021.00014

[26] P. Stodola and J. Mazal, "Architecture of the Advanced Command and Control System," 2017 International Conference on Military Technologies (ICMT), pp. 340-343, 2017, doi: 10.1109/MILTECHS.2017.7988781.

[27] L. Dodd and J. Q. Smith, "Devolving Command Decisions in Complex Operations," Journal of the Operational Research Society, 2013, doi: https://doi.org/10.1057/jors.2012.7

[28] S. Chan, "Prototype Resilient Command and Control (C2) of C2 Architecture for Power Outage Mitigation," 2019 IEEE 10th Annual Information Technology, Electronics and Mobile Communication Conference (IEMCON), pp. 0779-0785, 2019, doi: 10.1109/IEMCON.2019.8936241.

[29] Y. Chen, L. WAng, W. Wang, and Y. Lai, "Energy Scaling and Reduction in Controlling Complex Networks," Royal Society Open Science, 2016, doi: https://doi.org/10.1098/rsos.160064

[30] S. Chan, "Mitigation Factors for Multi-domain Resilient Networked Distributed Tessellation Communications," The Fifth International Conference on Cyber-Technologies and Cyber-Systems, p. 66-73, 2020, [Online]. Available from: doi: https://ssrn.com/abstract=3789770

[31] P. Benner and J. Saak, "Numerical Solution of Large and Sparse Continuous Time Algebraic Matrix Riccati and Lyapunov Equations: A State of the Art Survey," 2013, doi: https://doi.org/10.1002/gamm.201310003

[32] T. Summers and M. Kamgarpous, "Performance Guarantees for Greedy Maximization of Non-Submodular Controllability Metrics," 18th European Control Conference (ECC), pp. 2796-2801, 2019, doi: 10.23919/ECC.2019.8795800.

[33] I. Klickstein and F. Sorrentino, "The Controllability Gramian of Lattice Graphs," Automatica, vol 114, 2020, doi: https://doi.org/10.1016/j.automatica.2020.108833

[34] A. Hahn, M. Govindarasu, and C. Liu, "Vulnerability Assessment for Substation Automation Systems," Security and Privacy in Smart Grids, 2013, CRC Press, ISBN: 9780429110207

[35] Y. Liu, J. Slotine, and A. Barabasi, "Controllability of Complex Networks," Nature, vol. 473, 2011, doi:?10.1038/nature10011

[36] N. Kalinin, A. Guman-Saenz, Y. Prieto, and E. Lupercio, "Self-Organized Criticality and Pattern Emergence through the Lens of Tropical Geometry," vol. 115, 2018, doi: https://doi.org/10.1073/pnas.1805847115

[37] S. Roy and M. Xue, "Controllability-Gramian Submatrics for a Network Consensus Model," IEEE 58th Conference on Decision and Control (CDC), pp. 6080-6085, 2019, doi: 10.1109/CDC40024.2019.9030069

[38] F. Ludice, F. Garofalo, and F. Sorrentino, "Structural Permeability of Complex Networks to Control Signals," Nature Communications, vol. 6, 2015, doi: https://doi.org/10.1038/ncomms9349

[39] F. Cortesi, T. Summers, and J. Lygeros, "Submodularity of Energy Related Controllability Metrics," 53rd IEEE Conference on Decision and Control, pp. 2883-2888, 2014, doi: 10.1109/CDC.2014.7039832

[40] A. Viscardi, "Semi-regular Dubuc-Deslauriers wavelet tight frames," Journal of Computational and Applied Mathematics, 2018, doi: 10.1016/j.cam.2018.07.049

[41] S. Chan, M. Krunz and B. Griffin, "Adaptive Time-Frequency Synthesis for Waveform Discernment in Wireless Communications," 2021 IEEE 12th Annual Information Technology, Electronics and Mobile Communication Conference (IEMCON), pp. 0988-0996, 2021, doi: 10.1109/IEMCON53756.2021.9623140.

[42] R. Ehlers, "Formal verification of piece-wise linear feed-forward neural networks," Lecture Notes in Computer Science, vol 10482, Sep 2017, pp. 269–286, doi: 10.1007/978-3-319-68167-2_19.

[43] X. Zhang, J. Sun, and G. Yan, "Why Temporal Networks are more Controllable: Link Weight Variations offers Superiority," Physical Review, vol. 3, 2021, doi: 10.1103/PhysRevResearch.3.L032045.

[44] A. Shirin, I. Klickstein, and F. Sorrentino, "Optimal Control of Complex Networks: Balancing Accuracy and Energy of the Control Action," Chaos, vol. 27, Apr. 2017, doi: https://doi.org/10.1063/1.4979647

[45] Y. Zhu, J. Yan, Y. Tang, Y. Sun, and H. He, "The Sequential Attack Against Power Grid Networks," 2014 IEEE International Conference on Communications (ICC), pp. 616-621, 2014, doi: 10.1109/ICC.2014.6883387.

[46] F. Pasqualetti, S. Zampieri, and F. Bullo, "Controllability Metrics, Limitations and Algorithms for Complex Networks," 2014 American Control Conference, pp. 3287-3292, 2014, doi: 10.1109/ACC.2014.6858621.

[47] K. Grochenig and A. Rong, "Tight Compactly Supported Wavelet Frames of Arbitrarily High Smoothness," Proceedings of the American Mathematical Society, vol. 126, pp. 1101-1107, 1998.

[48] L. Zhou, C. Wang, and L. Zhou, "Cluster Synchronization on Multiple Sub-networks of Complex Networks with Nonidentical Nodes via Pinning Control," Nonlinear Dynamics, vol. 83, pp. 1079–1100, Sep. 2015, doi: https://doi.org/10.1007/s11071-015-2389-2.

[49] X. Zhu, Z. Cai, J. Wu, Y. Cheng, and Q. Huang, "Convolutional Neural Network Based Combustion Mode Classification for Condition Monitoring in the Supersonic Combustor," Acta Astronautica, vol. 159, pp. 349-357, 2019, doi: https://doi.org/10.1016/j.actaastro.2019.03.072

[50] W. Huang, J. Cheng, Y. Yang, and G. Guo, "An Improved Deep Convolutional Neural Network with Multi-Scale Information for Bearing Fault Diagnosis," Neurocomputing, vol. 359, pp. 77-92, Sep. 2019, doi: https://doi.org/10.1016/j.neucom.2019.05.052.

[51] A. Radford, L. Metz, and S. Chintala, "Unsupervised Representation Learning with Deep Convolutional Generative Adversarial Networks," 2015, [Online]. Available from: https://arxiv.org/abs/1511.06434

[52] T. Ohtsuka, T. Ikeda, K. Kashima, "Matrix Pontryagin Principle Approach to Controllability Metrics Maximization Under Sparsity Constraints," 2022, [Online]. Available from: https://arxiv.org/abs/2203.12828

Secure Publication Subscription Framework for Reliable Information Dissemination

Shugo Yoshimura
Graduate School of Information Sci. and Electrical Eng., Kyushu Univ.
Fukuoka, Japan
yoshimura.shugo.822@s.kyushu-u.ac.jp

Kouki Inoue
Graduate School of Information Sci. and Electrical Eng., Kyushu Univ.
Fukuoka, Japan
inoue.kouki.882@s.kyushu-u.ac.jp

Dirceu Cavendish
Graduate School of Eng. Kyushu Institute of Tech.
Iizuka, Japan
Dirceu_cavendish@yahoo.com

Hiroshi Koide
Research Institute of Info. Tech., Kyushu Univ.
Fukuoka, Japan
koide@cc.kyushu-u.ac.jp

***Abstract*—In this study, to make it easy for everyone to distinguish the right information from the wrong information, we suggest a new framework (Secure Publication Subscription Framework) that defines the reliability of publishers and provides it to subscribers. Nowadays, services like blogs and social media make available large amounts of information easily. On the other hand, there is a lot of unreliable information on the Internet. It is difficult to distinguish between true and false information. This problem is known as fake news and has become a serious problem. To solve this problem, we suggest a new framework for publishers and subscribers. The framework allows subscribers to easily confirm the authenticity of information by registering publishers and subscribers, and tracking publishers' reputation via a reputation score, guaranteeing the quality of the information that subscribers view. In this study, we show a proof of concept of a simple Secure Publication Subscription Framework and confirm that it is possible to implement a framework with the proposed functionality. We also confirm that the reputation score can be used as an indicator of the reliability of the information by using 1000 randomly generated articles within the framework.**

Keywords-dissemination; publication; social networking; authenticity of information; reputation score.

I. INTRODUCTION

In recent years, Internet technologies have made great progress, with the population of Internet users increasing rapidly. Thanks to services like blogs and social media, anyone can get a large amount of information easily. Nowadays, we can see what is happening around the world, no matter where we are.

On the other hand, there is a lot of unreliable information on the Internet. It is difficult to distinguish between true and false information. This problem is known as fake news and has become a serious problem. Fake news is fabricated information that mimics news media content in form but not in organizational process or intent [1]. It is not just a prank, but a serious problem. As an example, during the 2016 United Status presidential election, fake news was highly used and had a big impact on Twitter [2] [3].

To solve this problem, we suggest a new framework for publishers and subscribers. This framework allows subscribers to easily confirm the authenticity of information by registering publishers and subscribers, guaranteeing the publisher of the information that subscribers view, checking the information challenge from subscribers, and providing the publisher's reputation score that increases or decreases as a result of the authenticity of the information.

This framework consists of three parts, Publisher, Subscriber and Arbitrator. The main role of the Publisher is publishing articles or news. The Subscriber registers with the Publisher and subscribes for publications. The Arbitrator provides the Publisher's reputation and verifies the information challenge from the Subscriber.

The paper is organized as follows. Related work is included in Section II. Section III describes our proposed secure publication/subscription reference model. Section IV describes a proof of concept implementation of the reference model. Section V describes two experiments used to track the performance of the proposed publication/subscription model. Section VI presents the performance results and discussions. Section VII summarizes our studies and addresses directions we are pursuing as follow up to this work.

II. RELATED WORK

Previous research on publication/subscription systems have covered various areas, such as security, confidentiality and scalability.

Nakamura and Enokido [4] focused on a peer to peer publication/subscription model where multiple topics are supported. In that work, they propose a subscription initialization protocol to ensure that peers not authorized to have access to topics do not have access to them. They do not address the quality of the information exchanged within topics. In contrast, our framework addresses information quality on a

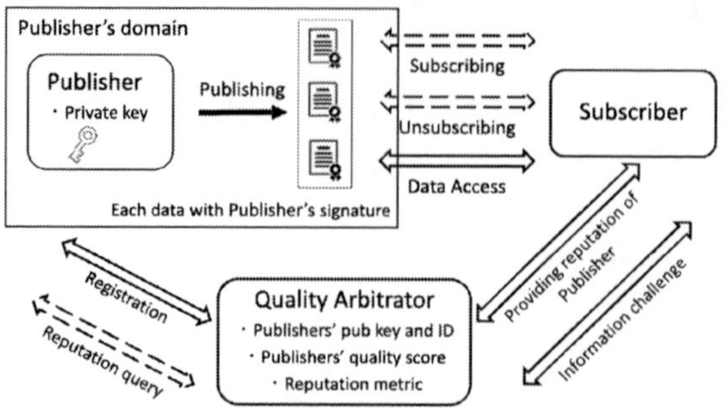

Figure 1. Secure Publication/Subscriber Architecture

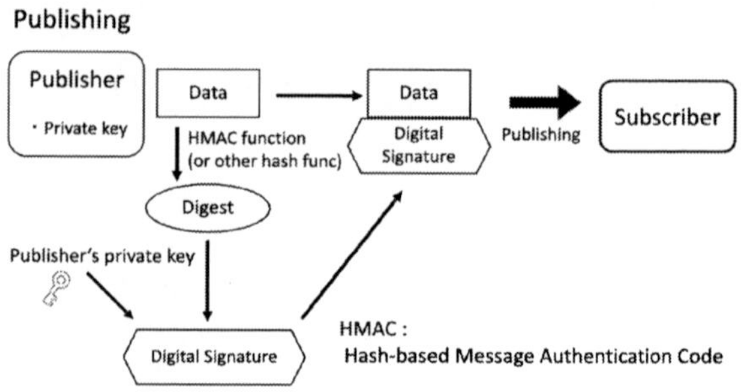

Figure 2. Signed publishing

generic publication/subscription architecture, not necessarily requiring a peer to peer model.

Salem [5] addresses the problem of authenticating users of a pub/sub system containing a message broker in a privacy-preserving way. The proposal supports mutual authentication in a scalable way, and may be adopted by pub/sub systems with a broker. In contrast, our work does not focus on anonymity of publishers/subscribers, although our pub/sub model could be adapted to include a broker, if necessary.

In Srivatsa [6], a secure event dissemination protocol is proposed where encryption and authorization keys are used on top of an IP network that does not provide confidentiality nor integrity of data. In contrast, although our pub/sub model supports integrity verification of data, our focus is on the control of the quality of data published.

Bovet and Makse [3] describe an information ranking mechanism to fight unreliable (spam) data in a pub/sub system model with a broker reference architecture. They propose to rank information as a way to avoid blacklisting. However, their ranking system is still based on participants voting. Although the purpose of the research is similar to ours, our solution to control quality of disseminated data is based on an arbitrator that is supposed to be able to verify data quality on specific domains, rather than relying on voting.

III. SECURE PUBLICATION/SUBSCRIPTION

This section describes the operation of the Secure Publication Subscription Framework in detail.

Figure 1 describes our proposed secure publication/subscription system architecture. Multiple publishers provide signed data contents to consumers, or subscribers. Data content quality is tracked by an independent quality arbitrator. The quality arbitrator provides publishers' reputation to subscribers. Also, the arbitrator may receive data truthfulness challenges from subscribers.

A. Sec Pub/Sub Components

Figure 2 illustrates how Publishers provide signed data contents. Publishers also produce a digest of the data content using standard asymmetric cryptography, using their private key to ensure data integrity.

Figure 3 illustrates publisher/subscriber interfaces. The subscriber requests subscription services from a publisher and receives the publisher public key used to verify data authenticity. Once the subscription service has been agreed upon, an information retrieval interface is used to request signed data from the publisher.

Figure 4 illustrates the subscriber's data processing of published data. Data processing includes data integrity verification and confirmation authorship. The subscriber verifies the digital signature and the digest of the data, using the publisher public key. In this process, the subscriber verifies the integrity of the received data and confirms the data's authorship.

Figure 5 illustrates publisher reputation tracking feature of the secure pub/sub framework. Each publisher registers first with the quality arbitrator, upon which its public key is passed to the arbitrator. The arbitrator then tests the publisher's possession of the corresponding private key as part of the registration. Each successfully registered publisher is associated with a reputation score metric, which can be queried by both the publisher itself as well as subscribers.

Figure 6 illustrates the subscriber/quality arbitrator interfaces. Subscribers can request publisher's reputation score from the arbitrator. In addition, subscribers can challenge publisher's trustfulness for each data received. The quality arbitrator, upon receiving the challenge, verifies data truthfulness, and adjusts the publisher reputation score according with data verification status.

B. Reputation Algorithm

The reputation score of a publisher is defined as $score =$ (the number of correct data) / (the number of all published data). However, as the quality arbitrator may not estimate correctly every and all data published, we introduce a noise model for data verification, as per Figure 7. In the model, p is the probability that a true piece of data be recognized as false, whereas q represents the probability of a false piece of information be admitted as true. In the experimental section, we exemplify the arbitrator score reputation tracking on two publisher scenarios: i- trusted publisher (all data is truthful);

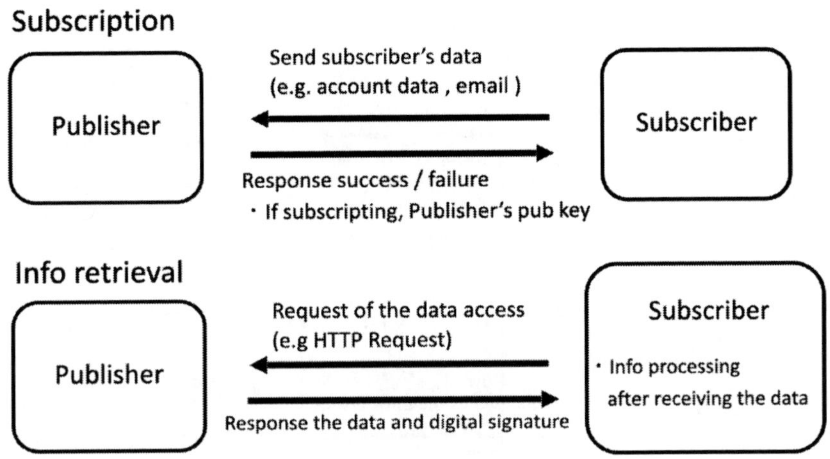

Figure 3. Subscription and Information Retrieval

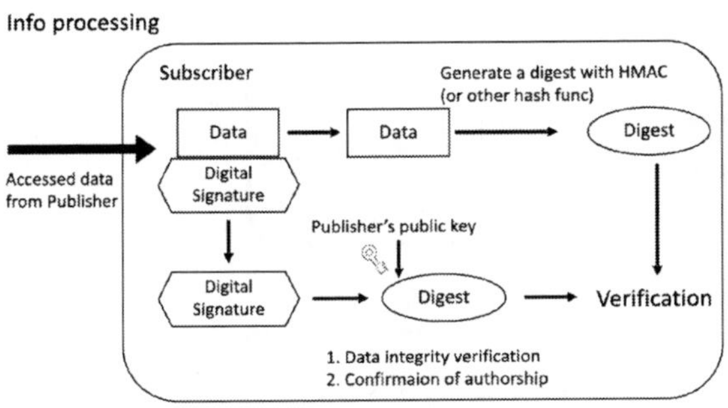

Figure 4. Data Integrity Verification

ii- untrusted publisher; Publisher produces up to 1000 data pieces (the data can be right or wrong).

IV. Implementation

In this section, we describe an overview of the implementation of Publisher, Arbitrator, Subscriber. We implemented the Publisher and the Arbitrator with Node.js and Express that is a JavaScript Web framework, and we implemented the Subscriber with Python3. The Publisher and the Arbitrator operate like a Web server, independently, and the Subscriber accesses them according to the scenarios. The versions used in the implementation are summarized in Table I.

A. Publisher

The Publisher is implemented with Node.js and Express, and it operates as a Web server. Figure 8 describes the implementation. The Publisher has subscriber registration, login, some data pages and digital signatures. In addition, it has a MySQL database that saves the Subscriber's name and hashed password. If it receives an HTTP Request from the Subscriber, it replies with an HTTP Response and sends the data.

TABLE I
Implementation

Application	Version
Node.js	12
MySQL	5.7
Python	3.9.12

B. Arbitrator

The Arbitrator is also implemented with Node.js and Express, and operates as a Web server. Figure 9 describes the implementation of the Arbitrator. The Arbitrator receives the Publisher's registration, reputation query, as well as information challenge and request for publisher's pub key. Additionally, the Arbitrator supports a MySQL database, which saves the Publisher's name, password, public key and Publisher reputation score. Firstly, the Publisher registers its name, password and public key. In our experiment scenarios, the Publisher's information is saved in initial state, so this step is omitted. If the Subscriber requests the Publisher's public key, the Arbitrator responds to it. If the Subscriber requests the Publisher's reputation score, the Arbitrator sends the Publisher's score. If the Arbitrator receives an information challenge from the Subscriber, it verifies data truthfulness, updating the score of the Publisher.

C. Subscriber

The Subscriber is implemented with Python3. It accesses the Publisher and the Arbitrator according to the different scenarios. During information processing, it verifies the integrity of received data and confirms data authorship (Figure 10).

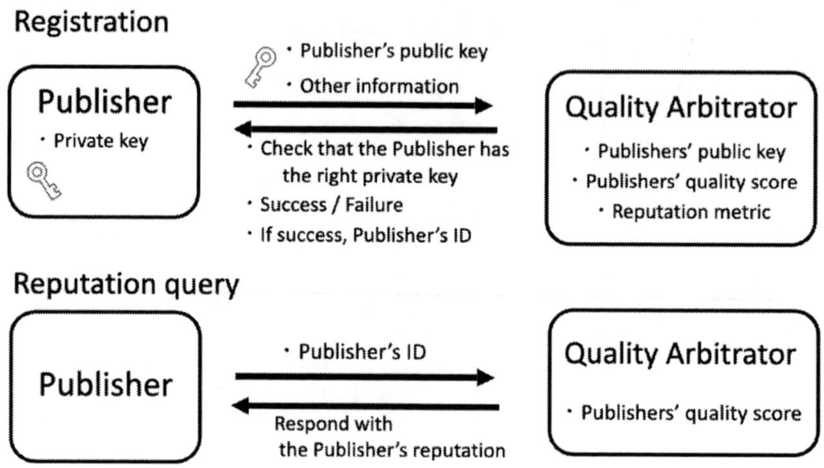

Figure 5. Publisher registration and Reputation Tracking

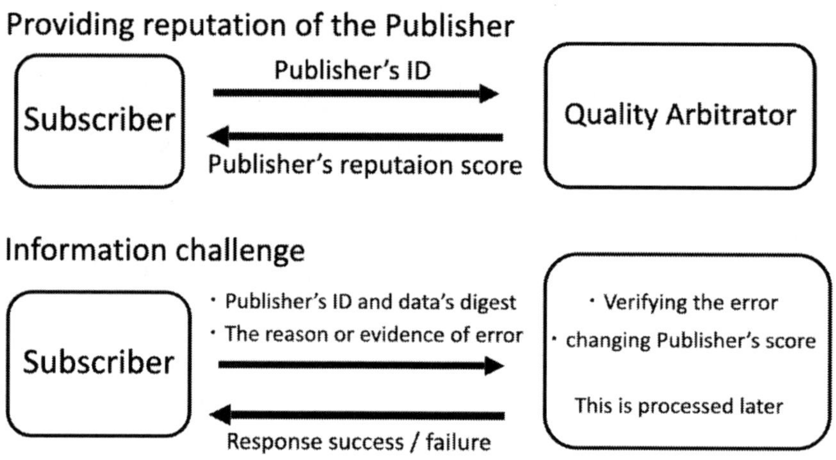

Figure 6. Reputation service interface

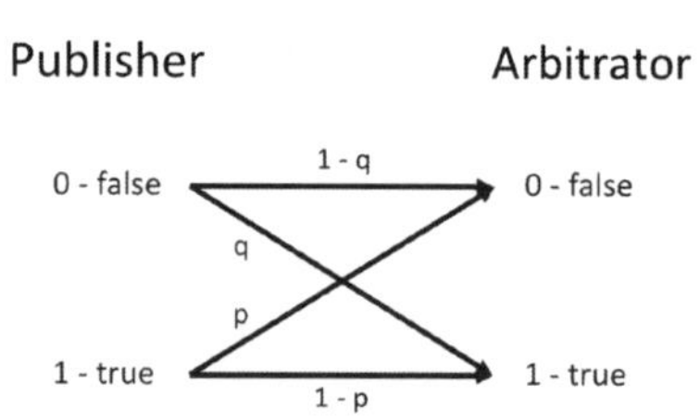

Figure 7. Noisy Channel Model

V. Experiment

This section demonstrates the evolution of the reputation estimator and reputation score for the Secure Publication Subscription Framework using 1000 randomly generated true and false data.

The resulting graph shows 3 lines:

- Actual reputation score: the reputation score actually obtained after going through the Secure Publication Subscription Framework,
- Expected reputation score : the expected value of the reputation score obtained from the actual truth of the data, p and q,
- True reputation : proportion of data that is actually true.

We exemplify the secure publication/subscription model with the following scenarios:

A. Scenario 1

1) Subscribers register and login in with the Publisher

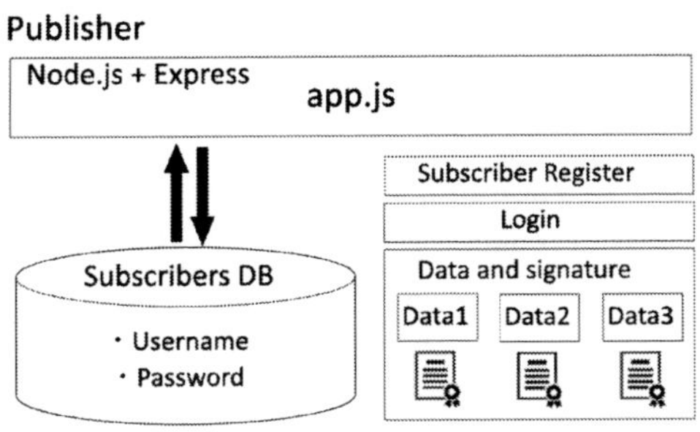

Figure 8. Publisher

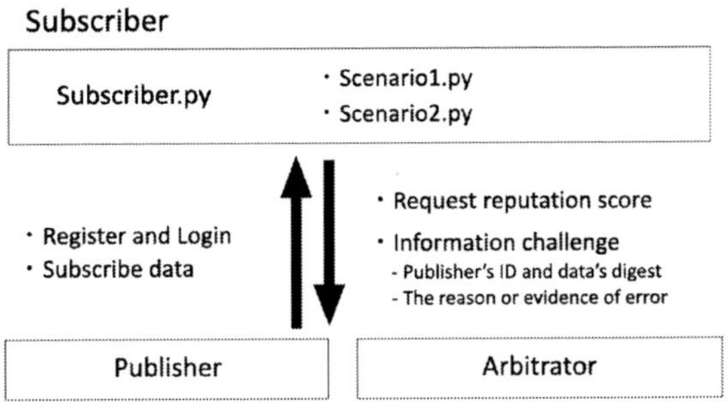

Figure 10. Subscriber

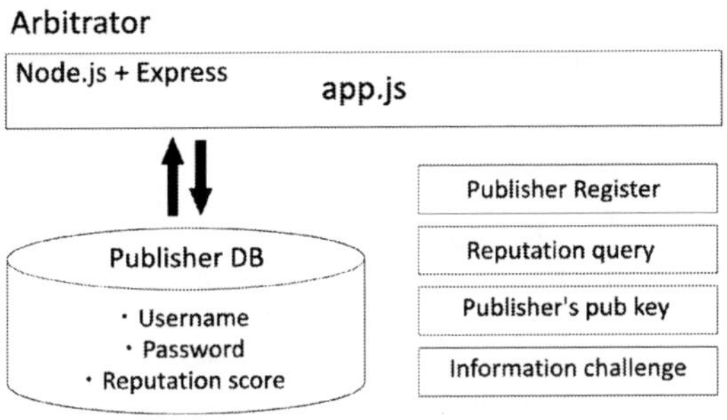

Figure 9. Arbitrator

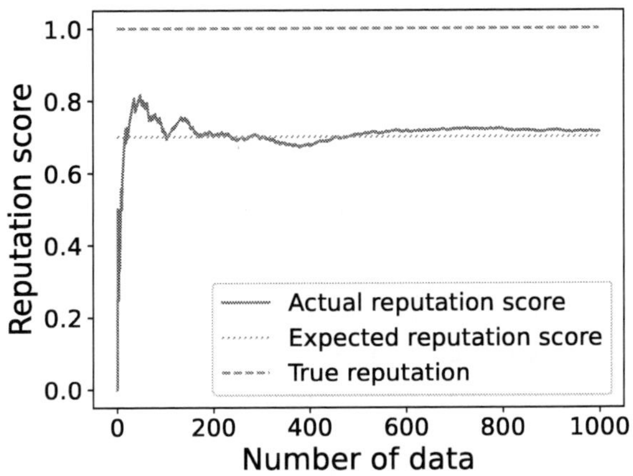

Figure 11. scenario 1

2) Subscribers subscribe to data from the Publisher
3) Subscribers retrieve the data
4) Subscribers send a query about the Publisher's reputation to the Arbitrator

In Scenario 1, the credibility of the Publisher's data is 100%, hence the Publisher's true reputation is 1. However, the expected reputation score is (1 - p) because there is a possibility that the Arbitrator will judge it to be false. In this experiment, the values of the p and q are set to 0.3 to check the reputation scores. To show that the accuracy of the reputation score does not drop even if the accuracy of the true/false discrimination is not so high, p and q were set to fairly low values. We think that there is still room for further study on this value.

Figure 11 shows the graph of the results for Scenario 1.

B. Scenario 2

In scenario 2, Publisher's data is not always true.

1) Subscribers register and login in with the Publisher
2) Subscribers subscribe to data from the Publisher
3) Subscribers retrieve the data
4) Subscribers issue an information challenge
5) The Arbitrator decides the data as false, and updates the Publisher's reputation
6) Subscribers query the reputation of the Publisher from the Arbitrator

Let a be the probability that the publisher's data is false. Then, the expected value of the true reputation is (1 - a), while the expected reputation score is $a * q + (1 - a) * (1 - p)$. In Scenario 2, step 1, 2, 3 are the same as in Scenario 1. However, the Subscriber carries out an information challenge in steps 4 and 5. The probability of judging the data to be correct was varied between 0.8 and 0.6, and p and q were 0.3 to check the reputation scores for each case.

The experimental results are shown in Figures 12 and 13.

VI. Performance Analysis

In this section, we present the reputation tracking results of our secure pub/sub system. In scenario 1, the final three scores obtained from the 1000 data points are shown in Tables II.

TABLE II
SCENARIO 1

Actual reputation score	0.713
Expected reputation score	0.700
True reputation	1.000

In scenario 2, the final three scores obtained from the 1000 data points are shown in Table III and IV.

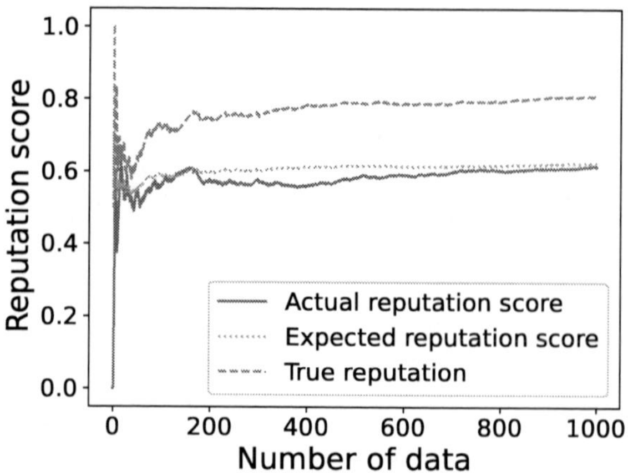

Figure 12. scenario2 data accuracy = 0.8

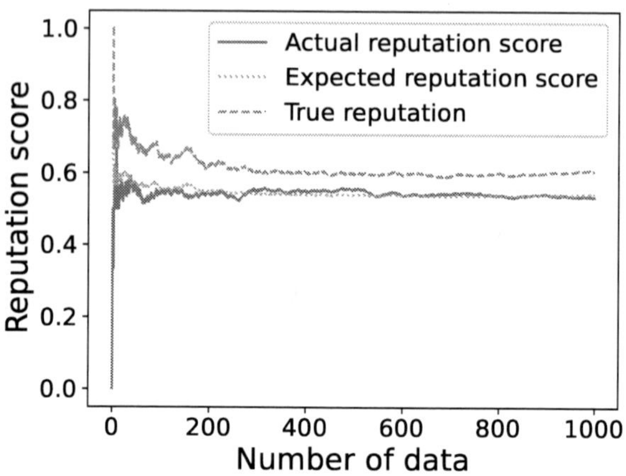

Figure 13. scenario2 data accuracy = 0.6

From these experimental results, with a sufficient number of data points and a certain degree of accuracy in determining the truth of the data, we see that the actual reputation score converges to the expected reputation score.

Moreover, we use a noise model for data verification, and we define the expected reputation to be $a * q + (1 - a) * (1 - p)$. So, if p and q are known, the Publisher's true reputation can be estimated from the actual score.

VII. Conclusion and Future work

In this study, we proposed a new framework (Secure Publication Subscription Framework) that allows subscribers to check the accuracy of information based on the authenticity of the publisher's historical data by checking the reputation score. In this framework, subscribers can check the reputation score of the publisher and challenge data reliability if the information is suspected to be unreliable. We also conducted experiments on the publisher's reputation score, and found that the actual reputation score approximates the expected

TABLE III
SCENARIO 2 DATA ACCURACY = 0.8

Actual reputation score	0.615
Expected reputation score	0.623
True reputation	0.808

TABLE IV
SCENARIO 2 DATA ACCURACY = 0.6

Actual reputation score	0.535
Expected reputation score	0.543
True reputation	0.607

value calculated from the probability of correctly judging the reliability of information.

With fake news becoming a major problem, it is important to have a system that allows subscribers to easily verify the authenticity of information. As such a system, our framework can be one of the promising options.

As future research, integration of AI(Artificial Intelligence) algorithms to automatically identify fake news with expert arbitrators is a promising path. Although the accuracy of discriminating fake news has been a challenge for AI technologies, our expert framework can aid by using AI algorithms to improve false positives/negatives. Combined with these technologies, we believe that a robust data reliability framework for publication/subscription platforms can emerge.

References

[1] D. M. J. Lazer *et al.*, "The science of fake news." *Science*, pp. 1094–1096, 2018.

[2] N. Grinberg *et al.*, "Fake news on Twitter during the 2016 US presidential election." *Science*, pp. 374–378, 2019.

[3] A. Bovet and H. A. Makse, "Influence of fake news in Twitter during the 2016 US presidential election." *Nature communications*, pp. 1–14, 2019.

[4] S. Nakamura, T. Enokido, and M. Takizawa, "Subscription Initialization (SI) Protocol to Prevent Illegal Information Flow in Peer-to-Peer Publish/Subscribe Systems," *19th International Conference on Network-Based Information Systems*, pp. 42–49, Sept. 2016.

[5] F. M. Salem, "A Secure Privacy-Preserving Mutual Authentication Scheme for Publish-Subscribe Fog Computing," *14th International Computer Engineering Conference*, pp. 213–218, Dec. 2018.

[6] M. Srivatsa and L. Liu, "Secure Event Dissemination in Publish-Subscribe Networks," *27th International Conference on Distributed Computing Systems (ICDCS '07)*, pp. 22–22, June 2007.

Recommendation Ranking Based on AHP Approach for Productivity Improvement in SME Context

Youcef Abdelsadek, Kamel Chelghoum and Imed Kacem
Université de Lorraine, LCOMS
F-57000 Metz, France
email: youcef.abdelsadek@univ-lorraine.fr, kamel.chelghoum@univ-lorraine.fr and imed.kacem@univ-lorraine.fr

***Abstract*—This work deals with a multi-criteria decision making problem that consists in providing recommendations, which can improve productivity in Small and Medium-sized Enterprises (SMEs) based on measures comparison. This problem is very interesting because it allows SMEs to benefit from the expertise of a panel of experts avoiding pitfalls and bad decisions. On one hand, SMEs must stay competitive. Therefore, it is crucial to adopt efficient productivity improvement using the best methods. On the other hand, it is often necessary to implement facilitators knowing that SMEs do not have enough resources and technological experience to implement several methods. Therefore, how to chose the most important method or measure? This work answers this question and an attempt has been made to compare and rank the well-known measures in Lean Production and Industry 4.0 by applying the Analytic Hierarchy Process (AHP). The obtained results show that the top three methods are Design of the value Stream, Continuous Improvement Processes and Material Replenishment, respectively. The on-line platform of the INTERREG Prodpilot project provides access to the proposed recommendations and the obtained ranking.**

***Index Terms*—Recommendation ranking; AHP; Productivity improvement; Lean Production; Industry 4.0; SME.**

I. Introduction

Several countries around the world try to support their companies with different economic programs to improve their industrial sector. The objective is to increase their productivity. This becomes more important nowadays with the free international trade [1] where companies have to be able to propose their products at competitive prices and with high quality. This implies that productivity must be improved to remain competitive and gain in performance.

Furthermore, on one hand, there is a quick increase in production demand with continuous markets expansion gaining lands against competitors, which force the industries, particularly the small and medium-sized enterprises [2], to use their resources to the maximum of their capacity in order to make the highest profit. On the other hand, industries can no longer afford spending time to try several methods to gain in productivity. This could lead to failure and seeing sales contracts going to the competitors, which implies loses in terms of money and branding.

Other important variables of this complex equation are the proposed products prices, which are influenced by the increase in the price of consumables and raw materials, such as fuel or semi-conductors. Industries tend to find out the most economic process in provisioning, warehousing, production and delivery to handle this variability.

For all these challenges, companies can rely on the progress that technology makes nowadays, such as Internet of Things (IoT) [3] [4], Artificial Intelligence (AI) [5] and Big Data technologies [6]. Indeed, new doors are opened and new facilities are now possible. The key words "*Smart Companies*" and "*Digitalisation*" are more and more widespread in the industrial sector [7]–[10]. Every company wants to follow the fourth industrial revolution and to integrate the industry of the future into their methodology and process. Several advantages emerge with the industry of the future, such as real-time accessibility and flexibility, data-driven analysis and self-adjusting production. Companies that want to perform better, should begin utilizing methods coming from Lean and Industry 4.0. Thanks to new technologies, companies can identify the capacity of their active resources to allocate them accurately and to better plan and forecast peak periods with production levelling [11].

It seems that there are several existing approaches for production enhancement, and it is not always easy to make a reliable strategic plan in the top management with regards to created value, flexibility and durability avoiding a bad decision. Therefore, companies have a challenge when dealing with this heterogeneous, dynamic and complex decision making. The purpose of this article is to overcome that, and it introduces a prioritized list of recommendations for productivity improvement of well-known methods in Lean and Industry 4.0 based on Analytic Hierarchy Process (AHP). A decision-maker can rely on this ranking to orient its decision by taking into account the opinion of a panel of experts in productivity. We point out that the development of the Maturity Model for measuring the advancement in Lean and Industry 4.0 of SMEs is not part of this work.

The remaining part of this paper is organized as follows. In Section II, we introduce more in detail the concept of productivity, Lean Production and Industry 4.0 used in this work. In Section III, a survey of the available measures for productivity improvement and also the description of the general framework for comparative evaluation are presented. Following that, Section IV is devoted to the comparison and the ranking of measures for productivity improvement and discussion of the obtained results. Finally, the last part of the paper includes the conclusion and offers the future perspectives.

II. Productivity, Lean Production and Industry 4.0 concepts

This section introduces more in detail the concept of productivity, Lean Production and Industry 4.0 used in this work.

A. Productivity

Productivity can be seen from different points of view, but commonly defined as the ratio between the output and the input used to product this output (see (1)), like goods or services [12] [13]. In general, productivity is an objective concept, where it measures how efficiently resources are used in the production process. For the industrial sector, productivity is expressed by the efficiency to transform inputs such as investments, raw materials, energy and labour into products. In other words, it is an overall measure of the ability of production per unit of used input. Other parameters can affect this equation like the supply chain reliability [14] and the efficiency of the delivery system or even also customers and employees satisfaction for a better quality of work life [15] [16].

$$Productivity = \frac{Outputs}{Inputs} \tag{1}$$

However, the productivity differs from production. The former is a quantitative relationship between the products and the converted inputs while the latter concerns the amount of outputs over a period of time. Furthermore, considering (1), higher productivity means either producing the same amount of products with less resources (i.e., smaller denominator) or producing with the same amount of resources more products (i.e., bigger numerator).

B. Lean Production

The Lean Production principle is to remove all unnecessary tasks from the production process, which waste resources without creating value and delaying the delivery time [17]. The base of Lean Production are continuous improvement (Kaizen) and Muda reduction (5S). It is built with two columns of Just-in-Time (JIT) [18] and autonomation (Jidoka) [19], which rely on 2 foundations production levelling (Heijunka) and standard working in order to absorb the demand fluctuations. Techniques like Single-Minute Exchange of Dies (SMED) and elimination of error causes (Poka-Yoke) are used to reach the delivery time, quality and costs objectives.

C. Industry 4.0

The fourth industrial revolution consists in integrating Data Science and Information and Communication Technology (ICT) in the process of companies digitalization [20]. Nowadays, with the technological progress, techniques and facilities can be categorized in three groups:

1) *Connectivity and data transmission*:
The Internet offers a large range of technologies to access information at any moment from any location, ensuring fluid communication between people, processes and equipment, especially IoT [21]. It is not longer necessary to invest in a large IT infrastructure to process big data thanks to Cloud and High-Performance Computing, which has contributed greatly to this information accessibility. Cybersecurity is another facet providing authentified connections in a trusted environment where the information can be transmitted without being intercepted by malicious third parties.
2) *Management and business intelligence*:
The use of software packages, like Enterprise Resource Planning (ERP), for business management has become more than a necessity. Such a generic tool is intended to manage different sections of the company including inventory, purchasing and sales for a centralized and irredundant information. Custom-made tools are more and more widespread in Intelligent Production relying on Effective Algorithms [22] and Machine Learning [23]. Those aim to provide an effortless and efficient tool to a decision-maker, which integrates its expertise in a user-centred algorithm, like in Active Learning [24], towards the optimized use of resources, pattern recognition in fault detection or accurate forecasting of product sales.
3) *Cyber-physical system*:
One can say that there is a bidirectional pipe between the real-world and the virtual world where devices can be used to enrich one world with information gathered from the other world. For instance, augmented reality with smart glasses for remote-guided maintenance [25] or improving manual production process [26]. On the other hand, sensors can be used for locating targets in indoor industrial locations [27] or in outdoor industrial locations, like GPS tracking of a fleet of trucks in order to optimize a real-time delivery system [28].

III. Measures and framework

This section presents more in details the measures that can be used in maturity assessments with the underlying enablers for productivity improvement, the general framework and the followed methodology.

A. Existing maturity models

Nowadays, almost all companies recognize what Lean Production and Industry 4.0 can bring to them in terms of progress. It has become a trend in this industrial era and every company wants to be part of it. Nevertheless, most of them cannot accurately determine their status-quo and do not really know how to adopt an appropriate transformation. In this context, a maturity model can be considered as a powerful tool to assess the degree of maturity and to define the next milestones. In this research field, there is no consensus regarding a common standard which characterizes the dimensions and the measures of the models. The objective of this article is not to make a survey of the numerous models, but a non-exhaustive list is presented in what follows.

In [29], the initial version of the Lean Enterprise Self-Assessment Tool (LEAST) is introduced. Based on a user needs identification, it is organized into three dimensions, namely Lean Transformation/Leadership, Life Cycle Processes, and Enabling Infrastructure Processes. Thereafter, other models are proposed including additional dimensions, like in [30].

Regarding Industry 4.0, Schumacher et al. propose an empirically grounded model to assess the Industry 4.0 maturity in the domain of discrete manufacturing [31]. Its main goal was to extend the dominating technology focus of the previous models by including organizational aspects. More recently, a 6Ps model for digital maturity has been introduced, which stands for Product-Services, Processes, Platform, People, Partnership, Performance [32].

Other models are assessing both Lean Production and Industry 4.0 aspects because they are intrinsically correlated. For interested readers, some surveys are given in [33]–[35].

B. Used maturity model - dimensions and measures

This article introduces a prioritized list of measures of a self-assessment tool providing recommendation for productivity improvement. This self-assessment tool is based upon Lean Production and Industry 4.0 principles with a SME scope. It is organized into five dimensions, 36 measures and 4 levels (beginners, intermediate, experienced and expert for each measure) illustrated in Figure 1. We point out that the development of the used self-assessment tool is not part of this work. For more details, we refer to the INTERREG Prodpilot project (040-4-09-104) [36].

C. Framework

In order to prioritize the measures for productivity improvement in a SME context, we adopt the Analytic Hierarchy Process (AHP) method as framework. AHP is one of the most widespread methods in Multiple Criteria Decision Making (MCDM) methods [37], offering to a decision-maker an effective tool for ranking alternatives based on quantitative comparisons. Indeed, a numerical scale reflecting qualitative superiority/inferiority can be used to solve complex decision problems with conflicting alternatives. AHP was introduced by Saaty in 70's and its major strengths are to consider several criteria simultaneously and making subjective trade-offs to arrive at a consensus [38]. To obtain this ranking, an Eigen value problem is solved using as input the pairwise comparison matrix. Thus, the first normalized Eignen vector represents weights (prioritized alternatives) while the Eigen value represents the Consistency Ratio (CR). The latter expresses the degree of cohesion through transitivity when the expert is filling in the comparison matrix. The closer this ratio is to the value 1, the more randomly the comparison matrix has been filled.

AHP can be applied in various complex decision issues, such as raking solution techniques for reactive scheduling [39], evaluating flexible manufacturing systems [40], management of construction projects [41], healthcare research [42], supplier selection [43] and choosing ERP Systems [44].

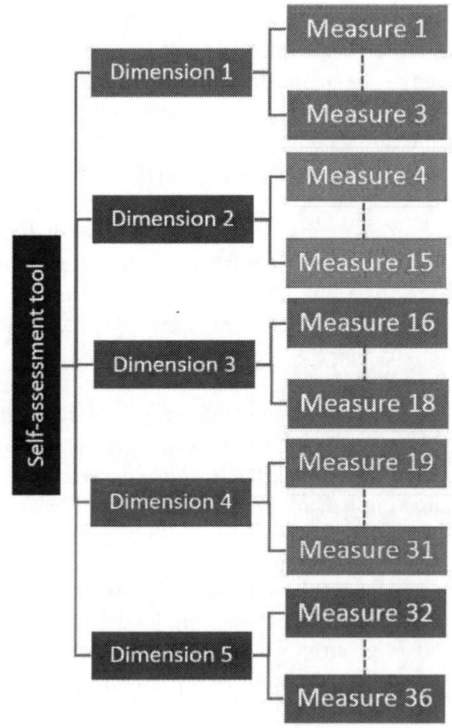

Figure 1. Self-assessment tool.

In this field, building an appropriate hierarchical structure of the addressed problem (i.e., goal, criteria and alternatives) is the cornerstone of an accurate prioritization. Figure 2 shows the different levels of the proposed AHP hierarchy to rank the productivity improvement measures. In Level 3, it is envisaged to compare 14 preselected measures (alternatives) of the aforementioned self-assessment tool. The root of the hierarchy represents the objective, which is the most effective measure for productivity improvement in the SME context. The intermediate level represents the criteria on which the experts will rely to make their judgements and rank measures for recommendation.

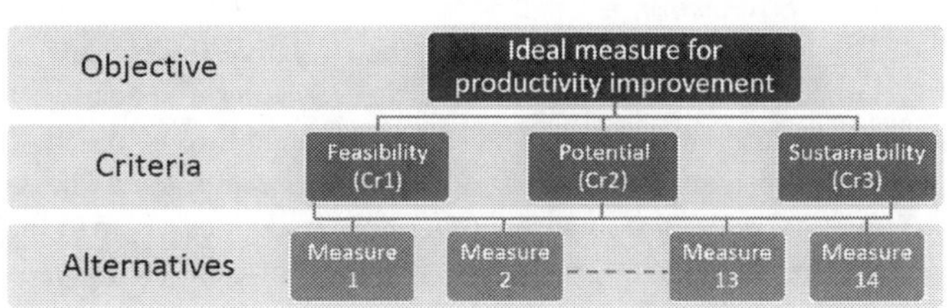

Figure 2. Defined hierarchy for AHP.

Each criterion is defined accordingly to reach the targeted objective.

1) *Feasibility (Cr1)*:

In a SME context, there are not enough resources and technological experience to implement several methods. Feasibility stands for how easily a measure can be implemented by a company. How much does the company need additional resources or experience?

2) *Potential (Cr2)*:
This criterion refers to the degree of improvement in productivity that the company reaches after implementing a measure. To what extent the implementation of a measure allows for a noticeable progress in terms of productivity?

3) *Sustainability (Cr3)*:
Last but not least, sustainability represents the durability of an action over time before it becomes obsolete. Obviously, the longer the company benefits from the measures implementation, the better the measure.

D. Methodology

Figure 3 depicts the followed methodology for ranking measures as recommendation toward productivity improvement. An explication is given in what follows for the pre-processing steps in contrast to AHP steps.

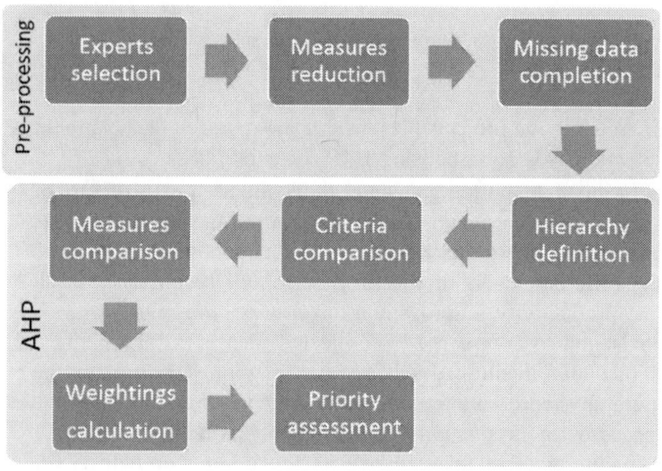

Figure 3. Pre-processing and AHP steps.

- *Experts selection*:
The criteria and measures with their relative importance impacting productivity are investigated using a specially designed questionnaire. The self-assessment tool is joined with the questionnaire for an explanatory purpose. The experts pool is composed of either academics or manufacturers with at least 5 years of experience in Lean Production and Industry 4.0.
- *Measures reduction*:
It is obvious that providing consistent pairwise comparison of 36 measures of the initial self-assessment tool is not a task that a human can perform. We asked the experts to keep only the most important 14 measures according to them, and to determine which are the most representative of the 5 dimensions. After the reduction step, the most preselected 14 measures is considered as the ideal set of measurements. Therefore, $\simeq$ 80% of the aggregate comparison matrix was filled in because the experts did not necessarily select the same measures during the reduction step. Nevertheless, this shows an agreement among the experts concerning measures reduction giving rise possibly to a shorter self-assessment tool for productivity improvement in SME context.
- *Missing data completion*:
One question might be raised, namely, how to fill in the $\simeq$ 20% of missing data. To answer this question, the first approach consists to apply the Harker's method. The idea is to replace the missing values in the comparison matrices with the most consistent values, which minimize CR [45]. However, it is not recommended to apply Harker's method when all entries of a row in the comparison matrix are missing. In this case, bias could be introduced in the data. The second approach relies on the Shannon's entropy principle of the Information Theory [46]. In particular, having no prior knowledge, the entropy is maximal for a source whose symbols are all equi-probable. Analogously to our context, having no prior knowledge regarding the superiority/inferiority of one measure over the others for an expert, then the relative measures are equi-important. The latter approach is used in this work for missing data completion.
- *AHP steps*:
The described hierarchy in Figure 2 is utilized as AHP hierarchy structure. Furthermore, the criteria and the preselected measures are compared with each other using the comparison scale [1-9]. Indeed, 1 denotes equal importance, 2 low importance and 9 extreme importance.

IV. OBTAINED RANKING

This section describes the obtained results by applying the framework presented in Figure 3. Table I shows the importance of each criterion with the respective weightings.

TABLE I
PAIRWISE COMPARISON OF CRITERIA WITH RESPECT TO THE IDEAL MEASURE FOR PRODUCTIVITY IMPROVEMENT

Criterion	**Importance** *Level*	*Weighting*
Feasibility (Cr1)	Hight importance	0.505
Potential (Cr2)	Moderate importance	0.301
Sustainability (Cr3)	Low importance	0.192
CR		**0.094**

According to the experts, the feasibility criterion is the most important, followed by potential and finally the sustainability criterion. This could be argued by the fact that SMEs suffer from lack of resources and technological experience to implement or adapt all measures. Indeed, compared to larger companies having an Research and Development (R&D) department where processes are continuously optimized and where new technologies are supported at all hierarchical levels, the feasibility is not as important as in a SME context. Furthermore, the potential of productivity improvement has an intermediate level of importance in the SME context, which can clearly be considered as the highest level of importance by larger companies. Finally, sustainability has obtained relatively the least important degree due to technology obsolescence for which companies of all sizes are aware.

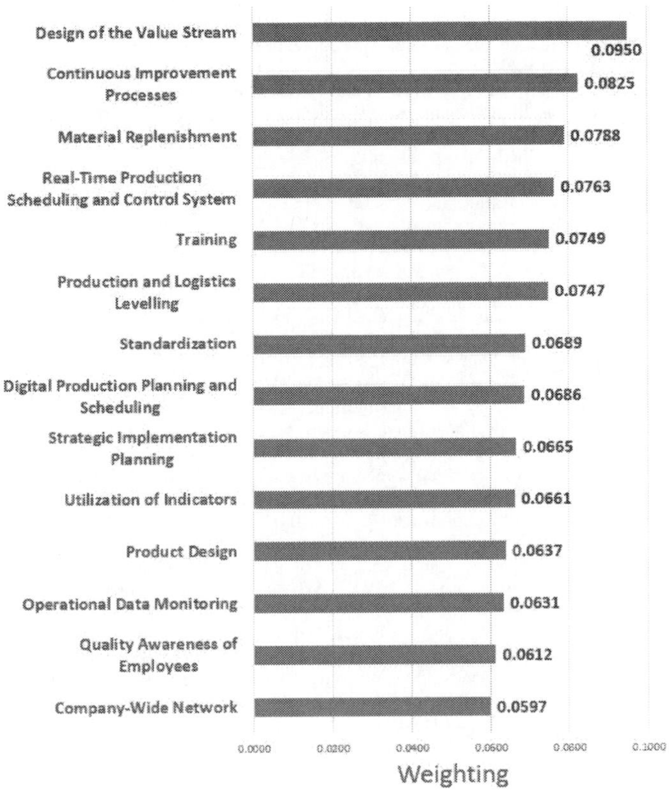

Figure 4. Ranking of measures for productivity improvement taking into account Cr1, Cr2 and Cr3.

Figure 4 presents the obtained prioritization of the 14 measures for productivity improvement considering the criteria. The recommendations based upon experts' opinions places Design of the Value Stream (DVS) at the top followed by Continuous Improvement Processes (CIP) and Material Replenishment (MR), respectively. Table II presents the potential pitfalls and the related aspects to be tackled for the top three measures.

Obviously, the above subjective ranking is very sensitive to experts opinions. Therefore, the choice of the pool of experts is a very important step to achieve an effective and qualitative recommendation based on AHP for which the researchers must pay attention. Moreover, the cohesion ratio is acceptable ($CR < 0.1$, see Table I) knowing that incoherence is part of the experts' judgement. Of course, the CR could be lowered by reinterviewing experts whenever inconsistency is observed. However, automatic methods should be avoided to reduce CR because they may alter the pairwise comparisons leading to unrepresentative data [47].

TABLE II
TOP THREE MEASURES, POTENTIAL PITFALLS AND THE ASSOCIATED ACTIONS

	Potential pitfall	*Action*
DVS	Persisting non-value added tasks	Continuous analysis and optimization of the whole value chain from the supplier to the customer end to reach the desired value-added percentage
CIP	Unstructured complex problem solving	Problem structuring and utilization of intelligent tools like Active Learning
MR	High inventory and material stock-out	Optimization of material stocks via collaborative tool involving different parties of supply chain

V. CONCLUSION

This work deals with recommendation making for productivity improvement in the SME context. The obtained prioritization is based upon experts judgements to rank the important measures in Lean Production and Industry 4.0 with respect to three criteria, namely feasibility, potential and sustainability. Companies can rely on these recommendations to adopt efficient productivity improvements and to choose the most important measure according to the experts in their strategic action plan. Particularly, in a SME context, there are not enough resources and technological experience to implement several measures. Therefore, the resulting measures ranking by applying AHP is presented in this paper and can be also accessed via the on-line platform of the INTERREG Prodpilot.

Regarding the perspectives, this work could be extended and it will be worth to consider other criteria to rank measures for productivity improvement, such as the reticence of SMEs regarding some measures.

ACKNOWLEDGMENT

This work is supported by the Interreg PRODPILOT V A project (040-4-09-104). The authors would like to thank the interviewed experts in Lean Production and Industry 4.0 for their valuable inputs.

REFERENCES

[1] *Centre for the Study of Living Standards (CSLS), International Productivity Monitor.* OECD Publishing, 2017.
[2] T. Munyai, B. Mbonyane, and C. Mbohwa, *Productivity Improvement in Manufacturing SMEs: Application of Work Study.* Taylor & Francis, 2017.
[3] I. Lee and K. Lee, "The Internet of Things (IoT): Applications, investments, and challenges for enterprises," *Business Horizons*, vol. 58, no. 4, pp. 431–440, 2015.
[4] S.-L. Chen, Y.-Y. Chen, and C. Hsu, "A New Approach to Integrate Internet-of-Things and Software-as-a-Service Model for Logistic Systems: A Case Study," *Sensors (Basel, Switzerland)*, vol. 14, pp. 6144–6164, 2014.
[5] A. Burgess, *The Executive Guide to Artificial Intelligence: How to identify and implement applications for AI in your organization.* Palgrave Macmillan Cham, 01 2018.

[6] E. Raguseo, "Big data technologies: An empirical investigation on their adoption, benefits and risks for companies," *International Journal of Information Management*, vol. 38, no. 1, pp. 187–195, 2018.

[7] R. Y. Zhong, X. Xu, E. Klotz, and S. T. Newman, "Intelligent Manufacturing in the Context of Industry 4.0: A Review," *Engineering*, vol. 3, no. 5, pp. 616–630, 2017.

[8] E. Hofmann and M. Rsch, "Industry 4.0 and the current status as well as future prospects on logistics," *Computers in Industry*, vol. 89, pp. 23–34, 2017.

[9] S. Mittal, M. A. Khan, D. Romero, and T. Wuest, "Smart manufacturing: Characteristics, technologies and enabling factors," *Proceedings of the Institution of Mechanical Engineers, Part B: Journal of Engineering Manufacture*, vol. 233, no. 5, pp. 1342–1361, 2019.

[10] P. Zheng *et al.*, "Smart manufacturing systems for Industry 4.0: Conceptual framework, scenarios, and future perspectives," *Frontiers of Mechanical Engineering*, vol. 13, pp. 137–150, June 2018.

[11] P. Rewers, A. Hamrol, K. Zywicki, M. Bozek, and W. Kulus, "Production Leveling as an Effective Method for Production Flow Control – Experience of Polish Enterprises," *Procedia Engineering*, vol. 182, pp. 619–626, 2017. 7th International Conference on Engineering, Project, and Production Management.

[12] J. Gordon, S. Zhao, and P. Gretton, *On productivity: concepts and measurement.* Productivity Commission Staff Research Note, Canberra, 2015 Feb.

[13] C. Syverson, "What Determines Productivity?," NBER Working Papers 15712, National Bureau of Economic Research, Inc, Jan. 2010.

[14] S. Nallusamy, A. M. Muhammad Umarmukdhar, and R. Suganthini Rekha, "A Proposed Supply Chain Model for Productivity Enhancement in Medium Scale Foundry Industries," *International Journal of Engineering Research in Africa*, vol. 20, pp. 248–258, 1 2016.

[15] J. Liker, *The Toyota Way : 14 Management Principles from the World's Greatest Manufacturer.* Business/ Management, Mcgraw-Hill, 2003.

[16] M. Rother, *Toyota Kata: Managing People for Improvement, Adaptiveness and Superior Results.* McGraw-Hill Education, 2009.

[17] Y. Monden, *Toyota Production System: An Integrated Approach to Just-In-Time, 4th Edition.* A Productivity Press book, Taylor & Francis, 2011.

[18] R. McLachlin, "Management initiatives and just-in-time manufacturing," *Journal of Operations Management*, vol. 15, no. 4, pp. 271–292, 1997.

[19] D. Romero, P. Gaiardelli, D. Powell, T. Wuest, and M. Threr, "Rethinking Jidoka Systems under Automation & Learning Perspectives in the Digital Lean Manufacturing World," *IFAC-PapersOnLine*, vol. 52, no. 13, pp. 899–903, 2019. 9th IFAC Conference on Manufacturing Modelling, Management and Control MIM 2019.

[20] H. Lasi, P. Fettke, H.-G. Kemper, T. Feld, and M. Hoffmann, "Industry 4.0," *Bus Inf Syst Eng*, vol. 6, pp. 239–242, 2014.

[21] S. Kumar, P. Tiwari, and M. Zymbler, "Internet of Things is a revolutionary approach for future technology enhancement: a review," *J Big Data*, vol. 6, pp. 1–21, 2019.

[22] Y. Abdelsadek and I. Kacem, "Productivity improvement based on a decision support tool for optimization of constrained delivery problem with time windows," *Comput. Ind. Eng.*, vol. 165, p. 107876, 2022.

[23] I. H. Sarker, "Machine Learning: Algorithms, Real-World Applications and Research Directions," *SN COMPUT. SCI.*, vol. 2, no. 160, pp. 1–21, 2021.

[24] J. M. Rozanec, E. Trajkova, P. Dam, B. Fortuna, and D. Mladenic, "Streaming Machine Learning and Online Active Learning for Automated Visual Inspection," *IFAC-PapersOnLine*, vol. 55, no. 2, pp. 277–282, 2022. 14th IFAC Workshop on Intelligent Manufacturing Systems IMS 2022.

[25] W. Vorraber, J. V. Gasser, H. Webb, D. Neubacher, and P. Url, "Assessing augmented reality in production: remote-assisted maintenance with Hololens," *Procedia CIRP*, vol. 88, pp. 139–144, 2020.

[26] A. Szajna, R. Stryjski, W. Woniak, N. Chamier-Gliszczynski, and M. Kostrzewski, "Assessment of Augmented Reality in Manual Wiring Production Process with Use of Mobile AR Glasses," *Sensors (Basel, Switzerland)*, vol. 20, no. 17, p. 4755, 2020.

[27] M. A. Khan, M. A. Khan, A. U. Rahman, A. W. Malik, and S. A. Khan, "Exploiting cooperative sensing for accurate target tracking in industrial Internet of things," *International Journal of Distributed Sensor Networks*, vol. 15, no. 12, p. 1550147719892203, 2019.

[28] L. Salhieh, M. Shehadeh, I. Abushaikha, and N. Towers, "Integrating vehicle tracking and routing systems in retail distribution management," *International Journal of Retail & Distribution Management*, vol. 49, no. 8, pp. 1154–1177, 2021.

[29] D. J. Nightingale and J. H. Mize, "Development of a Lean Enterprise Transformation Maturity Model," *Inf. Knowl. Syst. Manag.*, vol. 3, no. 1, pp. 15–30, 2002.

[30] M. A. Maasouman and K. Demirli, "Assessment of Lean Maturity Level in Manufacturing Cells," *IFAC-PapersOnLine*, vol. 48, no. 3, pp. 1876–1881, 2015. 15th IFAC Symposium onInformation Control Problems inManufacturing.

[31] A. Schumacher, S. Erol, and W. Sihn, "A Maturity Model for Assessing Industry 4.0 Readiness and Maturity of Manufacturing Enterprises," *Procedia CIRP*, vol. 52, pp. 161–166, 2016. The Sixth International Conference on Changeable, Agile, Reconfigurable and Virtual Production (CARV2016).

[32] M. Spaltini, F. Acerbi, M. Pinzone, S. Gusmeroli, and M. Taisch, "Defining the Roadmap towards Industry 4.0: The 6ps Maturity Model for Manufacturing SMEs," *Procedia CIRP*, vol. 105, pp. 631–636, 2022. The 29th CIRP Conference on Life Cycle Engineering, April 4 6, 2022, Leuven, Belgium.

[33] C. Leyh, S. Martin, and T. Schffer, "Industry 4.0 and Lean Production a matching relationship? An analysis of selected Industry 4.0 models," in *2017 Federated Conference on Computer Science and Information Systems (FedCSIS)*, pp. 989–993, 2017.

[34] S.-V. Buer, J. O. Strandhagen, and F. T. S. Chan, "The link between Industry 4.0 and lean manufacturing: mapping current research and establishing a research agenda," *International Journal of Production Research*, vol. 56, no. 8, pp. 2924–2940, 2018.

[35] L. S. Angreani, A. Vijaya, and H. Wicaksono, "Systematic Literature Review of Industry 4.0 Maturity Model for Manufacturing and Logistics Sectors," *Procedia Manufacturing*, vol. 52, pp. 337–343, 2020. System-Integrated Intelligence Intelligent, Flexible and Connected Systems in Products and ProductionProceedings of the 5th International Conference on System-Integrated Intelligence (SysInt 2020), Bremen, Germany.

[36] "Interreg prodpilot project (040-4-09-104)." http://prodpilot-plateforme.lcoms.univ-lorraine.fr/. (Date last accessed 22-July-2022).

[37] A. Ishizaka and A. Labib, "Review of the main developments in the analytic hierarchy process," *Expert Systems with Applications*, vol. 38, no. 11, pp. 14336–14345, 2011.

[38] R. W. Saaty, "The analytic hierarchy processwhat it is and how it is used," *Mathematical Modelling*, vol. 9, no. 3, pp. 161–176, 1987.

[39] V. Farrokhi, I. Kacem, and L. Pokordi, "Ranking the solution techniques for reactive scheduling problem in operating room," in *2014 International Conference on Control, Decision and Information Technologies (CoDIT)*, pp. 001–006, 2014.

[40] O. Bayazit, "Use of AHP in decision-making for flexible manufacturing systems," *Journal of Manufacturing Technology Management*, vol. 16, no. 7, pp. 808–819, 2005.

[41] H. Doloi, "Application of AHP in improving construction productivity from a management perspective," *Construction Management and Economics*, vol. 26, no. 8, pp. 841–854, 2008.

[42] K. Schmidt, I. Aumann, I. Hollander, K. Damm, and J.-M. G. von der Schulenburg, "Applying the Analytic Hierarchy Process in healthcare research: A systematic literature review and evaluation of reporting," *BMC medical informatics and decision making*, vol. 15, p. 112, 2015.

[43] A. K. Kar, "An approach for prioritizing supplier selection criteria through consensus building using Analytic Hierarchy Process and Fuzzy set theory," in *2013 IEEE International Conference on Signal Processing, Computing and Control (ISPCC)*, pp. 1–6, 2013.

[44] L. He and C. Li, "A Method for Selecting ERP System Based on Fuzzy Set Theory and Analytical Hierarchy Process," in *2009 WRI Global Congress on Intelligent Systems*, vol. 1, pp. 329–332, 2009.

[45] P. T. Harker, "Incomplete pairwise comparisons in the analytic hierarchy process," *Mathematical Modelling*, vol. 9, no. 11, pp. 837–848, 1987.

[46] C. E. Shannon, "A mathematical theory of communication," *The Bell System Technical Journal*, vol. 27, no. 3, pp. 379–423, 1948.

[47] T. L. Saaty and L. T. Tran, "On the invalidity of fuzzifying numerical judgments in the Analytic Hierarchy Process," *Mathematical and Computer Modelling*, vol. 46, no. 7, pp. 962–975, 2007. Decision Making with the Analytic Hierarchy Process and the Analytic Network Process.

Advances in Sensors and X-ray Spectroscopy for Agricultural Soil Analysis

Paulo E. Cruvinel
Embrapa Instrumentation, São Carlos, SP, Brazil
Post-Graduation Program in Computer Science - Federal University of São Carlos, SP, Brazil
Email: paulo.cruvinel@embrapa.br

Abstract— **This paper presents a study regarding sensors development and the use for X-ray spectroscopy. In fact, we include not only a novel discussion on sensors since the X-rays discovery, but we also present a prospective about the future. X-ray-based spectrometry is an analytical technique to determine the elemental composition of different materials. For agricultural soils, either soft or hard X-ray spectroscopies have been shown to improve agronomic competitiveness and agroecosystems sustainability. This review in X-ray sensors considers their use in both X-ray fluorescence and particle induced X-ray emission techniques, i.e., highlighting new materials, accuracy, resolution, efficiency, energy response, and related methods.**

Keywords—X-ray Sensors; Radiation-matter Interaction; Spectrometer; Intelligent Instrumentation; Soil analysis; Decision making.

I. INTRODUCTION

Currently, it is possible to estimate that agriculture represents around 3 trillion USD of the global economy. This considers the planet's growing population, the increased interest by consumers in the origins and quality of food, and challenges brought on by climate change, sustainability, and circular economy. Besides, it is becoming clear that the future of agriculture relies on technology and on technological advancement. In fact, the world already has experienced four waves of agricultural technologies, i.e., Mechanization (first wave, 1700–1940s); Agricultural chemistry, biochemistry, and genetics (second wave, 1940s–1990s), which has included synthetic fertilizers, pesticides for pest control, and Genetic Modified Organisms (GMOs), created through genetic engineering and available to consumers; and Precision farming (third wave, 1990s–2014), that brought the huge use of Global Positioning System (GPS), smart sensors and instrumentation to support decision making in agriculture. However, beyond that, in recent times, the agricultural world has been using advanced sensor-based methods on the interaction of the electromagnetic radiation with matter, as well as big data and artificial intelligence, all to better understand and manage the complex system soil-plant-atmosphere, i.e., not only for gain in production, but also looking for non-invasive operation and the resilience of the ecosystems [1][2]. Such a scenario has become the newest wave in the agricultural industry.

In the context described above, technology development and innovation lead farming operations to be more productive, harvesting more crops per area and yielding higher quality products. In such a context, non-invasive sensors play a vital role in this technological revolution [3]. For example, sensors in a smart agriculture technology are essential in the measurement of soil pH, which is related to the availability of nutrients and essential to plant growth. In addition, Global Positioning System (GPS) sensors, which are typically associated with tractors and other machineries, including wireless communication on farms, are useful for plant harvesting and related farming techniques, including highly precise machine guidance systems, i.e., reducing process overlap and the amount of time required to complete and optimize management tasks [4]. Likewise, temperature sensors based on the use of infrared radiation are crucial for ambient condition monitoring and mechanical asset monitoring. Similar to the use of temperature sensors in predictive maintenance, wireless accelerometers are being widely utilized to predict and assist with required maintenance. Primarily used on moving components and motors, the wireless accelerometers detect slight variations in movement and vibration inconsistencies and predict when standard maintenance is required, which is quite useful to prevent failure and improve reliability [5]. Such accelerometers are also used in a variety of automated systems and tracking methods, such as, for instance, to monitor the status of an adjustable spray nozzle on the end of a fertilization beam. In more recent applications, they also have been used with Unmanned Aerial Vehicles (UAVs) for inertial measurement, i.e., to track motion, speed, undesirable events, and position in space [6].

Further, the use of smart cameras operating in several bands of frequencies (multispectral or even hyperspectral) has been adopted for a variety of smart agriculture applications, i.e., to detect either crop vitality or even families of weeds and other plant locations to automatically and accurately decrease the use of herbicides and improve sustainability.

Furthermore, for soil quality evaluation, it is advantageous to have a large availability of sensors that are able to detect a set of elements and allow their measurement in a wide range of concentration values [7]. Such elements play an important role for plant growth. Actually, many of these elements have a quite well-known function with plant uptake, while others are still under investigation and demand scientific research. In such a context, the current elements that can be observed from an agricultural soil are macronutrients such as nitrogen (N), phosphorus (P), potassium (K), sulfur (S), calcium (Ca), and magnesium (Mg), as well as micronutrients, such as boron (B), chlorine (Cl), copper (Cu), iron (Fe), manganese (Mn), molybdenum (Mo), nickel (Ni), and zinc (Zn), all of which are based on natural resources or come from soil inputs, like fertilizers. To obtain such information, it is necessary to perform soil analysis, which is a valuable tool for food production as it determines the inputs required for efficient and economic production. A proper soil analysis will help ensure the application of enough fertilizer to meet the requirements of the crop while taking advantage of the nutrients already present in the soil. It will also allow the farmer to determine lime requirements and can be used to diagnose problems in the crop areas. Soil analysis is a requirement for farms that must complete a nutrient management plan.

Currently, there are several techniques available for soil chemical analysis [8]. The most common ones are spectrophotometry in the uv-visible and colorimeters, atomic absorption spectrophotometry, atomic emission spectrophotometry, inductively coupled plasma and High-Performance Liquid Chromatography. However, despite being efficient, most of them have a high cost, not only in terms of instrumental infrastructure, but also in relation to sample preparation, which in general is based on chemical processes. Also, the analysis is highly time consuming, which is a critical factor.

Based on the reasons mentioned above, the use of ionizing radiation for X-ray spectroscopy, which also allows elemental analysis of soil samples, has been considered even more for scientific research and innovation for soil analysis.

Soil analysis is the only method that allows, before planting, to identify the ability of the soil to provide the nutrients that are needed by plants, in addition to having a basis for recommending the necessary amounts of correctives and fertilizers to intensify crop productivity and, consequently, obtain the best return on investments and increased profit. When carrying out the soil analysis, the producer also allows monitoring the changes in the fertility of the production area. This is because it offers the possibility of increasing production and plant resistance, reducing expenses with pesticides (insecticides, herbicides and fungicides) and consequently, also promoting a reduction in environmental impacts.

The intelligent agriculture industry is expanding quickly, presenting new solutions to farmers practically daily. Methods and devices aggregate sensor data, relay critical information to farmers and are focused on the optimization of the agricultural processes for food, energy and fibers production.

This paper presents advances in sensors and potential applications in X-ray spectroscopy for analysis, i.e., based on the applications of both X-ray Fluorescence (XRF) and Particle Induced X-ray Emission (PIXE) in agriculture.

The rest of the paper is structured as follows. Section II presents the evolution of sensors for these two case studies, as well as their state-of-art and future prospective. Conclusions are presented in Section III.

II. SENSORS FOR XRF AND PIXE

X-rays were discovered in 1895 by the German scientist Wilhelm Conrad Röntgen [9]. These rays could pass through the heavy paper covering and exciting phosphorescent materials. One of Röntgen's first experiments late in 1895 was the use of a photographic film as a sensor. Current radiographic films are based on polyethylene teratalate (polyester). The Roentgen's discovery lead to the development of the X-Rays Fluorescence (XRF) spectroscopy which has become a powerful and versatile technique for the analysis and characterization of materials. Pioneering work in XRF has been led by William Lawrence Bragg and William Henry Bragg [10]. This work distinguishes different elements present in a sample according to the characteristic X-ray energies they emit and helps in determining their respective concentrations. Figure 1 presents a basic arrangement for a typical XRF instrument.

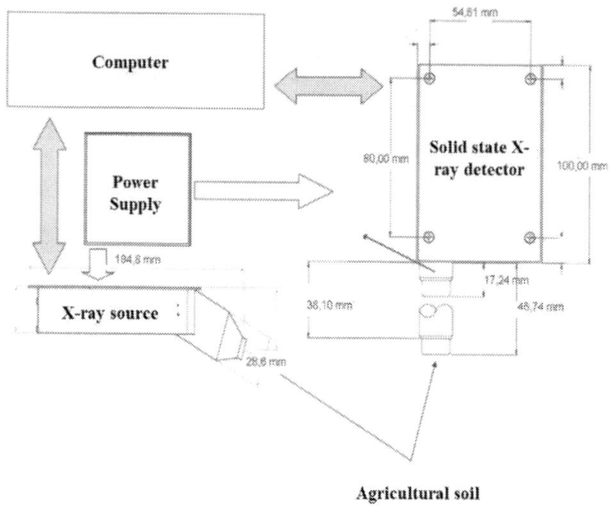

Figure 1. Instrumental arrangement for a typical XRF spectrometer.

In fact, X-ray spectroscopy is a technique that detects and measures photons of light that have wavelengths in the X-ray portion of the electromagnetic spectrum. There are different X-ray spectrometers configurations and associated methods that can be used for several disciplines and fields of application. In 1996, Pessoa and co-authors presented one of the first arrangements based on XRF for agricultural soil and plant analysis [11].

More recently, the definition for XRF has been expanded to include the study of the interactions between particles such as protons, electrons, and ions, as well as their interaction with other particles as a function of their collision energy. In such a context, one may use particles and their acceleration for the ionization of the atoms of a sample with subsequent X-ray emission, characteristic from the present elements, i.e., a technique named Particle Induced X-ray Emission (PIXE). The number of X-ray photons of a given element provides information on the quantity of that element. Pioneering work in PIXE has been first proposed in 1970 by Sven Johansson of Lund University, Sweden, and developed over the next few years with his colleagues Roland Akselsson and Thomas Johansson [12]. With this technique, samples can be analyzed with weight in the order of 10-12 g for solids and volume in the order of 1 mL for liquids. Such a technique allows the simultaneous detection of all elements with an atomic number above Mg, and the inorganic matrix of the sample during its preparation for analysis is maintained. Figure 2 illustrates a typical arrangement for PIXE analysis.

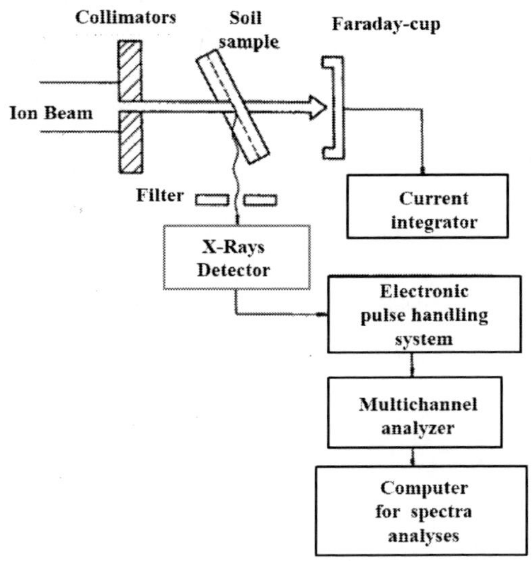

Figure 2. Instrumental arrangement for PIXE analysis.

In 1993, Cruvinel and Flocchini presented the first arrangement based on PIXE for agricultural soil analysis [13]. PIXE has allowed a very quick soil analysis. For instance, considering the X-ray induction by 4.0 MeV protons, the emergent X-rays have been obtained using the cross section as a function of the ionization energy, and the analysis of a set of soil samples was carried out. Further, additional arrangements using a particle accelerator either like a Cyclotron or a Pelletron, and an alfa source have allowed accurate analyses and configuration of portable PIXE instruments [14]. In fact, for both XRF and PIXE techniques in the quantitative analysis of agricultural soils, corrections are required, for the diameter size of the particles or aggregates of a certain composition. In addition, corrections are required for X-ray transmissions through filters, which are used with sensor-based detectors.

For the X-ray sensors, a significant evolution has been observed since the first experiment organized by Röntgen in 1895 using a photographic film. The Röntgen's original method remained important because it was widely available. In the 1900s and the 1910s, several rival techniques of chemical coloration evolved which were easier to use because no development was required. The discoloration of pastilles left on a body receiving radiotherapy would by comparison with a color chart give a measure of the dose applied. Such techniques were good enough if the precision required was not great. The rational radiotherapy of the 1920s required greater precision, however, driving the development of instrumentation that required no judgment by the human eye. The instrument eventually chosen was an elaboration of that with which Ernest Rutherford and the Curies had conducted their experiments in radioactivity [15]. The idea was that radiation ionized air in a chamber and the ions were counted by measuring the current they produced across an electric potential. However, this was greatly dependent on the size of the chamber and the material of the walls, and also on the relative positions of the X-ray tube and chamber, and it was not until 1928 that an international X-ray intensity standard was fully accepted, a standard that specified the behavior required to achieve the required precision. For the first time, X-ray researchers had confidence that numbers could be compared between laboratories [16], i.e., considering metrological bases aspects.

New X-ray detectors are being developed since the 1940s, with the emergence of proportional and scintillation counters and the electronics needed for signal processing. With an extensive use of tubes, solid-state counters have also been incorporated since they are less expensive, have high collection efficiency and there is no need for moving parts.

The smaller counters have not only enabled portability in the 1980s, but also improvements in the analytical techniques related to XRF and PIXE. In fact, there are different detectors, especially based on single crystals [17]. For the X-ray detectors, many corporations can make their commercially available ones, including Silicon (Si) photodiodes, and Charge Coupled Devices (CCD) cameras, among others. In the low energy X-ray region called the soft X-ray region from a few hundred eV to about 20 keV, direct detectors such as Si PIN photodiodes (PIN layers: P, I, and N, where the P-layer is doped with a trivalent impurity, and its terminal acts like anode, the I-layer is undoped or very lightly doped, and N-layer is doped with a pentavalent impurity, and its terminal acts like cathode), Si with the transistor Active Pixel Sensors (Si APS), and CCD area image sensors are utilized. The PIN structure allows high quantum efficiency and fast response for detection of photons in the 400 nm to 1100 nm range [18]. All of these X-ray detectors can provide high energy efficiency and high energy resolution and can be useful for elemental analysis of agricultural samples. On the other hand, for the hard X-ray region with energy higher than 20 keV is sensors based on high penetration efficiency through samples or objects are utilized. For such a context, scintillator detectors are still widely used, i.e., they are able to convert X-ray into visible light and detect this visible light to detect the X-ray indirectly. Likewise, one may find expressive diversity in the X-ray detectors currently in use for spectrometers; however, the majority of these are already semiconductor-based detectors. This occurs because of the outstanding combination of high speed, spatial resolution, and sensitivity, as compared to other types of detectors, such as those based on gas and photomultiplier tubes with single crystals [19].

As we have seen, the use of semiconductor materials to detect electromagnetic radiation has been developed extensively during the last forty years [20]. Within this period, for instance, the Lithium Silicon (Si(Li)) detector [21] of a particular shape and size has been the preferred choice for detecting low energy X-rays. These include XRF systems, among other applications. Within the last years [22], it has become known about the usefulness of

Germanium (Ge), as well as its advantages in relation to the use of Si. However, even though the technology based on the use of Ge is known for X-ray detectors, there are still customization and development needed for a wider range of experiments based on the use of high energies, such as those required in imaging. In fact, major attention has been employed for the development of these Ge detectors as devices for high resolution energy dispersive XRF.

Gallium arsenide (GaAs) is also used in diodes, Field-Effect Transistors (FETs), integrated circuits, as well as for X-ray sensors. For such devices, the charge carriers, which are mostly electrons, move at high speed among the atoms. This makes sensors based on GaAs components useful at ultra-high frequencies. GaAs devices generate less noise than most other types of semiconductor components [23].

On the other hand, Cadmium telluride (CdTe) is also a semiconductor with favorable characteristics for spectrometer-based X-ray detectors. The band gap is sufficiently large so that only moderate cooling is required to obtain small leakage currents. The high density and high atomic numbers (Cd with Z=48, and Te with Z=52) result in efficient photoelectric absorption. This high-Z semiconductor material provides excellent stopping power, resulting in superior detection efficiency even at high X-ray energies. The manufacturing quality and the availability of Schottky contacts allow achieving adequate energy resolution over one useful workable range. The detrimental spectral tailing due to the comparatively short lifetime can be limited by applying large bias voltages. As an example, the CdTe thickness of 1000 μm provides high quantum efficiency for hard X-ray energies up to 100 keV, and it can be capable of operating high X-ray fluxes [24].

In addition, in terms of the state-of-the-art and the future, it is possible to find commercially available Silicon-Drift-Detector (SDD), which incorporates two different design concepts, one based on an integrated FET and the other based on a discrete external FET [25]. Figure 3 shows a typical relation between efficiency and energy for the SDD. The performance of the SDDs provided by these two technologies can provide advantages and disadvantages, depending on the application and needs.

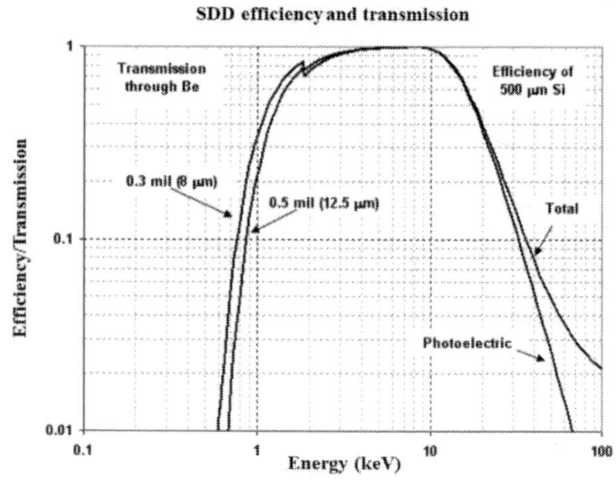

Figure 3. Efficiency versus energy for a typical Silicon Drift Detector (SDD).

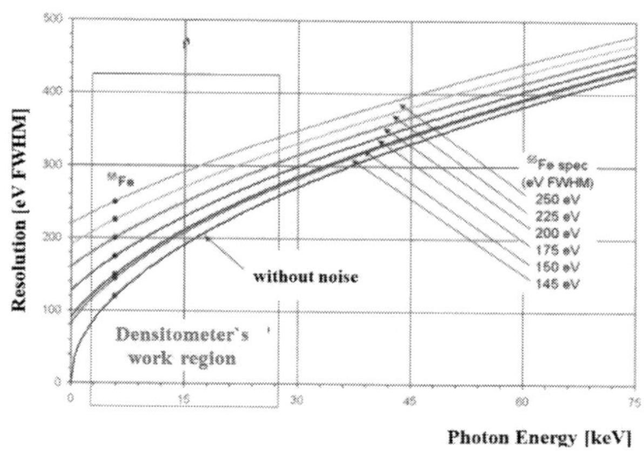

Figure 4. An example for one solid state sensor working region evaluation based on 145 eV resolutions.

Figure 4 illustrates, as an example, the evaluation of a high-performance semiconductor sensor that operates with a resolution in the order of 145eV in a wide working region, i.e., from 4keV to 30.0 keV.

The SDD sensor with integrated FET considers integrating the FET into the sensor design as part of the anode assembly. This way, the capacitance of the anode-FET combination can be minimized. Besides, the high resistivity material used is very different from the lower resistivity material that has typically been used to optimize gain and noise for discrete FETs. Therefore, since it has lower voltage noise, a good resolution can be achieved at the minimum possible process time with the highest possible count rate. However, in such a set-up, part of the sensor is susceptible to irradiation by incident X-rays and the electrostatic fields surrounding the FET result in performance losses at low energies. To overcome this issue, the shape of the sensor can be re-designed to place the anode and FET at the margins protected by a collimator. Likewise, the drift rings are designed in a tear-drop shape so the electrons drift towards the anode.

The SDD sensor with a discrete external FET uses a dedicated feedback capacitor and a well-proven method of pulsed charge restoration. This allows stability and provides more accurate X-ray measurement. It also means FETs can be designed and manufactured separately and the materials can be chosen to maximize their performance. The advantage of this arrangement is that the bonding between anode and FET introduces higher capacitance than with integrated designs. Therefore, the speeds at which the best resolution can be achieved are lower, although still much faster than what can be achieved with Si(Li). Such a sensor can also provide reduction on the rise time effects, and excellence in low energy performance even with large area sensors.

Beyond the SDD detectors, one prospective opportunity for the future is related to the use of conductive polymers for X-ray sensors. Conductive polymers present numerous advantages such as high sensitivity, short response time, room temperature operation, and the possibility of tuning both chemical and physical properties by using different substituents [26][27]. Therefore, sensors based on conductive polymers and their composites have attracted much attention from researchers. The conductive polymers used for sensors mainly consist of polyaniline, polypyrrole and poly (3,4-ethylenedioxythiophene), among others. In fact, conductive polymers composites combine different advantages in relation to other sensing materials such as carbonaceous materials, metal oxides, as well as they may lead to both high sensing characteristics and performance due to the synergistic effect of the components.

Furthermore, the field related to X-ray sensors for spectrometry is still under a promise revolution, i.e., there are challenges related to the improvement in multiple energies response and resolution, size, non-invasiveness, operation at room temperature, low-power consumption, reliability, detectable limit, and methods for customization based on the application, among other aspects. Despite that, it is also important to observe that sensors are only one important part of a spectrometer into the analysis chain. The nuclear pulse processor and the additional electronics associated with the software design are equally important to achieve a reliable system not only for high but also for low count rates.

III. Conclusions

Even though different detectors are widely used in X-ray spectrometry, there are still challenges related to the need for improvements for both soft and hard X-ray detection. For such matter, several studies have been performed in the last decade, all of which are looking to new possibilities for advanced X-ray detection based on new materials and intelligent electronics for signal processing, and other decision-making computational support related developments. As shown, a new line of spectrometry and related methods have been generated focused on agricultural demands and analysis, i.e., related to food production and environmental protection. The concepts of physics and the analysis tools available or developed by various branches of knowledge and engineering have allowed advanced use of XRF and PIXE in agricultural sciences. One challenge is linked to the integration and interpretation of the results at different scales

Another major challenge requiring continuous scientific and instrumentation effort is the development of on-the-go and portable X-ray sensors-based spectrometers, which can be taken to the field to carry out in-situ measurements. These could allow not only the measurements of stationary elemental concentration values, but also dynamic studies in relation to soil nutrients availability and uptake by plants. In addition, they could help with real-time soil fertilization at a variable rate based on the use of precision agriculture concepts.

Acknowledgment

This research was partially supported by the Brazilian Corporation for Agricultural Research (Embrapa).

References

[1] M. K. Sott et al., "Bibliometric network analysis of recent publications on digital agriculture to depict strategic themes and evolution structure", Sensors, vol. 21, pp. 7889-7916, 2021.

[2] M. Liebman and L. A. Schulte, "Enhancing agroecosystem performance and resilience through increased diversification of landscapes and cropping systems", Elementa: Science of the Anthropocene, vol. 3, pp. 000041-000048, 2015.

[3] G. Agati et al., "In field non-invasive sensing of the nitrogen status in hybrid bermudagrass (Cynodon dactylon × C. transvaalensis Burtt Davy) by a fluorescence-based method", European Journal of Agronomy, vol. 63, pp. 89–96, 2015.

[4] Z. Zhai et al., "Decision support systems for agriculture 4.0: Survey and challenges", Computer and Electronics in Agriculture, vol. 170, pp. 1052- 1057, 2020.

[5] P. E. Cruvinel et al., "Real-time evaluation of failure and reliability in agricultural sprayers using embedded sensors and controller area bus protocol", International Journal on Advances in Systems and Measurements, vol. 13, pp. 161-174, 2020..

[6] K. S. Hatamleh et al., "Development of a specialinertial measurement unitfor UAV application", Journal of Dynamic Systems, Measurement, and Control, vol. 135, pp. 011003-011013, 2013.

[7] R. I. Donahue, R. W. Miller and J. C Shickluna, Introduction to Soil and Plant Growth, 5th Edition, Library of Congress: New York, USA, 1983.

[8] J. R. Okalebo, K. W. Gathua and P. L. Woomer, Laboratory methods of soil and plant analysis: a working manual, 2nd Edition, Nairobi Tropical Soil Biology and Fertility Programme: Kenya, Africa, 2002.

[9] F. Nüsslin, "Wilhelm Conrad Röntgen: The scientist and his discovery", European Journal of Medical Physics, vol. 79, pp. 65-68, 2020.

[10] W. H. Bragg and W. L Bragg, X-rays and Crystal Structure, Bell and Sons: London, England, 1915.

[11] J. D. C. Pessoa et al., "Preparation of soil and plant samples for determination of macronutrients by X-ray fluorescence", in Proceedings of the Symposium on the interaction of photons and electrons with matter (SAIFEM 96), São Carlos, SP, Brazil, pp. 9-10,1996.

[12] T. B. Johansson, R. Akselsson and S. A. E. Johansson, "X-ray analysis: Elemental trace analysis at the 10^{-12} g level", Nuclear Instruments and Methods, vol. 84, pp. 141–143, 1970.

[13] P. E. Cruvinel and R. G. Flocchini, "Determination of Se in soil samples using the proton induced X-ray emission technique". Nuclear Instruments and Methods in Physics Research Section B, vol. 75, pp. 415-419, 1993.

[14] P. E. Cruvinel et al., "Elemental analysis of agricultural soil samples by particle induced X-ray emission (PIXE) technique", Nuclear Instruments and Methods in Physics Research, Section B, vol. 150, pp. 478-483, 1999.

[15] A. Hessenbruch, "Rutherford's 1901 experiment on radiation energy and his creation of a stable detector", Archives for the History of the Exact Sciences, vol. 54, pp. 403-420, 2000.

[16] A. Hessenbruch, "The origins of exact x-ray dosage", in Proceedings of the Emergence of Modern Physics, Università degli Studi di Pavia, pp. 81-87, 1996.

[17] F. C. Miguens et al., "A new protocol to detect light elements in estuarine sediments by X-ray microanalysis (SEM/EDS)J", ournal of Electron Microscopy vol. 59, issue 5, pp. 437–446, 2010.

[18] C. Z. Zhou and W. K. Warburton, "Comparison of silicon pin diode detector fabrication processes using ion implantation

and thermal doping", Nuclear Instruments and Methods in Physics Research, Section A, vol. 378, issue 3, pp. 529-530, 1996.

[19] K. Laqua et al., "Detection of radiation" Pure and Applied Chemistry, vol. 67, no. 10, pp. 1745-1760,1995.

[20] Tru-Q™ – Making accurate analysis a reality for all application: Available through the Oxford Instruments: [Online]. Available from: http://www.oxinst.com/products/x-ray-microanalysis.

[21] D. Newbury, "X-ray Mapping in the Spectrum Image Mode at Output Count Rates above 100 kHz with the Silicon Drift Detector (SDD)", Microscopy and Microanalysis vol. 12, pp. 1380-1381, 2006..

[22] J. Y. Zevallos-ChaHvez et al., "Response function of a germanium detector to photon energies between 6 and 120 keV", Nuclear Instruments and Methods in Physics Research, Section A, vol. 457, pp. 212-219, 2001.

[23] G. Lioliou and A. M. Barnett, "Gallium Arsenide detectors for X-ray and electron (beta particle) spectroscopy", Nuclear Instruments and Methods in Physics Research, Section A, vol. 836, issue 11, pp. 37-45, 2016.

[24] D. Krasikov et al., "Why shallow defect levels alone do not cause high resistivity in CdTe", Semiconductor Science and Technology, vol. 28, 125019 (7pp), 2013.

[25] P. Lechner et al., "Silicon drift detectors for high count rate X-ray spectroscopy at room temperature", Nuclear Instruments and Methods in Physics Research, Section A, vol. 458, issues 1–2, pp. 281-287, 2001.

[26] H. Shirakawa et al., "Synthesis of electrically conducting organic polymers: halogen derivatives of Polyacetylene (CH)x", Journal of the Chemical Society, Chemical Communications, vol. 16, pp.. 578 - 580, 1977.

[27] E. C. Venancio et al., "Line patterning of graphite and the fabrication of cheap, inexpensive, `throw-away´ sensors", Sensors & Actuators, B: Chemical, vol. 130, pp. 723-729, 2008.

International Academy, Research,
and Industry Association (IARIA)
412 Derby Way
Wilmington, DE 19810

ISBN 978-1-7138-6959-7

CURRAN ASSOCIATES INC.
proceedings.com

Thirteenth International Conference on Digital Society and eGovernments (ICDS 2019)

Held at DigitalWorld 2019

Athens, Greece
24 – 28 February 2019

IARIA